OMDURMAN DIARIES
1898

OMDURMAN DIARIES
1898

Eyewitness Accounts of the
Legendary Campaign

Edited by

JOHN MEREDITH

with a Foreword by
HENRY KEOWN-BOYD

LEO COOPER

In memory of my mother

MARY ELINOR MEREDITH
1899–1973

First published in Great Britain in 1998 by
Leo Cooper Ltd

an imprint of
Pen & Sword Books Ltd
47 Church Street, Barnsley, South Yorks
S70 2AS

ISBN 0 85052 607.8

A CIP record for this book is available
from the British Library

Typeset by Phoenix Typesetting, Ilkley, West Yorkshire

Printed in England by Redwood Books Ltd, Trowbridge, Wilts.

CONTENTS

Foreword vi
Acknowledgements viii
Glossary ix
Maps x, xi
Author's Note xii
1. Ordered to the Front 7
2. Waiting to Advance 28
3. Towards Atbara 47
4. The Battle of the Atbara 78
5. The Waiting Begins 101
6. The Long Hot Summer 125
7. Final Preparations 149
8. The Battle of Omdurman 166
9. Back to Cairo 193
Epilogue 204
Bibliography 207
Index 208

FOREWORD
by
HENRY KEOWN-BOYD

John Meredith has skilfully woven the quite recently discovered journal of Private George Teigh of the Lincolns together with the those of three other participants in Kitchener's re-conquest of the Sudan.

For the son of a Victorian farm-labourer, Teigh was remarkably literate (primary school education in his day must have been better than it is now), but the most graphic of these diarists was Lieutenant Meiklejohn of the Warwicks. There is little doubt of the accuracy of these records as, where two or more of the diarists are recounting the same incident, there are only the most minor differences in their accounts.

While the two major battles of the campaign, the Atbara and Omdurman, are vividly described, especially by Meiklejohn, the most indelible impression with which the reader is left is of the acute discomfort and hardship endured by all ranks during the long approach marches and in camp throughout the sweltering summer of 1898.

Despite the alarmism of the British Brigade (later Divisional) commander, Gatacre, which so greatly added to the physical and mental weariness of his troops, Kitchener's Anglo-Egyptian army was never in any great danger from the Mahdist enemy. Its principal foes were heat, disease, boredom and the parsimony of the British and Egyptian treasuries. Neither the home government nor Cromer, the de facto ruler of Egypt, were enthusiastic about the campaign and Kitchener knew that his job depended on running it on a shoe-string – or, more appropriately, on a boot-lace, the possession of which humble commodity was much prized by the troops.

Teigh, unlike most British soldiers, was not a grumbler and seems to have accepted his lot with philosophical resignation, but it is clear that he and his comrades were inadequately fed on rations of the most basic standard (although the medical orderly Skinner seems to have done better). Fortunately, "luxuries", like tins of sardines, were available from the Greek and Syrian traders who set up shop whenever and wherever the army halted, so, as no alcohol, except an official rum ration, was allowed, the troops spent most of their meagre pay on food.

The two battalions with which we are principally concerned here, the 1st Royal Warwicks and the 1st Lincolns, were highly regarded county regiments of the line. Teigh expresses little criticism of his officers, but Lieutenant Cox of the same regiment has no time for his colonel, Verner, writing "THE COLONEL HAS GONE!!! GOOD OH!!!" in his diary after the unfortunate man had been wounded at the Atbara and invalided home!

Gatacre, a highly-strung and hyper-active martinet, was unpopular with all ranks, especially the officers, as he combined extreme recklessness (not only with his own life) in battle with pernickety interference in every detail of routine and discipline on the line of march and in camp. In stark contrast, although he appears little in these pages, was the Egyptian divisional commander, Hunter, described by Churchill, with perhaps a rather curious choice of noun, as the "darling of the Egyptian Army". On the Sirdar, Kitchener, we get little comment from the diarists, although Teigh does remark upon his rugged appearance. No doubt all four were too junior to have had much contact with this Olympian figure.

The ruthlessness and lack of consideration with which the British soldier of the day was treated by his government is illustrated by the fact that even officers, for example Meiklejohn, could not expect home leave after a rigorous campaign. As for Private Teigh, he was immediately shippd off to India where he remained almost until his engagement had expired in 1905.

This book is a valuable historical document, for, although John Meredith keeps us abreast of the progress of the campaign with periodic bursts of his own narrative, we are seeing it for the first time almost exclusively through the eyes of junior combatants.

Henry Keown-Boyd

ACKNOWLEDGEMENTS

Since I have been involved with Private Teigh's Journal for at least sixteen years many people have, often unwittingly, helped me. I apologize for unmentioned helpers. In no particular order I thank Graham Teigh, Private Teigh's grandson, who brought the diary into a history lesson, and his son-in-law, the late Mr Kenny, who gave me particulars from the Family Bible and other recollections: Philip Ziegler, whose *Omdurman* helped me understand the campaign, and who kindly corresponded over some biographical details: D. Bateman, for help with research at the Public Record Office: Jan Fretten, Bampton Library, for helping me find source material: Roy Barratt, for photography: Captain J. Lee, BEM, the Royal Lincolnshire Regimental Museum, for introducing me to Lieutenant Cox's diary and for much other help: Dr P. Boyden, National Army Museum, for much advice and suggesting a publisher: Henry Keown-Boyd, whose *A Good Dusting* inspired me to continue, who suggested illustrative material and offered help at all times. Tom Hartman read the manuscript and his many recommendations have been most valuable. Leo Cooper exercised extreme tact with an impatient author and nurtured me through a fascinating experience. Finally Graham Newman, who has kept my computer going, and Derrick Mason, who has endured non-stop progress reports on an idea which has finally become a published book.

The drawing of General Kitchener is reproduced by kind permission of the Marquess of Cholmondeley; the photograph of the Nile steamer was taken by Mrs Henry Keown-Boyd and is reproduced with her kind permission. Illustrations nos 7–16 are reproduced by permission of the Billie Love Historical Collection.

GLOSSARY

Ally Sloper: A sauce which took its name from a popular comic
    paper
Angoreeb: native bed
APD: Army Police Department
ASC: Army Service Corps, also known as Ally Sloper's Cavalry
AVD: Army Veterinary Department
Beasty/Bhisti: water carrier
BM: Brigade Major
BSO: Brigade Signals Officer
Dahabiah/dahabiyeh: a large passenger-carrying boat peculiar
    to the River Nile
Devil/dust devil: a moving sand-spout
Donga: A ravine or watercourse with steep sides
Fantassa: water container carried by camels
Friendlies: Tribesmen loyal to the British
GOC: General Officer Commanding
Gyassa: A sailing barge
Jaalins: Friendly tribe massacred by Mahmud in June, 1897
Jedahiya: Literally, 'Warriors of the Holy War'
jibah/jibber: coloured robe
Khor: A dry gully
OSD: Ordnance Survey Department
picquet: small body of troops on guard
PMC: President of the Messing Committee
PMO: Principal Medical Officer
QMS: Quartermaster Sergeant
rub: literally quarter (¼). A unit of the Mahdist army varying
    from battalion to brigade strength
Tukkle: A thatched hut
zariba: a defensive enclosure of thorn bushes

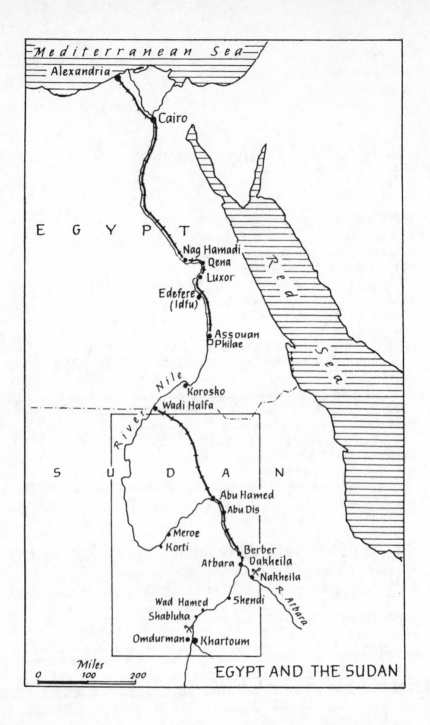

EGYPT AND THE SUDAN

x

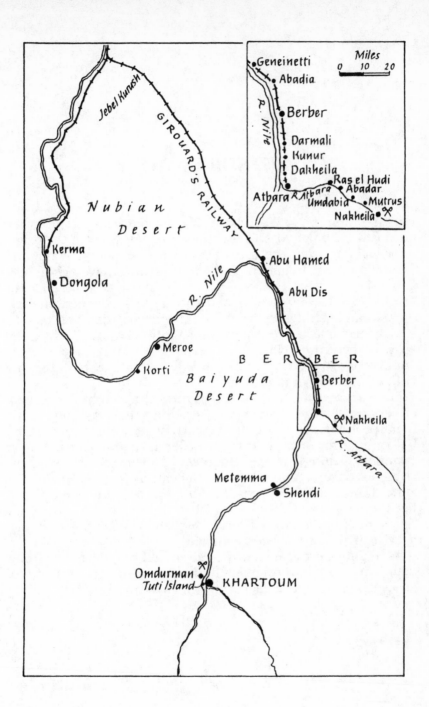

AUTHOR'S NOTE

This is mainly a book of extracts from diaries written either during a campaign or shortly afterwards. At times in the originals writing and spelling deteriorate, especially that of Lieutenant Cox. In general, where difficulties have arisen, the general sense has been followed. In extracts from Private Teigh's Journal, his own vocabulary has been retained, though occasional spelling errors, which are clearly copying errors, have been corrected and some punctuation has been added for ease of reading. Names, wherever possible, have been confirmed from Army Lists, and most ranks and initials of Officers are shown in the index.

Many extracts tend to use different spellings for place names, either because the writers were spelling them as they heard them pronounced, or because the transliteration from Arabic led to a different spelling. In order to avoid confusion, a common spelling has been adopted. The word *zariba*, a defensive enclosure of thorn bushes, appears in every conceivable variant; indeed Teigh spells it *zebera*. For convenience this has been standardized throughout. It is interesting to note that Teigh and Skinner always write Dervish, while the officers use dervish. This has not been changed.

As might be expected, entries are sometimes given the wrong date. This was a natural result of the circumstances at the time, and such entries have been retained as written.

OMDURMAN DIARIES 1898

Private George Teigh was a member of 'F' Company, the 1st Battalion, the Lincolnshire Regiment; Lieutenant Samuel FitzGibbon Cox was in 'B' Company of the same Battalion; both were stationed at the Citadel, Cairo. Lieutenant Ronald Forbes Meiklejohn was at Alexandria with the Royal Warwickshire Regiment. Corporal George Skinner was with the Medical Staff Corps, also at the Citadel.

Early in January, 1898, they received orders to move south towards the Sudan and each kept an account of the campaign.

George Teigh was the third child born to James and Letitia Teigh of Money Bridge in the parish of Pinchbeck, near Spalding, Lincolnshire, on 5 April, 1874. His parents had married in 1867. George was five years younger than his elder brother, and eventually eighteen years older than his youngest. His parents had nine children in all. His father was an agricultural labourer, who appears never to have left the area.

At the age of 18 years and 10 months, on 20 February, 1893, George took the 'Queen's Shilling', giving his trade as 'Labourer'. It is likely that he had walked to Spalding, where there was a depot of the Lincolnshire Regiment. Quickly transferred to Lincoln, he passed the necessary medical examination two days later, weighing in at 10 stone, only 5 feet 6 inches tall with a chest measurement of 36 inches, which with a good breath he could expand by a further 2 inches! His complexion was fair and his eyes hazel. Not unnaturally he was Church of England.

Until the end of January, 1895, he served in England, before being sent with the 1st Battalion to Malta. In February, 1897, the Battalion moved to Cairo, where it was stationed in the Citadel.

Samuel FitzGibbon Cox was born on 3 June, 1870, in Belfast, and joined the Militia on 10 December, 1887, aged seventeen. As a member of the Militia, which was the 'back door' to an army career, and a commission, he was attached to the 3rd Battalion, the Royal Warwickshire Regiment. On 28 June, 1890, he transferred as a 2nd Lieutenant to the Lincolnshire Regiment, becoming a lieutenant in 1892. On 28 September, 1895, he arrived in Malta, before moving on 4 February, 1897, to Egypt. His records show that his father was

Lieutenant-General J.B. Cox, who had been in the Indian Army and fought in the Afghan war. So the Army was very much in his blood.

Ronald Forbes Meiklejohn was born in 1876. His father was a Colonel in the Royal Horse Artillery, and he was sent to Rugby before entering the Army in 1896 to serve with the Royal Warwickshire Regiment, stationed by the beginning of 1898 at Alexandria.

George Skinner was older than the other three, being a thirty-year-old former teacher, serving with the Medical Staff Corps, soon to become the Royal Army Medical Corps. Born in 1867, he had lived in Kingston on Thames at Ingleley Cottage, Elm Road, with his father, before becoming a Pupil Teacher at St John's School in 1883, when he was sixteen. He remained there for four years, and then in 1889 joined the Medical Staff Corps at Aldershot. George Skinner was only just 5 feet 4 inches tall, of fresh complexion, with bluish-grey eyes and brown hair. He too was Church of England. He had served as a Private until 1896 when he was promoted to Lance Corporal and later Corporal, before being sent, in March, 1896, to Egypt.

* * *

The slave trade had originally caused Britain to take an interest in the Sudan, where it continued to flourish long after its abolition in the British Empire. Under a series of treaties the Khedives of Egypt ruled the Sudan and other areas to the south. This they did with considerable financial support from the European powers, principally Great Britain and France. By 1880 Egypt was, in effect, if not in name, under British rule. This led to pressure being put on the Khedives to suppress the slave trade between them and other Arab countries. This caused serious disturbances for Egypt in the Sudan, since it was economically damaging, and there was no suggestion in the Koran that it was unacceptable. The Soudanese Arabs were unified by the attempts to stop the trade, and the emergence of a focus for this came in the appearance of a Mahdi el Muntazer or Expected One, a phenomenon not unknown in Muslim countries.

The Mahdi, Mohamed Ahmed, claimed descent from the prophet, and many of his followers sincerely believed in his holiness. Others took the opportunity to jump on the bandwagon. Egyptian opposition to him was feeble, and "in under four years he had acquired a tenuous mastery over all but the extremities of the Sudan, an area of nearly one million square miles. He had killed or captured some forty thousand Egyptian troops. He had defied successfully the greatest power on earth, Great Britain, killed one of her national heroes and forced her soldiers, perhaps the finest in the world, to withdraw. Aided only by harsh climatic conditions, an inhospitable terrain and the natural fighting instincts of his followers, he had accomplished all this without military training, with few modern weapons and no outside allies. Furthermore, and perhaps even more astonishing, the precarious and ramshackle edifice which he had erected survived under a less charismatic successor for another thirteen years".[1]

After the death of General Charles Gordon at Khartoum in 1885 at the hands of the Mahdi, the British Government saw no immediate necessity to re-enter the Sudan. It was realized that militarily it was a difficult area, where troops could easily be overcome by heat, thirst and fear. In addition lines of communication were extremely difficult to establish and keep open. There was a requirement to make sure that Egypt was able to look after its own defence, which could be achieved by British support for the Egyptian Army, largely staffed by British Officers. In terms of public relations there could be no overt withdrawal from the region, since the failure to relieve Khartoum was seen as a national disaster. But there was no willingness to become involved in any action which would incur financial cost.

The Egyptian Army had been rebuilt by Sir Evelyn Wood, who was called the Sirdar, or Commander-in-Chief, and some successful joint British-Egyptian actions had bonded the two armies, both before and after Khartoum. The backbone of the Khedive's Egyptian army were black Soudanese troops, mostly former slaves, or descended from slaves. While these troops were difficult to train, when they were trained they became a fighting force of considerable strength.

Only five months after the death of Gordon, the Mahdi, who, on the withdrawal of the British armies, had become the absolute master of the Sudan, died. Just before his death he declared Khalifa Abdullah his successor. The Mahdi had bequeathed a position which could only be maintained over the numerous smaller groups,known collectively as the Dervishes, by the sword. For thirteen years the Khalifa used every device by which other Oriental rulers had bolstered a perilous sovereignty. Self-preservation was paramount, and all real or potential rivals were removed. Since Khartoum had been mostly destroyed, he set up his power base at Omdurman, only a short distance away and with the advantage of communication along the Nile. This capital housed the Mahdi's tomb in a square white building, surmounted by a hexagonal block, and crowned by a dome, in all eighty-five feet high. In time it became a holy shrine.

At first the Khalifa's attentions were directed to the south, toward Abyssinia; but in the early 1890s clashes between the Italians and the Dervishes began with raids into the new Italian colony of Eritrea. In 1893 and 1894 the Italians inflicted several defeats on the Dervishes, but then in 1896 suffered a disastrous defeat at Adowa on 1 March, 1896, which left them asking Egypt for help. The presence of another European power in the area necessitated some response from the

---

[1] Henry Keown-Boyd, *A Good Dusting*.

3

British government, however reluctant. Both the British and Egyptian governments knew that eventually they would have to go on to re-occupy Khartoum, but both were terrified by the possible costs. The campaign which was to follow was one of the most miserly campaigns ever initiated.

However, the control of the upper reaches of the Nile had a considerable, if not a paramount, bearing on Egypt, and when in 1896 the French, smarting under the feeling that Great Britain had stolen a march in influence over the Khedive, decided to lead a small military expedition to the Upper Nile and raise the Tricolor at Fashoda, British Ministers were forced to act. In March, 1896, it was decided that a limited campaign of reoccupation of the Sudan should be set in motion, in the name of the Khedive. The Province of Dongola, an area immediately to the south of Egypt around the Nile and the northern part of the Sudan, was to be reoccupied. This was a reluctant decision on the part of the British Government, and of Lord Cromer, British Agent and Consul General in Egypt. Cromer had spent many years putting the financial affairs of Egypt in order and was most reluctant to see his work undone by military extravagance. General Kitchener, his nominee as Sirdar in 1892, was a proven economizer, and so ideal to lead the expedition. By the end of 1897 Dongola Province was in the hands of the British, though nominally the Khedive, ruler of Egypt.

In January, 1898, General Kitchener decided it was time to mount a further expedition and to send troops up the Nile. The move was not entirely comfortable for those concerned, and was a mixture of train and boat. Private Teigh, Lieutenants Cox and Meiklejohn and Corporal Skinner were all ordered to the Front.

1st Battalion Lincolnshire Regt
Ordered to the Front 2/1/98

On the 2nd of January 1898 Two Companies to start
on the 4th at 7.15 pm that was B & F Companies
the remainder of the Battalion to follow on in a
few days time. We fell in on the Barrack square
at the time noted above had just shaken hands
with many of our comerades we was leaving
behind some of them for a few days and then
they will join us again others going to the
old country, altogether it was a splendid
sight and when we moved off you could
hear nothing but cheering amongst us all
the troops played us to the Station just before
starting through the City of Cairo Major
Simpson who was in charge halted us and said
he was proud to be in charge of the first
body of British troops up the Nile he would
be pleased if we would keep a little quite
going through the city. So his orders were
obeyed untill we got to a large English Hotel
called Shepherds and there was a lot of tourists
there who cheered us so we had to return
the compliment of course we broke the order
given to us by Major Simpson but we
could not help it on hearing good old English
voices this was close to the Railway Station as
we were marching along the platform large
crowds of English were there shaking hands with
us all and telling us to give the Dervishes a
good shaking up as we got seated in the

1

ORDERED TO THE FRONT

2ND JANUARY 1898:

Teigh: Two Companies to start on the 4th at 7.15 pm, that was 'B' and 'F' Companies, the remainder of the Battalion to follow on in a few days time. We fell in on the Barrack Square at the time noted above; had just shaken hands with many of our comrades we were leaving behind, some of them for a few days and then they will join us again, others going to the 'Old Country'. Altogether it was a splendid sight and when we moved off you could hear nothing but cheering amongst us. All the drums played us to the station.

Just before starting through the city of Cairo, Major Simpson,[1] who was in charge, halted us and said he was proud to be in charge of the first British troops up the Nile. He would be pleased if we would keep a little quiet going through the city. So his orders were obeyed, until we got to a large English hotel called Shepherds [*sic*], and there was a lot of tourists there, who cheered us and so we had to return the compliment of course. We broke the order given to us by Major Simpson, but we could not help it, hearing good old English voices. This was close to the Railway Station. As we were marching along the platform, large crowds of English were there shaking hands with us all, and telling us to give the Dervishes a good shaking up. As we got seated in the train, the General came along and we cheered him. As we were shifting off the Drums started playing 'Auld acquaintance be forgot' and so on. It was pretty dark as we left the station. I was fortunate enough to get along with my comrades, which I like very much. The great attraction was a very small boy on the Drums, who

---

[1] Simpson, Charles Rudyard: attached Lincolnshire Regiment 1874; Major 1893; 2 i/c 1st Battalion, 1896; Brevet Lt-Col, 1898; later 1900 to Middlesex Regiment; General, 1908.

belongs to my Company. He is the pride of the Regiment. He gave us a few tunes on his flute and a few bugle marches.

After that we had a little singing and we all began to feel a little sleepy, but unable to get a sleep owing to being so closely packed up. I was in a corner leaning against the back of the carriage and my comrade by my side was resting his head against me. He was very soon off to sleep. I think I got about 2 hours' sleep. When I woke up, I was stiff and tired. I tried to ease myself without disturbing my comrade, but do what I could, I could not get no rest in such a cramped position. At last the morning came and we were still steaming along in the train.

Cox: Forrest stopped me and said that we were off up the Nile. I said rot!

3RD JANUARY

Cox: Rumours confirmed; orders arrived for us to proceed up the Nile.

4TH JANUARY

Cox: 'B' and 'F' Companies started today. Doctors would not let me go owing to poisoned fingers, the result of sores got out shooting at Xmas.

Meiklejohn: We were all sitting in the Mess at Mustapha Pasha barracks, Ramleh, Alexandria, on New Year's Eve, when someone dashed in excitedly, saying, "Have you heard the latest? We are off to the front in a week". There was wild confusion and excitement for a few minutes, then we settled down to discuss things more quietly. Two days later we heard that we were to start on Sunday, 9th January, so we had plenty to do, mobilizing, selling ponies, getting kit, paying farewell calls, etc.

7TH JANUARY

Skinner: Left Cairo by train at 11 pm. A great many of the visitors, as well as the native population, was at the station to see us off. . . . The bands of the 21st Lancers and Cameron Highlanders were formed up on the platform and played us out of the station with tunes that brought back to us all memories of old England and friends.

5TH JANUARY

Teigh: About 9 am the train stopped at Maraut and we got out here for five minutes, and were very glad to ease ourselves. I bought one piastre of oranges and some I gave away, the remainder I ate myself. We got into the train and we were soon off again. We passed several small stations too numerous to mention. We arrived at the end of the line (Nagh Hamadi) about 2 pm, where we had to carry our arms and kit bags on to the small barges. Then we had the ammunition and baggage to carry on board. As soon as everything was on, we were attached to a Nile paddle boat and started off at 3.30. Shortly afterwards we were issued out with a small portion of cooked meat and we had a little bread in our haversacks that we got before leaving Barracks, and it went down very dry. That was the first that we had to eat since leaving Barracks, but we had to be content. We had our blankets thrown all over the deck and we had to lay down the best we could. We were packed worse than cattle. We got to Kenat [Qena] at 10 pm and stopped there for the night.

Cox: Sat tight, rather sick about fingers, spreading up my arm. On board with us Dr Adamson and Braddell, Major Friend R.E., Smith A.V.D., Officer O.S.D., Officer A.S.C. (don't know their names yet), Smith A.P.D.

6TH JANUARY

Teigh: We went on shore and Major Simpson informed us that we were going for a run along the Kenat road, where our Regiment came during the engagement with Napoleon Bonaparte in the year 1801. Before embarking on the barges again, we did physical drill at 10 am. We embarked and passed some splendid scenery as we sailed along. The banks were well cultivated and there were high hills on each side. About 10 pm we arrived at Luxor and disembarked for an hour. There were

9

the ruins of a very big place just where we landed. We had a walk for exercise. There was a village here which Major Simpson led us through and found a good beer shop so any one that wished for any could buy it. But no lemonade could be bought anywhere. The price for the beer was 5 piastres a bottle. That is ½d in English money for a pint bottle. We embarked again at 11 pm and sailed all night.

Cox: Sat tight and packed all the morning, feeling generally seedy. Afternoon went out and did all my shopping. Couldn't get half the things I wanted, all warlike stores having been bought up. Doctors said I could go tomorrow – much pleased!

7TH JANUARY

Teigh: About 6 am we passed another large village, which is called Matana. All along the banks the land was cultivated, chiefly sugar canes and some parts were very paddy. Lots of natives were working along the banks of the Nile, partly naked, only just a little covering around their loins. We passed a couple of Cook's pleasure boats making their way up the Nile. Of course we had several duties to do on board, and it was my turn for guard, which was over the ammunition and stores, but these duties were easy on board. About 3.30 pm we passed a great deal of date trees and a lot of natives on the banks cheered as we went past them. At 4 pm we arrived at Edefere, where the two companies went ashore and I was fortunate to be on shore with them. The Major took us to a very ancient building, which was called some gate. I remember he told us it was built 4 thousand years before Christ. There were some wonderful large figures upon the walls. The Cook's pleasure boat was staying at Edefere, so we had a chance to talk to the tourists on shore. It was exciting when we arrived back again to the boat. Policemen were there with large whips keeping the natives off our boats.

There were two water wheels, home-made, drawing water from the Nile to keep the land in a state of cultivation. They work by oxen and a native driving behind. Quite ancient they seemed. We remained on shore about an hour. The Drummers played all the way there and back.

Well then, when we got back, it was bedtime and we seemed somewhat tired and we were soon asleep; but I could not rest and I kept having a wink now and again. I did not feel as though I had been to sleep but a few minutes when the bugler on the steamer sounded Reveille. So I got up and had a wash, and I felt somewhat sleepy the remainder of the day.

Cox: Regiment marched out of Citadel at 8.15. Tremendous reception passing Shepheard's, ladies in evening dress, waving handkerchiefs. 21st [Lancers] and 79th [Cameron Highlanders] bands playing – only 2 men drunk. Never seen such a sight, men cheering, . . . the station absolutely packed with the elite of society, much weeping and gritting of teeth. 21st Officers handed round cigars and champagne in silver cups, people seem to be much upset at our leaving. Personally, never knew how damn popular I was before!! Trains left at 10.30 pm amidst absolute howls from everyone. Adamson our doctor to stop with us throughout. 18 hours train journey in front of us. 5 officers in our carriage. No dinner tonight but got some stuff from the Club.

Skinner: The railway journey was a very long and tedious one, the dust flying up very thick, everyone looking more like niggers in the morning than anything else, and to help matters to make us more comfortable we were packed like sardines in a box, almost unable to move, so sleep was therefore almost impossible. Our small party had supplied ourselves with a supply of whisky.

8TH JANUARY

Teigh: I was upon the deck as usual and it was a very nice sight to gaze along the banks of this part of the Nile. When we came to another part called Assouan we halted. At 10.20 the guard had to get out of the boat and look after the luggage. Whilst we were taking if off the boat and putting it on the train, our cooks got dinner ready for us. This is where we left our English friends and the Cook's steamer sailed away up the Nile. But before they left us there was an English Lady who gave the Major 2 pounds to distribute between the men of the 2 Companies in refreshments. While we were at dinner a lot of convicts came. I finished loading our train and by 2.30 the train was all loaded and started about 3 pm. For about 2 miles the ground was nice and green with corn just coming up nicely. A little further on there was an old 1882 graveyard, and in it was a large cross. On the right a small village with about 500 camels; and about 100 native women turned out to cheer us as we passed by and making a great noise with their mouths. The country was very rocky. After this we neared the first cataract, but when we got there it was a splendid sight. The rocks were built in some nice shapes. When we got here, we landed just alongside of the boat. There were another 200 convicts here to help us remove the great quantity of stores we had with us upon the train. But our Major said they could let them go back as it would do us good to do a bit of work, and so we did, for we got a good load on here. We received a different lot of barges. The ones we formerly had were Cook's, but these belonged to the Egyptian Government. We had one on each side of the steamer, which was a curious make. The paddle wheel was behind. We had more room on these boats than we had at first. We were ready to start at 9 pm, but did not start till 10. It was a nice moonlight night. We had not got far before I was in bed and I had the best night's rest that I have had during the voyage. I woke up with the sounding of the bugle at 7 am.

Cox: Got to Naja-Meli [Nagh Hamadi] at 3.30 pm and detrained and embarked at once in two of Cook's steamers each towing two barges. Everybody very comfortable but men rather squashed. Cook running the officers for 8/- a day inclusive of everything. Flotilla started at 7.30 by moonlight. Cook's steamer passed us full of tourists – more weeping! Most curious scenery, rather pretty in places, established signals between the boats. Tied up at 10.30.

Skinner: The messing good, in fact the vegetables we were getting were far superior to what we had been used to in Cairo. Our rations here consisted of 1lb. of bread, 1lb. of fresh meat mostly goat, ½lb. of onions, 1lb. of potatoes, ½oz. tea, 2ozs. sugar, ½oz. salt, $^{1}/_{36}$ oz. of pepper.

9TH JANUARY

Teigh: I could see nothing but hills on either side, about 100 feet high. About 9 am we met one of Cook's steamers full of English tourists, who cheered us as we passed and we gave them a hearty cheer in return. We got the order for church at 10 and the officers Commanding Companies read a little to us and then we sang three hymns accompanied by the drums playing their fifes, and then we finished up singing the Queen. I may say that there were no distinctions between the different Religions. We all went to the same. There was no clergyman on board. The Major afterwards came round to see if we were alright. We passed a few mud villages on our right and also the Gavian hills. On our left there was a lot of trees and green corn. Just here I see a pair of book cap slippers go overboard and was soon out of sight. It was very nice all the way along. Just then the first post sounded, so we turned into bed. We got the order to parade in drill order the next morning at Korosko. There is much I could say concerning Korosko, but time will not permit me. It used to be one of the greatest places of importance for the tourists. Wonderful history it holds and this is where the Equator runs, so you may be sure it is wonderful hot here.[1]

Cox: Started again at 6 am and tied up for half an hour at 9 am to issue rations. Men all appear happy but beastly grimy – nobody seems to know what our destination is – 6th [Royal Warwickshires] ought to start today and 79th [2 Bn. Queen's Own Cameron Highlanders] next Friday. Just been into the saloon and found it full of maps to be issued to us. Spent afternoon reading Scallywag sent to me by mother. Whist after dinner, tidied up at 11 pm and turned in.

Meiklejohn: We fell in [at Alexandria] at 10 am. I am very lucky, since, being the junior 2nd Lieutenant, I should really have been left. Also I have a fairly nasty go of jaundice (from a chill), but, though my eyes are bright yellow, I got through the Medical exam and got treatment from a civilian doctor. I did not dare go to the M.O.!
    We wore khaki breeches, red coats, and Sam Browne belts. We are taking the red coats with us, as the dervishes have learnt to respect the "thin red line" and refer to us as the "fighting red Inglesee". The band played us to the station where an immense crowd had collected to see us off. . . . Uncle Gus gave me a

---

[1]   He may have meant the Tropic of Cancer. Korosko is 22.5°N.

splendid hamper with wines, Cherry Brandy, etc. This I put aside, as I can't eat much except plain food.

We left about 7 pm and had a most unpleasant night in the train. It was bitterly cold, and we had no rugs, only greatcoats. A van caught fire during the night, but was promptly extinguished.

10TH JANUARY

Teigh: The boat got there earlier than it was expected, so a few men were ordered out of bed to get two days' rations and some wood. I was one of the party but we had not the chance to see much. There was a nice village on the left. There were two English graves, 1801, and the scenery along here was grand. One of the Medical Officers on board here, Dr Carr, gave us instructions how to use the field dressing, which we had in our pocket. There is one of them in the khaki jacket on purpose to just fit the parcel in, and he took one to pieces and showed us how they were used.

Further on after that we got issued with half a stick of tobacco each. Then we gathered together for a nice smoke and chat, which was profitable to us all. We were warned to be careful about the sand banks about here, as they were too numerous. At 4 pm we ran aground on a sand bank, but we got off again very quick.

Cox: Ripping good night. Woke up at 7.30 and found that we had tied up at Luxor. Stopped about 2 hours to take in provisions and issue rations. Most interesting place Luxor, wonderful temple close to river, went over it, statues and hieroglyphics, saw Thebes in the distance. Some half doz. tourist dahabiahs tied up alongside. Wish we had more time to do the sights. Scenery getting more mountainous. Fingers much better, got rid of one of the bandages. Storks and all sorts of strange birds appearing on the banks. We had great revolver practice before lunch all forming up on the port side and shooting at bottles thrown over. Tied up for half an hour about 2, about 6 fellows took their guns out, had quite a go at pigeons of which there were hundreds, but rather startled the villagers, think they must have thought we were going to attack them. Glorious moonlight night, looks beautiful on

14

the water, marked increase in the temperature. Turned in at 10.30.

Meiklejohn: We reached Nagh Hamadi on the Nile at 10 am and detrained. Then embarked on the Cook's tourist steamer *Hatasoo*. A very strenuous day, unloading and loading all the baggage and stores. The *Hatasoo* is a most ancient and out-of-date looking craft, and had two barges full of men alongside to tow up stream. We heard she had been out of commission for some months, and used as a landing stage! Cockburn (my Major) and I were just sitting down to our supper (we had Company messes) when somebody remarked that we were going DOWN stream! To our surprise we saw this was so. Then the Captain came and said that the engines would not work so we were drifting with the current. We also noticed with some uneasiness that we were going straight into the Nagh Hamadi railway bridge and must be overturned if we struck it! Major Cockburn cheerily remarked that if we were all going down we might as well have a good supper first and finish my hamper, and that probably I need not worry about my jaundice. . . . The anchors were got out, but could not hold and we got perilously near the bridge. The men in the barges very gallantly cut them loose. One was rescued by a small boat taking a rope to the shore: the other very luckily brought up against one of the spans of the bridge without upsetting. Our anchors finally caught on some firmer ground and held, but we did not know if this would last. In addition we sprung two leaks, and the Captain, hardly a cheery optimist, remarked that it would be lucky if we remained afloat till the morning. Major Etheridge drily commented that the Khalifa would be really pleased if he could see us. A native fireman got his arm in the engines and dashed on deck moaning and yelling and covered with blood. We undid our boots ready to swim for it if necessary, and slept in our clothes. A weird and unpleasant night, and we did not bless Thomas Cook.

11TH JANUARY

Teigh: We got to Wadi Halfa about 11 am. This is the garrison for the Egyptian Army. As we neared the landing stage the drums played us a few tunes and, as we landed, there was cheering and shaking hands, both by Officers and men, by

15

Sergeants and Officers that had left us and joined the Egyptian Army Staff. How pleased they seemed to hear of the British Brigade coming to help them in the taking of Khartoum.

Then we had about 2 hours of hard work unloading our stores. When the work was completed, we marched into Wadi Halfa and formed up in line with fixed bayonets. Just then General Kitchener was in sight. As he got near us, the Major in charge gave the command, "British troops shoulder arms", and the General inspected us. He is a well built, smart looking soldier; a man that you could see has had to rough it. He was very well pleased with us. We were then marched to the mud huts, called Barrackrooms. Then the Major came around and said we had worked very hard and he would get us some minerals [soft drinks] and he did so very soon. Then we had dinner. Of course it was a bit rough, cooked in a sort of a copper. That was about 2 pm, and we had to shift at 3 pm. We had but a few yards to go to the train. We had to wait 2 hours and then we had to get into the trucks, similar to coal trucks in England, 30 men in each truck and we were very much crushed up. General Kitchener came along and our Major shouted 3 cheers for the Sirdar and we gave him 3 hearty cheers and then we moved off.

We had a lot of blankets thrown into the trucks. We started at 5 pm and we all laid down but could not get much rest, as there was not room to turn oneself round. We halted 130 miles from Wadi Halfa in the morning, 7.30 am.

Cox: Going ahead when I woke up. Adamson and Marsh called out of breakfast, they couldn't open the cabin belonging to Orderly Room Sgt Haines, and on bursting in found him on the floor with his throat cut, dead, cabin swamped with blood, no apparent reason; inquest at once, suicide, temporary insanity – great nuisance to Marsh being a young Adjutant and stranded thus – burial tonight at 10.30 pm anywhere we happen to tie up – C.O. in a hell of a rage – naturally. Passed tourist steamer and two private dahabiahs with English people on board – more tears! Funeral took place at 10.30, beastly weird by moonlight, tourists couldn't understand what was going on until stretcher and blanket appeared – then they retired. C.O. officiated. Turned in at 11 pm. Wrote home.

Skinner: At 6 am I was called to a cabin in the aft part of the boat occupied by Sgt Haines of the Lincolns, who was found on the floor with his throat cut from ear to ear, severing the head almost from the body; it was evidently done with his own razor, as it was found firmly grasped in his right hand; he had evidently done it over night, as he was quite cold and the blood almost dry. We sewed his body up in a blanket . . . parts of the service were read over by Colonel Verner, commanding the regiment.

12TH JANUARY

Teigh: We made a big fire and had some tea. As soon as we had had our breakfasts, we got into the trucks again for another long and dreary ride. But me and one of my comrades got sat down in a corner and had a nice smoke and chat to ourselves, as there was nothing to look at only desert. But some places we could see skeletons, but I thought they might be camel bones scattered about.

We got to Abu Hamed about 3.30 pm, the place where there was a big fight about September, 1897. This is 231 miles from Wadi Halfa. About 1 mile further up we passed the grave of Lieut. Fitzclarence and Captain Sydney on our left, who got killed at the Engagement here.[1] We went on 19 more miles to camp [Gurheish] and the cooks made dinner while we unloaded the trucks. By the time we got done, dinner was ready, that was 5.30 pm. We could not see what we were eating, but we were very hungry, so we did not feel at all particular, but the meat was as tough as a piece of leather. There was some lemonade to be obtained here and I bought some and me and my comrades enjoyed it heartily. We brought it from Wadi Halfa with us. Then we had a job to find our tents it was so dark and about a mile from the line. But we arrived there at last. Me and my comrades managed to get together again. We received a good night rest.

---

[1] At the Battle of Abu Hamed on 7 August, 1897, which had been part of the occupation of Dongola and a forerunner to the Omdurman campaign, the 10th Soudanese had come under heavy fire and the C.O., Major Sidney, and Lieutenant Edward Fitzclarence of the Dorsets had been killed. They were the only two British Officers to be killed directly under fire in the campaign of reconquest [1896–98]. Fitzclarence was a reputed great-grandson of King William IV.

17

Cox: Awoke up this morn at 5.30. Had to tie up to put the vet on board the horse barge astern – a fever of sorts broken out amongst them. Hachett Thompson's died last night and had to be put ashore, Simpson's also sick. We got to Assouan at 3.30, disembarked and entrained on a luggage train, men sitting on top of luggage, and went round the cataract where we embarked in 3 stern wheelers and 8 barges in the dark – confusion pretty considerable. However, we have left baggage till tomorrow morning. No more decent grub, we started bully beef tonight. Heard tonight that we go straight on to railhead. That means bivouacking for a good time. Saw one last white fish tonight at Assouan. Country much wilder and dervish like. Going to turn in at 10.30.

13TH JANUARY

Teigh: Reveille sounded at 6.30 am. We had a bathing parade at 7 o'clock. Two or three good swimmers were told off as bathing picquet to look after anyone who caught the cramp or was not able to swim very well, or in case anyone was carried away with the tide, for it was very strong here. I ventured in the water as usual and had a swim out, and when returning to get dressed, I heard some one shout out that a man had gone down. There were a lot trying to save him, but his heart utterly failed and he was gone. I made for the spot, but I was only just in time to see the top of his head. There was much diving, but all in vain. He could not be found. He was only about 8 yards from the bank. Lieutenant Peters, who is an officer of my company, is the tallest man in the Regiment, and he undressed and tried to bottom it, but he could not. Two or three men were told off to watch for the body, being relieved by one another every two hours until the body came to the top. The man's name was Simcoates (3532). There were native divers sent for, and they dived and tried to get him with nets, but it was all no use. It was very warm sitting on the banks of the Nile all day watching for the man's body.

Cox: Reveille went at 5 am, light at 6. Turned out men to unload and ship baggage. Officers split up amongst the three steamers, only 2 doctors and paymaster on board with us now. Scenery rugged. Isle of Philae, one of the best sights I've seen, most beautiful ruins and very picturesque. C.O.'s horse left behind sick with fever, likewise Simpson's, vet says he won't live; all the English horses going to the dead, Arabs all right. Getting decidedly hot and smelly as we on the steamer are hemmed in by men on 4 barges alongside, also 32 mules and 5 horses. Men behaving excellently. Have started a beard! Steamers going day and night, we passed through a small cataract about 9 pm and went ashore three times but no damage. Feeding on rations now but got a native as mess cook, who turns out quite a respectable dinner. Got my whisky sneaked and smoked my last cigarette for some time to come. I expect to bed 10.15.

14TH JANUARY

Teigh: While on picquet at 5 pm we had a parade for exercise in field operations and we had it rather stiff. Our shirts were wet through with sweat.

Cox: Nothing exciting today, had some more revolver practice at birds on the bank. Tied up at 10 am to issue rations. Other boats out of sight, much quicker than we are. Rather exercised in my mind about brigade signaller. Should have brought a horse up with me. Expect to get to Korosko midnight tonight. Turned in at 10 pm.

15TH JANUARY

Teigh: Still on picquet. They held an inquest during the day.

Cox: Another dull day – been ashore twice – tied up Korosko at midnight only for a few minutes to take on rations. Spent all the morn shooting at birds with rook rifles and revolvers – total bag nil! Expect to reach Wadi Halfa tomorrow at 9 am. Wrote home.

16TH JANUARY

Teigh: I was on guard. I mounted at 9 am and was 3rd relief. Our detachment had an open air service. A few hymns were sung and, all over, my guard passed away all right. But it was very cold at night and hot during the day.

Cox: Arrived at Wadi Halfa at 9 am. Found Sirdar and staff. Unloaded ships and left with two companies by train, officers in carriages, men in trucks. Beastly cold at night. Fairly in the desert, saw some sand grouse and few gazelle. Getting rather fed up with travelling. Toothache.

17TH JANUARY

Teigh: While our two Companies were down bathing, they saw the drowned man floating on the top of the water. So Pte. Wilcox of my company, 'F', went in and fetched him ashore. He was wrapped in a blanket and carried under a tree close to the camp. At dinner time our company escorted him to the grave. I was one of the firing party, but we did not use any ammunition. Our Captain read the burial service, as we have not got a clergyman with us. We sang a hymn and then were dismissed.

Just then the Battalion arrived and we had plenty of work to do.[1] We had to pitch a fresh camp nearer the line. We had all our things to shift. I had just got settled down when I came across James Williams and a few more comrades. We had a chat together and we went down the Nile for a wash and some of them told us about the sad news of the Orderly Room Sergeant, who had cut his throat one night in his bunk, and was buried on the right side of the Nile. This was another of my Company. We had a walk for a short time and then we felt inclined for a rest, so we bid each other good night.

Cox: Passed Abu Hamed about 10 am, saw Sidney's and Fitzclarence's graves. Arrived here, (Gurheish) railhead about 22 miles south of Abu Hamed, found Egyptian cavalry and 1 battery camped near. Pitched camp, mountain service tents, 2 officers in one tent, Boxer my companion. River about ½ mile off. Open desert beastly cold at night – got cold in my jaw, all

---

[1]   This would have been the arrival of Cox and Skinner.

my teeth aching. Hear we stop here for a fortnight, then shift on with the railway. Am afraid we are in for two or three months "sitting tight" with nothing to do. Turned in at 8 pm with infernal toothache.

Skinner: We pitched our hospital on high ground close to the Nile, the Regiment being on our left front. On the same evening of our arrival here a funeral took place of Pte. Simcoates 'B' Coy, Lincolns. After this the usual routine of camp life began in earnest.

18TH JANUARY

Teigh: At 6.30 am Reveille sounded. The Battalion paraded under the Officer Commanding at 10 am. He gave us a lecture and warned us about the women in this area, but it is not necessary for I never saw any here. He also said that we would have a shift towards the front as soon as the railway was put down. They are very hard at it now. He said that he was pleased that the Regiment had worked very hard. Then he dismissed the parade.

Then some men went out and trimmed up Simcoates' grave with large stones, so that the natives could not shift them to interfere with the corpse. For these people would do anything for a blanket.

In the afternoon we did our washing and after that I wrote a letter home. At night we were issued with two pieces of white linen to put on the sides of our helmets. The Lincolns was the white, the Warwicks red, and the Camerons blue. This is so they can distinguish the different Regiments at a distance.

Cox: Up at 7.30 am. Damn busy day, general settling down and wood cutting fatigues. Our mess is beastly cramped and won't hold us all, so it's a case of first come first served. My teeth won't let me eat. We are very lucky each officer having a tent each. Mine is quite comfortable considering, with all the signalling store panniers as tables. Can't get any ammunition for my rifle, and can't get hold of a horse as charger, d—d fool not to have brought one up.

19TH JANUARY

Teigh: We had to parade early to wash our feet and face. It was very cold in the morning, but it always gets hot in the daytime. We got two loaves of bread to each tent. That was to ten men, as we were bound to be satisfied.

Cox: Up at 7.30 am. Whole holiday. Another tent added to the mess, which makes things much more comfortable. Jaw much better thank GAUDE. Spent most of the day fishing with Adamson with no result. Nile 'Salmon' evidently don't think much of British rations.

20TH JANUARY

Teigh: We had Commanding Officer's parade. He told us what he expected. The Warwickshire Regiment came up today and would like us to join them in their work. So I was put on fatigue making a latrine for them, and that lasted till dinner time. After dinner they arrived and we unloaded the waggons for them and we were soon settled down. The Warwickshires laid on our left facing the line. I then went for a wash. After I came in I had a read and then we had a chat till bed time and I didn't feel as though I'd rest much.

Cox: Up at 7.30 am. Jaw a bit better. No parade, general fixing up of camp. 6 Comps. of the Warwicks arrived at 2.30 pm. Also our post with no letters for me! except a beastly bill from Shepheard's. To bed early with the blues.

Mountain Service Tent. 8 Men — 2 Officers.

Meiklejohn: We reached the railhead (Gurheish) at Abu Hamed at 3 pm where we found the Lincolnshire Regiment encamped. Pitched tents and had tea with them. I managed to get an angoreeb for 10 piastres (2/-).

GENERALS, GUNS AND BOOTS

Horatio Herbert Kitchener was born in 1850 in County Kerry, Ireland, the son of Henry and Frances Kitchener. His father had been a Lieutenant-Colonel in the Worcestershire Regiment, but overseas service did not suit his wife and he settled in Ireland. Herbert decided on an army career at an early age, but preferred the Royal Engineers to the Cavalry, which his father wished. He had been educated by tutors, and a cousin complained that "He had never known a boy more totally devoid of any groundwork of education". His mother died when he was fourteen and he spent a short time at a school in Switzerland before entering the Royal Academy, Woolwich, in 1868.

Two years later he passed out and was posted to the School of Military Engineering, before seeing service in Egypt and becoming fluent in Arabic. During the next fourteen years he saw varied service in the Eastern Mediterranean, before becoming a Major in the Egyptian Army, which was mainly commanded by British Officers. Kitchener never married and found fulfilment in his work, allowing no distractions. This placed him at an advantage with his fellow officers, but did not always bring popularity.

During General Wolseley's expedition to relieve Gordon at Khartoum, Major Kitchener did much useful work, but the result was a failure. Thereafter he was appointed first Adjutant-General of the Egyptian Army and then in 1892 Sirdar or Commander-in-Chief with the rank of Major-General, although by seniority he should not have been considered; the reaction in Cairo was one of dismay and disgust.

"Few major figures of the epoch can have been less prepossessing than Kitchener. This dour, lowering figure seemed unable to relax or to establish true friendship with any human being, to show feeling or derive pleasure from any pursuit outside his chosen profession. Arrogant with his inferiors, uneasy with his peers; he was obsequious only with those who might advance his career, and even here his churlishness sometimes got the better of discretion. His physical appearance – the coarse, beefy face; heavy, empurpled jowls; glazed, rolling eyes; opulent yet disciplined moustache – seemed somehow to reflect his character; strong, brutish, inflexible. 'He may be a general, but never a gentleman,' wrote Churchill to his mother, and if the word 'gentleman' be taken to assume some sensitivity to and respect for the feelings of others, then the stricture was wholly justified."[1]

General William Forbes Gatacre, who was to command the British Brigade, and later the British Division was born in 1843. His father, always known as 'The Squire', lived at Gatacre in Shropshire. In 1860 he entered the Royal Military College, Sandhurst, and without much distinction left to join the 77th Foot, later the Middlesex Regiment.

For over thirty-five years William Gatacre saw service in India, except for a short period when he was an instructor in surveying at the Royal Military College, Sandhurst, returning in late 1897 to take command of a Brigade at Aldershot. During the New Year break the War Office sent a telegram to Aldershot which ran:

> "Please send General Gatacre and Major Snow, Brigade Major, here as soon as possible; may be wanted for foreign service."

In less than two days Gatacre had left for Egypt. He reached Wadi Halfa on 28 January, 1898, and there met the Sirdar for the first time. Gatacre was universally unpopular and, though respected, had a number of enemies. Kitchener, however, got on well with him. "He was an electric-saw man – rasping, fretting, perpetually active – whose ambition was to do every job in the Brigade himself. From an indecently early dawn until late at night his spare, wiry form was everywhere, nagging, interfering, supervising every facet of the daily life of an army on the move. The men called him 'General Back-acher', but recognized that his activities were generously benevolent and on the whole thought well of him. The officers called him 'Fatacre', bitterly resented his inability to let them get on with their jobs in their own way and considered him a tactless and aggravating bounder. Kitchener appreciated him. He liked a subordinate who would not interfere in the higher strategy or expect a large share of the glory, he respected industry and efficiency and did not care twopence for the injured sensibilities of his officers. Indeed, on the whole, he probably thought that their sensibilities were the better for being outraged: a complacent officer was well on the way to being an idle and an inefficient one."[2] Whatever else the men may have thought of Gatacre, his decision to make the expedition teetotal was unpopular, and brewing and drinking tea became an important task, frequently recorded by Private Teigh.

During the campaign that was to follow many problems arose from the quality of the boots issued. It was being conducted on an exceptionally small budget, and supplies were never of the best. It will be seen that Teigh was later to be without boots for several days, and then

[1] Philip Ziegler, *Omdurman*.
[2] ibid

obtained a pair from someone in hospital. W.H. Steevens, the Correspondent of the *Daily Mail*, reported that, "The brigade had only been up river about a month. We have been campaigning in the Sudan off and on for over fourteen years; we might have discovered its little peculiarities by now. The Egyptian army uses a riveted boot; the boots of the British boys were expected to march in had not even a toe-cap. So that when the battalions and a battery arrived at Berber hundreds of men were barefoot: the soles peeled off and instead of a solid double sole revealed a layer of shoddy packing sandwiched between two thin slices of leather. It is always the same story; knavery and slackness strangling the best efforts of the British soldier."

The issue was raised in Parliament, and, in respect of the reply given by the War Office, Steevens wrote: "It is a strange sort of answer to say that a military boot is a very good boot only you mustn't march in it." The soldiers suggested that they were soled with cardboard!

A second equipment problem arose from the rifles and bullets issued. The army had been equipped with Lee-Metford .303s, but the bullets issued were not as effective as the generals had hoped. Gatacre wrote:

"The present-shaped bullet .303 Lee-Metford rifle has little stopping power. Well, we have this class of ammunition, so I am altering the shape of the bullet to that of the Dum-Dum bullet, which has a rounded point. I do this by filing the point off. Before I left Cairo I provided four hundred files and small gauges to test the length of the altered bullet, and daily we have 2,800 men engaged on this work. I borrowed fifty railway rails and mounted them flat side uppermost, to form anvils on which to file. We have a portion of men unpacking, and another portion packing, so that the same men are always at the same work. The men are getting very sharp at it; it would make a capital picture. . . . The men are working very well; we have no drink, and therefore no crime or sickness. I am getting on well with altering the ammunition. We have 3,000,000 rounds to alter, but are making good progress, altering 80,000 rounds per day."[1] Fortunately, more effective bullets were issued later.

The Generals also came to rely much on the Maxim machine guns. Hiram S. Maxim, an American, had invented a machine gun and tested it in 1884. It was not immediately adopted as it was thought, at £5 per minute, to be too expensive. There was also some confusion as to whether it was an infantry or artillery weapon. As late as 1894 General John Adye, an artillery officer, had said that machine guns 'had not, in my opinion, much future in a campaign against a modern army' and that they 'would add considerably to the impedimenta of troops in the field.' They were water-cooled .303 calibre, weighing

---

[1] *General Gatacre 1843–1906*, B. Gatacre.

26

40lbs, and firing 600 rounds per minute. Much destruction was to be caused to the Dervishes by these guns.

These were the Generals whom Private Teigh, Lieutenant Cox and the British Brigade were to serve under, with boots in which they could not march and bullets which were ineffective.

2

WAITING TO ADVANCE

21ST JANUARY

Teigh: We had a big parade across the desert for exercise in field drill.

Cox: Parade at 9 am. Always to be at 9 am to get men fit and to practise 'dervish' tactics. Bathing parades daily at 7 am, whole battalion double down to river, bathe and back again. Tried fishing again this afternoon with Adamson, no result, but had rather fun washing for gold, lots of it in the sand on river banks but not enough to make it pay. To bed at 10 pm.

22ND JANUARY

Teigh: Paraded as usual, but on returning to Camp it was very hot, and the men were all of a sweat. The Commanding Officer halted us and told us not to drink much water for it would harm us. It was a pretty hard job to get a drink but there was soon a party sent to the Nile to fetch some water. After dinner I went to the Nile and when I was a coming back my Company's call sounded for pay, and I was paid out 50 piastres. That was 8s 5d I have had this month. Then we assembled for a chat till bedtime.

Cox: Decidedly warmer today, fellows' complexion beginning to hover between a chestnut and a boiled lobster, and all faces infernally sore, shaving tortuous. Very sweaty parade for three hours in the morning. Slept in afternoon and had a tub. Walked over to Gyppy [Egyptian] lines with Plunkett in the evening and got some Sudan stamps. To bed at 10 pm.

23RD JANUARY

Teigh: Parade for bathing at 7 am this morning. I chanced a swim. We have to double down to the Nile and back every morning. This gives us a good appetite for our breakfast, but I can never get enough to eat. At 10 am we had church parade on the Square. Our Colonel constructed the service, read the prayers and we sang a few hymns and then dismissed.

Cox: Got leave for the day, up at 5.30 and off with Hill to the other side of the river with rifles after gazelle, sighted a herd of 15 at 11 am, followed them for 2 hrs. but they were far too wild; however, got in three shots at 400 yards, one over and one under, one wide, result nil. Most fatiguing day. Sun too hot for that sort of game in uniform. To bed at 10 pm. Got letters from home today: Father said, "Fear nothing and thank God." Mother said, "For God's sake do nothing rash." Wrote home.

24TH JANUARY

Teigh: We had a swim in the morning. Then we had to unload a few trucks of flour, and we had to change our tents in the dark.

Cox: Up at 7 am. Usual parade at 9. Outpost duty, Signallers got rather damned, collared the two best by the way for the telegraph office. Afternoon ammunition fatigue and general post as to officer's tents – am doubled up with Boxer now in order to reduce 10 to 8 men in a tent, rather a nuisance, but I suppose all's fair in love and war. To bed at 10 pm.

25TH JANUARY

Teigh: As usual in the morning. As we were parading at 9 am to go out in the desert, the Cameron Highlanders came in. On arrival of the train 3 companies of our Regiment went to give them a hand to unload. The remainder of us had a run across the desert. We heard the news that their Quartermaster shot himself the night before they left Cairo. Nearly all the Camerons were in the Nile for a swim as soon as they got settled down.

Cox: Up at 6.30. The 79th arrived in two trains at 9 and 2 and with them Brigade Major Snow. G.O.C. Gatacre comes on Friday from Halfa. Union Jack hoisted in our camp. 20 rounds served out to men and 2 companies in force out for the future day and night outposts. Hill in bed with a touch of sun fever. Two companies inlying picquet with boots on for the future. Sun getting terrific. Got to mount an outpost tomorrow at reveille. To bed at 9.30 pm. Saw a most extraordinary "devil" going up into the sky and only about 3 feet thick.

26TH JANUARY

Teigh: We had early morning parade. It was too cold to swim. It was an awful day. The dust blew terrible. I had to wear my glasses. We could not hardly see any one close to us, but we kept in our tents nearly all the day.

Cox: Up at 5.15. Mounted outpost duty. Most infernal sandstorm blowing. Can hardly see 50 yds. Very cold at night, after midnight. Had to bivouac[1] behind zariba made out of stones – dust awful.

27TH JANUARY

Teigh: The dust was nearly as bad, but we had a parade on the desert. In the afternoon we had some of the Warwicks, which arrived from Cairo and Mr Watson, the Church of England minister. I was tent orderly that day and had to fetch some water from the Nile for to make early morning breakfast.

Cox: Dismounted off outposts this morning at 6 am; sandstorm still growing strong. Can't shave, face too sore from sun and wind – eyes all bloodshot from sand. Camp in a filthy state.

---

[1] 'Bivouac' here means not having tents for cover at night.

28TH JANUARY

Teigh: I was on fatigue carrying General Gatacre's baggage from the train to his tent.

Cox: Up at 5.30 on duty. Sandstorm worse than ever. Tent simply full of sand. Washing quite out of the question. Food beastly, like eating sandpaper. Heard of raid at Korti. 300 men going to be held in readiness. Glad I'm not on outpost duty tonight but see they have got fires burning. G.O.C. arrived tonight at 7 pm. Completed mess hut with stone walls – much more comfortable. Can't shave, razors all gone 'fut', also face too sore.

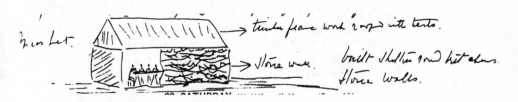

Skinner: General Gatacre and his staff arrived. We soon found out that this was to be a teetotal expedition and of course the troops began to moan, especially when it was known that the officers were getting as much as they wanted, anyhow we had to content ourselves with pure Nile Water.

29TH JANUARY

Teigh: Our Company was on wood fatigue all the morning cutting wood for the bakery where they bake our bread.

Cox: Up at 7. The usual parade at 9 – practice at building bivouacs and zaribas. G.O.C. spoke a few encouraging words to us in the shape of telling us to sleep in our boots. He appears a very fair chap and knows his work but first impression seems a bit "fussy".

Meiklejohn: Gatacre our General arrived. He had a talk to us and announced his intention of making everyone keen and on the

31

"Qui vive". He said we were all to sleep in clothes and boots every night now, which is universally condemned as bad for the men's feet, and unnecessarily wearing for us all. He will have "Night alarms" and take us out for a march at any moment. He then asked us all what we would do. Skipwith unguardedly said "Sketching" and was told he would be given one to do soon. As a result the rest of us disclaimed any ability. This camp is called "Gurheish" – the watering place of small donkeys.

30TH JANUARY

Teigh: Our Company was on picquet. We had to turn out at 5.45, drill order with 20 rounds of ammunition in our pouches. As we were inspected by the Field Officer, we were told to take off none of our things and not to leave our tents, as we might be called out any moment. There is a Company of each Regiment on outpost duty. If we were attacked, we were to turn out at once. It did not take our Company for church but the remainder fell in at 10 am for church, drill order, and formed up in rear of the camp and the General gave them a lecture. We had to turn out again at 5 pm to be inspected again and were told we had to sleep with all our things on, and have our rifles by our sides.

Cox: Church at 10 am after which the G.O.C. addressed the men, started by jumping on them for not singing 'God Save the Queen', he included officers. He talked for about 20 minutes. I think he is a rather sound chap, he certainly has taken the men. Afternoon rode out about signalling business, saw B.M. about B.S.O. He is going to see G.O.C. Simpson told off to do a survey.

Meiklejohn: The last ¾ hour was taken up with a speech from General Gatacre. He said that when we meet the enemy we must go through them like a pat of butter. If he held up his hand we must go through even a stone wall. We wondered how! Altogether a "blood and thunder" oration.

31ST JANUARY

Teigh: We had bathing parade at 9 am and the Commanding officer told us that any one feeling sick was to report sick at once without delay, as there was one of our Comrades in Hospital dangerously ill and he might have been with us now if he had but reported sick sooner, but he recovered. Then he marched us to the banks of the Nile to learn how to make ropes out of palm leaves and they make very strong ones too. They are getting on well with the railway, as there is a lot of rails passing through here daily. The General stopped a load of rails and we had to unload them. There was 12 rails issued to each Battalion to put around the square. While we were doing this the Warwickshire Regiment buried a man that died in the Hospital.

Cox: Up at 6 on woodcutting fatigue for bakery until 11.30. Got a fine old fatigue on now, viz to file down the heads of 1,000 cartridges. Man of the 6th (Warwickshires) died today from pneumonia – one of ours bad with enteric. Native came in with a gazelle, which he had shot and presented it to the mess – a great addition to our rations. My filter gone 'fut'.

1ST FEBRUARY

Teigh: We had a big route march; we paraded at 7 am. The General is always present on parade with us and he does pull us through. We arrived back at our camp at 12 noon and rested for the remainder of the day.

Cox: Up at 6. Didn't have much of a night as I slept in all my clothes barring boots. Should have had them on, but can't go the whole hog straight off. Brigade field day from 7 to 12. C.O. got damned long lecture in the afternoon on the subject of filing down cartridges – discovered that, when altered, magazines cannot be used. However, G.O.C. says he doesn't care, in fact says its rather a good thing. Don't know that I agree with him.

2ND FEBRUARY

Teigh: I was on woodcutting for the bakery in the morning. After dinner I was filing bullets till tea. That is what the rails were put round the square for to hold the bullet firm against till we filed off the top of the bullet. We commenced to turn into bed earlier as the first post sounded at 7.20 pm; last post 8 pm. I have been very hungry since I have been here, in fact everyone has and we cannot buy anything. We have had bread since we have been in this camp and they gave us ½lb extra tonight. We were very glad of it. I ate mine before I went to bed. There is nothing we are able to obtain except a few dry dates.

Cox: Up at 7. Ammunition fatigue the devil, all available men and officers 6 hours daily for 30 days to file off the tops. Makeshift anvils made out of inverted railway lines resting on stone pins with mud as mortar. Simpson, Peters and Johnson left with the survey party. Inlying picquet tomorrow, outlying next day! No lack of work anyhow! Collared some rounds for my rifle, shall go out on Sunday. 9 pm, just going to turn in with boots and fully equipped.

Meiklejohn: The General says that our bullets have not got sufficient "stopping power" for savages, so we are to file off the tops to make them expand. Gauges have been issued and every bullet has to be gauged by an officer. When Gatacre was standing near, Colonel Longbourne audibly remarked of these gauges, "Damned things are all a different length". An evident fact, but the General was clearly annoyed and said we must judge for ourselves. Then the General discovered that the men had no glasses to drink from, so we have to collect all empty bottles which we must cut with string dipped in vinegar to improvise tumblers! We soon got into the way of this, but the men won't use them. Gatacre also says that all Officers must turn out on the first note of reveille and see that the men do the same. This assumes that we all sleep in full kit!

3RD FEBRUARY

Teigh: Each company got five boxes of ball ammunition to file and when we had finished that, we had done our task. We got finished at 12 noon. In the afternoon at 3 pm the General came round and inspected the boots of the whole Regiment in their turn.

Cox: Up at 5.30. Inlying picquet paraded at 6.45. Slept fully equipped, most beastly but must get used to it. Bullet fatigue as usual. Canteen started for mess today, I hear it is bought clean out tonight, the men are full of money and nothing to spend it on. Soda machine in working order, a great boon! Outpost tomorrow for me. Had long and touching letter from May Bateman. Really think G.O.C. is a bit off his head, he called on the mess this morning at 6.30! Found fault with the glasses of last night being on the table. However, he has given us another marquee for an ante-room. To bed early.

4TH FEBRUARY

Teigh: We had another route march and we did a few formations of attack. Then marched home. When we were marching in camp our commanding Officer seemed very lively and he said, "Sing up men", and we did. In the afternoon there were some dried goods came and we had them to unload. Then there was a dry canteen opened and what an awful rush there was. I managed to get ½ lb of cheese, which cost me 8 piastres.

Cox: Outpost duty; up at 5. Built zariba and general defences only got an hour's sleep at night.
Certain cure for headache – Emerson's Brown Seltzer.

5TH FEBRUARY

Teigh: We had a bathing parade at 6 am and a drill parade at 7 am. The General said we laid in bed too long and he meant to have us up earlier. We paraded again at 9 am. For bullet filing in the hot sun, we had 8 boxes instead of 5, so we had to work again after dinner.

Cox: Dismounted from outpost duty at 5 am. Usual bullet fatigue at 9 am and wood cutting in the afternoon. Adamson followed a gazelle all the afternoon with my rifle but didn't get him, hope I have better luck tomorrow. Very hot day with no wind. To bed early rather tired. Wrote home.

6TH FEBRUARY

Teigh: On wood cutting for the bakery again and picking up stones to make a line around the camp. There was a party of

A.S.C. arrived today and 30 bakers. But up to now we have had our own Regimental bakers.

Cox: Had rather a rotten day. Got up at 4, crossed the river in a palm tree hollowed out and walked about 15 miles, but only saw one gazelle which I couldn't get near. Sirdar comes tomorrow. One officer up at reveille every morning per company to see the men out. To bed at 9 pm.

7TH FEBRUARY

Teigh: The alert sounded about 3.30 am. We all turned out in front of our camp, but it was only an alarm, so we were dismissed again till 6, when we fell in for wood cutting for our Regimental cook-house. At 8 the Company paraded again for bullet filing and got finished at 12 noon. Just then the Sirdar, General Kitchener, arrived in camp and we had to turn out and have a field day. It was very hot. After dinner bullet filing again till tea time, which was at 4.30 pm. At 5.30 my Company paraded again for picquet under the Field Officer.

Cox: The G.O.C. sounded the alarm at 3.35 this morning – the regiment turned out in 8 minutes, all except that beauty the C.O. and we have suffered in consequence. I don't think I have ever seen him so bad, even at Aldershot. Bullets at 9 am and we had a sudden parade at 11.45 for the Sirdar who arrived this morning, the C.O. let off steam after parade. Bullets at 3 pm.

Meiklejohn: An awful affair last night. All the Colonels and the Medical people disapprove of the idea of sleeping every night in full kit, so we have gradually got into pyjamas again. We had given up all thoughts of a night alarm, though strangely we had discussed it at supper, and some decided to sleep fully equipped. Still it seemed a silly idea at bed time, so we all turned in. Brewis, however, put a match box near his head, and I a candle by mine. About 1 am we were awakened by all the bugles sounding "Alert" followed by "Fall In" and "Double", while Earle, our Adjutant, came dashing round telling us to fall in at once! Pandemonium ensued! I trod heavily on the candle, while Brewis discovered that the match box was empty. We wasted a few valuable seconds exchanging remarks, then scrambled into such scanty kit as we could find, and dashed wildly into the darkness. Brewis took my sword belt by mistake, and his was far too large for me. There was a scene of some confusion. Officers and men tripping over tent ropes: frantic searching for boots and articles of kit: and the most lurid language. I made for our "falling in" place, with Brewis' sword dangling about my feet, and remember a momentary feeling of surprise at hearing strong remarks issuing from the depths below me. Next instant I repeated the experience at Korti by stepping into space and landing at the bottom of a deep ditch which Gatacre had made us dig for no apparent reason. (Somebody suggested it was with the idea of trapping locusts!) My fall was broken by landing on the top of a distinguished Field Officer and his remarks were distinctly personal and shattering. One was "Thank God some other . . . idiot has done the same!" I crawled out weakly and got to my Company. Poor 'F' even in the darkness looked a subdued and ragged crowd, and it was evident that things were far from well. Whispered remarks such as, "'Oo's got two right boots?" "Any bloke with two large a 'elmet pass it along. This . . . one won't go on me 'ead," etc. We took 8 minutes to fall in, instead of Gatacre's limit of three. Caldecott was easily first, and was congratulated by the General, who failed to notice that he was in pyjamas under his greatcoat and only had one puttee! Poor Colonel Verner of the Lincolns was actually one of the very few sleeping in full kit, but, being a little deaf, did not hear the bugles, and his Adjutant forgot to call him! Luckily we did not march any distance, since practically nobody was properly dressed, and some men had no boots. We hear some men have reported sick, having damaged their feet, but the P.M.O. is tactfully ascribing their indisposition to accidents and chill due to being turned out in the darkness. Quite a busy morning resorting kit!! We now all *have* to sleep in boots and putties, a most unnecessary hardship.

8TH FEBRUARY

Teigh: 30 men of my Company were for outpost duty, which took No 1 Section, and the Captain of the Company bought 5 piastres of dry dates and gave them to the men. They boiled down and made jam of them for tea. They told us they were very nice, so of course I had to try them. They remained on outpost till the following morning at 6.

Cox: On duty. Up at reveille 5.15. Brigade parade at 7. 5-mile march and the deuce of an attack at the end. Very hot, got rather a head from the sun, perspired "orrid". Slept in the afternoon. Flies all getting a regular torment. Hear we move on by night march on Saturday. Hubbard, Woodcock and draft of 100 men arrived this evening at 7. Too dark to see what they looked like. To bed 10 pm.

9TH FEBRUARY

Teigh: I went down to the Nile and had a wash in the morning and brought up some water for breakfast at 9 am. Part of our Company was on wood cutting. I was on the covering party. We had a number of men with rifles to see the road was clear of the enemy, while the others cut the wood. At 7 pm we received a draft of 100 men and they were posted so many to each Company.

Cox: Up at reveille, 5.15. Parade at 6, bullets at 9 am. Ct Martial 2 to 4 pm. Dinner at 7 and so to bed.

10TH FEBRUARY

Teigh: I was on guard and how quiet it seems on the desert. I wrote a letter home.

Cox: Up at 6. Woodcutting from 7 to 11. The battalion finished their slice of ammunition today, so we will have a respite with that for a bit, thank goodness. Hear we shift to next camp next Monday. Another sandstorm all day. Paddled in the river getting my feet into trim for marching.

11TH FEBRUARY

Teigh: We had a big route march to a big hill opposite to our camp about 6 miles off. So when we got to this the General asked if any man wanted to fall out as he was going a few miles further and there was not one man fell out of our Battalion. So we marched 4 miles further, then came back making it 20 miles. We got the order to get 2 rounds of ammunition ready for firing. A few minutes later we fired 2 volleys. We thought we were near the Dervishes. We formed up into line and we all fired 2 rounds at some rocks in front of us. We arrived back about 2.30 pm and had a rest for the remainder of the day.

Cox: Up at reveille 5.15 am. Round huts and mounted Inlying Picquet at 5.45. Brigade parade at 7. Marched about 15 miles, practising surprises on the way – G.O.C. ordered two rounds to be served out per man and we attacked several rocks. Mail came in with papers from home, much appreciated, hope they will continue to come. On Outpost duty tomorrow.

12TH FEBRUARY

Teigh: Bathing parade at 6 am. After breakfast I did a little writing and played a few games at cards and in the afternoon cleaned my things.

Cox: Mounted outpost 5.45 am, recalled at noon. Warned for advanced party for new camp to parade this evening. Wrote home.

13TH FEBRUARY

Teigh: Church parade as usual. The Presbyterian minister arrived and the Wesleyans and Presbyterians went to the same service. We got the order to move camp and the tents were struck and put upon the train by tea-time. We then paraded at 5 pm with rolled coat and blankets each. We marched about ½ mile and bivouacked till 1.30 the next morning.

Cox: Paraded this morning at 1.30 am. 46 men + 79th (Cameron Highlanders) and 10 R.E. marched 10 miles by moonlight with G.O.C. and A.D.C., halted ½ hour for tea, then again 8½ miles to new site for camp, Abu Dis. Marked out camps, pitched some tents, built latrines, unloaded trains, and very tired. Men went very well. New site much nicer and looks much more gamey – railhead just close. G.O.C. stood breakfast. Got in this morning at 9.40 – average 3½ miles an hour including halts. Regiment bivouacking at old camp and marching tonight – glad I've done it. Beastly tired – but can't go to bed till rail and bakery train come in. Think march will tell on some of them tonight. R.E. Officer reported me for delaying them an hour, damn him. Took exactly 10 minutes – told G.O.C. so. Saw lots of sand grouse on the way.

14TH FEBRUARY

Teigh: We commenced marching again and marched until 7 am; in that time we had covered 16 miles, when we halted and got a drink of tea and ¼lb. of bread and a few dates, which were issued to us before we started. After this we started off again and arrived at Abu Dis about 9.30, covering the distance of 19 miles in all.

We had just got in when I was warned for guard and I got 3rd relief, so I got a rest before going on sentry. We got a tent and pitched it ourselves, whilst the remainder of the Battalion was unloading the train, which brought all the ammunition and some boxes of money containing 10,000£ belonging to the Paymaster, which we had to do sentry duty over. It was very cold and dusty, and cold during the night. I got relieved at 6 am the next morning and I was glad too.

Cox: Up at 5 am, prowled around with my rifle, shot a curious bird with a neck about a mile long. That infernal train came in this morning at 3 am, had to get men to unload it. Regiment got in at 10 am looking fit – C.O. cursed me for not having breakfast ready, but not my fault as camp kettles never came in time. G.O.C. apologised about the train, the train was delayed at his own camp, not mine. River very pretty here, small cataract with wooded islands scattered about, ought to be something to shoot, saw a baby crocodile but of course did not have rifle. 6th (Warwicks) come in tomorrow. The pitching of our camp was simply disgraceful, really C.O. absolutely incompetent.

15TH FEBRUARY

Teigh: I was glad to get my boots off, but I was soon called out for to go on fatigue. At 2 pm I paraded to see my Company Officer and he let the men off fatigue who had been on guard the previous day, and we were all soon off down the Nile to have a swim. For that was the first time we had had a chance for a wash since Sunday morning. Then after tea our Company was on picquet, which takes every man of the Company.

Cox: Actually had a Europe morning, up at 7 am. On fatigue at 9 to build a shelter round the bakery of trees and palm leaves to keep the sand off. There has been a sandstorm more or less all day. Went out with my rifle and Barlow this afternoon up the river, B. with gun, got a dove and quail, I got a goose, shot him on the water about 60 yards off and sent a native in to fetch him – also winged another – a very good long shot, but couldn't get him as he got into the cataract. C.O. apologised today about breakfast as it wasn't my fault. To bed at 9 pm.

16TH FEBRUARY

Teigh: I was unloading trains for the whole of the day.

Cox: Got leave and up early to shoot with Barlow, started at 4.30 am and walked up the river, and shot another goose, an eagle and two other furry black birds, all with rifle, which shoots very straight. One wants a boat to do it properly, as you have to send a native to fetch birds. No gazelle on this side of the river. Shifted 'A' & 'B' companies' lines after lunch and then lazed it, had a tub and so to tea. Weather lovely, cooler, light breeze and no sand thank goodness.

17TH FEBRUARY

Teigh: I was on canteen fatigue but that was very cozy. Private Perry of 'H' company died of fever and he was buried at 1 pm.

Cox: On duty up at 5.15 am. Bearded the Brigade Major with the result that I have been appointed signalling officer to the

41

force; don't know what the deuce to do about charger. Bought a crocodile skin. Man of 'H' Co. died of enteric.

18TH FEBRUARY

Teigh: Route march around another big hill nearly opposite our camp, and we fired three volleys at a big sandbank. After I got back I wrote another letter. We had tinned beef for dinner and at night the order came out that if anyone wanted any extra bread it could be obtained, and I think nearly all of the men of my company put down for an extra ½ lb. each.

Cox: Brigade day, but got off personally for woodcutting and had a real Europe night, slept in pyjamas and didn't parade till 8 am! Went out with rifle and Adamson in the afternoon. I got nothing this time; he got a sheldrake, too many guns out. Maxwell and Barlow got a doz. doves and 3 couple snipe. Went up to railhead camp and saw Plunkett; he has got on to a real loaf. Not settled about signalling, G.O.C. wants best man and doesn't know who to take.

19TH FEBRUARY

Teigh: Bathing parade before breakfast. 8 am made a pulpit for the church service. 2 pm making sentry boxes out of palm leaves and dry grass.

Cox: Up at 5 am inlying picquet. Rumours of dervish advance and forced march onto Berber but don't believe it. Outposts tomorrow.

FORCED MARCH

During the campaign of the previous year to re-establish a British presence in the Dongola Province, the Sirdar had reoccupied Abu Hamed close to Abu Dis, which Private Teigh and Lieutenant Cox had reached in mid-February 1898, and, further south, Berber, close to the confluence of the Nile and the River Atbara. As an aid to holding these places the railway had been extended southwards, and had reached Geneinetti. The Egyptian Army was stationed at Berber in considerable strength: three infantry brigades, eight cavalry squadrons and four artillery batteries.

However, the Khalifa's nephew, Mahmud, was determined to wreck the railroad, and to raid the country around Berber, if not the garrison itself. He was helped by Osman Digna, a much feared ruler of local tribesmen, who had been a thorn in the side of the Egyptian army since 1883. Now he was bringing in his 10,000 infantry, riflemen and spearmen with ten small rifled brass guns and 4,000 cavalry. Mahmud, it was believed, intended to cross the Atbara about thirty miles from Berber, swing round so as to attack the Anglo-Egyptian troops and cut the railway link. This was a serious threat to future plans, made more difficult as the true intentions of Mahmud were not clearly known to the British, and possibly not to Mahmud himself. Throughout the campaign disagreements among the Dervishes and with the Khalifa himself made planning of strategy difficult for Kitchener and Gatacre. The Khalifa's intelligence as to the British and Egyptian positions and strength was poor. Mahmud and Osman Digna disagreed as to the best action, and the Khalifa was wary of allowing them too much independent action.

In the early part of 1898 there had been much skirmishing with the Dervishes. Gunboats patrolled the Nile and exchanged fire with Dervish forts. Osman Digna constructed two new forts on the Nile at Shendi. But by mid-February it became clear that action further south from Abu Dis was a distinct possibility. Kitchener was moving south, and the British Brigade under Gatacre followed. However, Gatacre seems to have over-reacted to the possible danger to Berber, seeing his action as a 'Relief of Berber'.

Since speed was essential, in Gatacre's mind at least, the tents and heavy baggage were left behind as transport was difficult in a short period. The march was often undertaken in the heat of the day, but also at night to avoid the midday sun, and over ground rocky in places, or through soft sand. The infamous British boots found it hard to cope. Inexplicably the men carried their greatcoats, possibly to give them extra warmth at night, as well as a hundred rounds of ammunition. Halting during the day gave the men little sleep on account of the flies and lack of shelter.

The march is regarded in British military history as a great achievement. In six days, on one of which the Brigade halted, 140 miles were covered, showing what British troops could do when ordered. Whether it was a military necessity is open to question, but criticism of Gatacre may be unjust. Telegrams had passed between the Sirdar at Berber and the Brigadier at Abu Dis. On the day the march started the telegram received from Berber had been:

"News has come in that enemy in ten rubs[1] advancing. You can therefore move Brigade as arranged. – Sirdar."

To which the reply was:

"I shall arrive at Atbara Camp nine or ten o'clock on Wednesday second with Maxims and 2,000 men; guns and cavalry will arrive on first. – Gatacre."

These telegrams suggest that "Gatacre's Forced march" was not entirely of his own making.

The next few weeks were to give little rest for Private Teigh, Lieutenant Cox, or any of the British Brigade. Mahmud and Osman Digna were moving in a wide circle around Berber, but their precise intentions were not fully clear to Kitchener, who was, however, aware that at some point he must mount an attack. This was a tense time, since it was never clear how close the Dervishes were, and zaribas had to be constantly constructed as the units moved from place to place.

Having reached Berber, the Brigade moved the same day to Da Baka, where Gatacre erected grass shelters, since he expected a prolonged stay. However, the kit and heavy baggage which had been left behind started to come up the Nile, giving greater normality. On 12 March they moved on three miles south to the deserted village of Darmali. Four days later they joined two Soudanese Brigades at Kunur, a further five miles south. At this point the British Brigade was in place under the direct control of the Sirdar, together with the Egyptian Cavalry and Artillery. A further draft of Lincolns came from Cairo, and the 1st Battalion Seaforth Highlanders arrived. They did not have an easy journey from Wadi Halfa. First they were railed

---

[1] A rub was any number between 500 and 1,500 men.

across desert to Geneinetti. From there half the battalion was brought by steamer to Kunur, while the others were jolted across the desert on camels, an experience they had neither been trained for, nor had the right clothes.

At this stage rumour was always rife, and both the men and officers remained on alert. It was difficult to predict what was going to happen, the more so as Mahmud and Osman Digna were still in disagreement. When they reached the Atbara, Osman wanted to move away from the Anglo-Egyptian army in a south-easterly direction, believing the Sirdar would not follow. Mahmud, regarding this as an excuse to avoid battle, crossed the Atbara to the north-east side and moved towards Berber, without consulting the Khalifa and against Osman Digna's advice. However, when he reached Nakheila he stopped, and constructed a very large zariba, inside which he made a small village, surrounded by trenches. Here he waited for the enemy to come to him, rather than to continue to seek them out.

Meanwhile the Sirdar had moved from Kunur, when he heard that the Dervishes were leaving the Nile on the west, to Ras el Hudi on the Atbara, between Berber and Nakheila. This was another difficult march, in a sandstorm; ten miles was covered in five hours. On arrival, a zariba had to be constructed. However, the following day Kitchener decided to move even further up the Atbara, thus keeping Mahmud away from Berber and the railway to the north. Again the army moved another five miles closer to the enemy, to Ras el Hudi.

This constant moving, and the uncertainty as to whether an attack was imminent, caused considerable difficulty among the British Brigade. Gatacre was not the calmest of generals and his blood-and-thunder approach upset many. At times he was hardly articulate and made many alarmist speeches to his troops, who then became very jittery.

Ras el Hudi itself was a very pleasant place. The Atbara was a fast-flowing river only after the melting of the snow in Abyssinia. In March and April it was a dry bed of white sand about four hundred yards wide, but dotted with deep and very clear pools, alive with fish and crocodiles. Bird life was particularly colourful. This was the camp from which the Sirdar had to decide when to attack Mahmud and Osman Digna.

Pressure was being put on Mahmud in the hope that he would come out from his zariba. When he had moved from the Nile to come nearer to Berber, he had left at Shendi a small depot of surplus stores, as well as the wives of the Emirs. This was attacked by a flotilla of gunboats on 27 March, and infantry and guns landed. While the wives of the most important Emirs escaped to Omdurman, many others, including children, were captured, and much loot taken. Though the action had mainly been carried out by the Egyptian Army, its success gave the British Brigade heart.

Meanwhile they waited for the Sirdar to make his decision, and kept in readiness. Parades continued, though the area was not conducive to marching or for the cavalry. Outside the bush the ground was undulating and either stoney or cracked by the annual overflow of the Atbara. The heat during the day was oppressive; even under the grass huts or improvised tents the temperature reached 115° Farenheit.

Private Teigh, Lieutenants Cox and Meiklejohn and Corporal Skinner had endured both the 'Forced March' and then several moves of camp nearer to Mahmud. Now they had to wait for the Sirdar finally to form his strategy.

3

TOWARDS ATBARA

20TH FEBRUARY

Teigh: At 8.30 am church parade service and we had a very nice sermon given on the subject of faith, hope and charity. After service the General gave us a fine speech and told us he was pleased in the way the Brigade was working. He said he should have another Regiment here and the Maxim battery and all our transport. Then we should be able to go straight to the enemy. He said that the Dervishes had come from the other side of the Nile to this side. He said it was the belief of the Soudanese people that there would be a force come from the North to help them, and the commander would ride upon a white horse and he would take Khartoum. So he had bought one, and this caused the troops to laugh at him. He expected we would go up to our knees in blood shortly or rather he would be disappointed if it didn't go over our boot tops.

Cox: Up at 4.30 – outpost duty, G.O.C. came round and made me blow my whistle, the signal for alarm. The men did all right and then he told me that he had made me signalling officer to the force, so that's all right. Gun gone fut.

21ST FEBRUARY

Teigh: It is a very hot day. The whole Battalion is filing bullets and it is a tedious job.

Cox: Had my first brigade signalling practice with great success. Some on about forced march to Berber; we are to get 12 hrs' notice, someone to go back with all heavy kit, each officer to take nothing but as follows, have consequently bought a donkey, shared with Boxer, frightful price £6. Kit: 2 blankets, 1 shirt, 1pr socks, 1pr boots, 1 cup, brush, razor, notebook, knife, fork, spoon and cup on waterbottle strap – a nice little kit to exist for nearly three months.

22ND FEBRUARY

Teigh: Route march and every man had to carry 105 rounds of ammunition, but our Company was on wood cutting so we were not on the route march.

Cox: Up at 5. Brigade route march, beastly hot so G.O.C. didn't take us far. Out shooting in afternoon, crossed over to an island in a cut-out palm tree, which filled up with water half way – got a couple of geese and wounded another but couldn't get him. To bed 8.20.

23RD FEBRUARY

Teigh: Our company on picquet, Q.M.S. Freeman got reduced to the ranks for drunkenness while being in charge of the convoy of baggage, while on the line of march from the old camp. The 16th Company, Royal Artillery, arrived with 6 maxims and the remainder of our transport.

Cox: Europe morning. Bullet fatigue all day. 500 camels arrived today from Berber to take our baggage in case we have to go. I expect we shall be out of this soon. Everything has been got ready – G.O.C. awaiting a wire from Sirdar who has gone up to the Atbara. Still no nearer getting a horse.

24TH FEBRUARY

Teigh: I am on out post, but I was cook for the remainder and had nothing else to do. We got relieved at 6 next morning.

Cox: Up at 6. Brigade signalling in the morning. Strolled out with rifle in afternoon but saw nothing.

Teigh: The Brigade went on a route march, so my company was on fatigue all the morning, carrying water for the troops. When they got back at 2 pm it was very hot. Just as our Regiment got on the square, the Commanding Officer said give 3 cheers for our lads, just to let them know how well they had done the march, and not a man fell out, while the other Regiments had about 10 each. The General took 100 Donkeys with the troops to let the men ride that fell out.

We received the order then to pack up an emergency kit ready for marching and we had a decent job. We were only allowed to take a shirt and one pair of socks and a piece of soap. The remainder of our kits we left behind. We got served out with a piece of bread and meat. We had no time for any tea. We got into the trucks, 60 in each. Those that could not sit had to stand. After waiting for about 2 hours, we started. We got as far as the railhead, a distance of about 20 miles, arriving there at 9 pm. When we arrived there was a number of natives setting fire to palm trees around there to enable us to see. Also to get a bit warm as it was very chilly. We fell out and had a walk round and soon the whole place was on fire. It was just like the fireworks, and after an hour's rest we started to march again. I felt as though I was sleepy nearly all the way. We got a halt for every hour's marching and then I had a sleep. We started again and got to our resting camp at 6 am.

Cox: Forced march – no reports! A day missed somewhere.

Meiklejohn: Started at 5 am and marched towards railhead about 8 miles: breakfast there: then back, doing manoeuvres on the way. Very hot and deep yielding sand and everybody weary. On reaching camp we got the startling news that Mahmud, the Dervish Emir, was advancing rapidly on Berber, and that we had to start for the Atbara River (145 miles) as soon as possible to save the town. Gatacre made a speech in which he said that the lives of many women and children depended on our getting there in 4 days, so every man must do his utmost. After a hasty lunch we started packing up and striking tents and did not finish till 8 pm, being somewhat weary after our long march. We were only allowed a minimum of kit as the number of camels was limited. The rest is to go by boat up the Nile. . . .

Started in cattle trucks, crowded together and mostly standing, and arrived at railhead (20 miles) at 1.30 am. We then detrained and started off on "Gatacre's famous forced march" at 2, having now been on the move since 5 am. A really hectic 21 hours.

26TH FEBRUARY

Teigh: I got another lay down until the sun got too hot, so we had to shift in the shade and I felt as though I was sick for a few minutes, but I was soon alright again.

I was orderly man and we got some tea at 1 pm and our bit of meat for dinner. We fell in at 8.15 pm and the Commanding Officer told us we had to do a forced march of 93 miles, as the enemy has left Shendi and was trying to gain a fort called Atbara. If they did they would be able to regain Berber, so we would have to march 19 miles, 22 miles, 26 miles, 32 miles. So we started on the march at 12 noon 27th.

Cox: Up at reveille 5.15, brigade route march. We went 7 miles out, breakfast taken by camels, returned after breakfast. On return G.O.C. found wire ordering Brigade up to Atbara with all possible speed. Afternoon – fearful chaos – struck tent – stacked heavy baggage for Halfa – left 8 pm by train for railhead 17 miles – marched 10 more miles – camel transport – got to Atbara by forced marches in 4 days, 98 miles. A day missed somewhere.

26 SATURDAY

Cox: Arrived 27 miles S of Abu Dis at 10 am, bivouacked on ground for day. It appears dervishes are advancing on the Atbara. Paraded at 9.40 pm. Marched all night.

27TH FEBRUARY

Teigh: We had taken the wrong way and had got too far from the Nile and we ran short of water. There were about 500 men of the Brigade fell out and we marched 32 miles. As soon as I saw the Nile I made for it, for I felt very faint, but how much water I drank I cannot say. When the men saw the water there was no such thing as keeping them in the ranks. They strolled all over the shore, so you can bet how they felt. We stopped here for an hour and then marched another 5 miles in the heat of the sun. Officers and everyone were falling out. I stopped and made a drink of tea and had some cold meat. Then we started on again. When I got there I was pleased to have a rest. We had a japputtie, the same bread as the natives eat. After we got settled down a bit we got a ration of rum, two table spoonsful a man.

Cox: Got into bivouac today at 11 am after a forced march of 34 miles. I haven't closed by eyes since Friday at Reveille. Men marched splendidly, not a bit done at finish. My feet very sore – got 26 miles tonight – absolutely fell asleep while on march last night, my donkey going strong. Rather expect a fight Wednesday.

Meiklejohn: Marched till 6 am and then halted. Officers and men fell down flat at once and went to sleep as some had been dozing on the march and waking to find ourselves falling. Halted an hour, then on again till 11. A scorching hot day: very heavy going in patches of deep sand: boots wearing out on the flinty desert: no water and everybody suffering from thirst: all very exhausted and the men falling out in scores. These were brought on by camel. When at last we sighted the Nile again about 11 am there was a regular stampede for the water and we all waded in and drank, not caring whether it was pure or not. Then we had a little food and tried some sleep. There was no shade: the sun was scorching: and the flies awful. Started off again about 2.30 pm and marched 5 miles to Derea. By now most officers and men were utterly done up and we had to find out how many men could continue. All were very keen to try, as they did not want to miss the fight, but some had no soles on their boots, many had the skin off their feet and others were worn out. We left about 150 men and two officers (Caldecott and Christie): the Lincolns left 180: the Camerons 200: and these waited for two gunboats to arrive and bring them on. We had had no food for 26 hours and no sleep for even longer, so I crawled off eventually and tried to get a nap. Major Quayle-Jones, now commanding us, came and woke me and asked what I had had to eat. I said I had seen my men get their rations but had not anything myself as I only wanted to sleep. He said, "Come on at once and have something". I said I would rather

51

sleep, upon which he said, "I order you to come at once". He gave us all some brandy and we had a little food and tea, then slept till 1 am, about 3 hours. Started off again at 1.30.

28TH FEBRUARY

Teigh: We marched another 13 miles. After arriving there we had our own tea to make, which was issued to us the previous day and there we had a rest till 4.30 pm.

Cox: Actually had 3 hrs sleep last night. We paraded at 1.30 am and marched 12 miles to bivouac ground. I had to go with some stores, a convoy consisting of 500 camels. Egyptian R.A. battery passed up on way. 100 weakly men are coming by boat from last bivouac. My feet are beastly sore and I'm heartly tired. I should like to have a week in bed. Paraded again at 4.30, did another 15 miles and got in at 9.30 pm, bivouacked where we stood – couldn't sleep much – beastly tired. Had a ripping bath in Nile. G.O.C. told us we might get shot at by frightened inhabitants – that we were not to take any notice.

Meiklejohn: Was beginning to feel a bit shaky in the legs, as indeed did all of us. Major Quayle-Jones gave us all short rides on his pony. Had again to carry two rifles for men of my company who were finding it difficult to go on, and most of the fitter of us had to try and help in this way. Am still going as strong as anybody and my boots are lasting splendidly.

1ST MARCH

Teigh: I got a wash here just before starting. Men who thought they could not keep on marching fell out and came on after with a steamer. Our Company was advance guard and I was connecting file and had a good chat with the guide, an English Officer, who is on the Egyptian Staff. We done a good march until 10 pm. We had marched 18 miles and we saw plenty of dead camels by the way. There was plenty of singing all the way. The troops were very cheerful. This was half way and we got some tea and bread and a rest till 2.30 am.

When we marched off again my company was rearguard. We

1. George Teigh in middle age.

2. ...and in old age.

3. Samuel Fitzgibbon Cox.

4. General Kitchener, Sirdar
   1892-1900.

. The 'house' in which George Teigh is believed to have been born.

. A Nile steamer in the 1960s - almost identical to those used by Kitchener in the 1890s.

7. Lieutenant-General Francis Grenfell, whom Kitchener succeeded as Sirdar in 1892.

8. Major-General William Gatacre, Divisional Commander, Omdurman, 1898.

had not been started very long before we got the order to fix bayonets on approach of a large village. It was expected that the enemy was in the vicinity and that they might probably give us an attack. But we were in luck's way. They did not happen to be there.

Rearguard's duty is to pick up all the faint and sick and put them on camels and there was a lot of men fell out. I could hardly stick it myself. In fact everyone was done up. We arrived at our resting place about 5 am, which was about another 15 miles on a pretty good road. We passed a very big mud village and on the other side of the Nile, it was all green and cultivated. As soon as I made my tea, I went and had a swim in the Nile. It was very hot, so I kept my helmet on. Just as I was going up to camp, I saw my chum under a tree in the shade. So I soon joined him and we had a read of the newspaper. After we had a rest, we went down to the Nile and filled our mess-tins with water. We commenced to make a drink of tea and put it in our water bottles ready for the march. We fell in at 4 pm and our company was rearguard again.

It was a splendid route march and a splendid route too, but very tiresome. We went through a lot of villages. We kept on the march until 12.30 am, and we must have marched about 15 miles. There were a lot of men fell out. The sick camels were all loaded. I saw a Corporal in charge of a lot of camels get reduced on the march. He had not been marching right, so an Officer went up to him and pulled the stripes off. He was an Egyptian. We halted in a very nice place, just close to the Nile. The place is all cultivated here. I got some water melon, after that I had a drink of tea, which we made. Then we got a blanket and had a rest till 7 am.

Cox: Paraded this morning at 3 am. Marched off, did 11 miles and bivouacked for dinner. Johnson and Earle gone by steamer with men with sore feet – this march is a bit thick to say the least of it. Fight expected Friday. We are to go beyond the Atbara. Men doing well and sticking to it – everybody with a very dogged determined look – 7 blisters on my feet and agony to walk. Paraded at 4 pm and marched 15 miles to bivouac. 5 miles North of Berber – the most fatiguing march of the lot and soft dirty sand. Thank goodness a rest tomorrow – reveille at 7 am. Future movements depend on dervishes who are reported 20 mile south of Atbara. A man of the 6th fell dead on the march today and Toogood fell off a camel and hurt himself.

2ND MARCH

Teigh: We had a bathing parade. When we started on this Expedition we had 25 men in my section and there were only seven marched last night. All the N.C.Os. had to ride on camels. We got a nice bit of bread for breakfast this morning and had a good rest all day. We got plenty of water melons here, but it was a very sandy day. We got the order to fall in at 2.45 am . . .

Cox: Reveille at 7 pm – a gigantic blessing – barring my feet feeling much better after a night's rest. Spent morning in building straw huts for shelters against the sun. An awful black sandstorm on, everybody's kit in a filthy state. Bathed twice in the Nile today. The sun is getting so beastly hot.

3RD MARCH

Teigh: . . . and arrived at Berber about 5.30 am where we were met by three bands of the Soudanese Regiments. There were very strong bands and drummers in each. They also played some good marching tunes through Berber. The Soudanese and Egyptian Regiments were formed up in line, making a road. We marched through them, being continually cheered by them. I never saw any one so happy as they were. We passed General Kitchener on the way and each company cheered him as we passed.

After passing through Berber, which is about 5 miles long and all mud houses, we came to a large open place, so we formed up in line and the three Soudanese bands got in front of us, and General Kitchener gave the order "Three cheers for Her Majesty the Queen". So while they played, we raised our helmets and cheered, and then marched off again.

We got to our resting place about 8 am, where we were met by the 11th Soudanese Regiment who gave us a good drink of tea. We had marched 12 miles. We left this camp again at 4 pm, and got to another camp (Da Baka) close to the Nile about 9 pm, distance of about 9 miles. After a drink of tea, we lay down for the night. I was soon off to sleep, but I was very restless with my knees always shaking. We had a bathing parade at 4 am and I was very glad of it.

Cox: Paraded at 3 am. Marched through Berber and bivouacked for dinners on South side of it. Quite disappointed in Berber – a long straggling collection of mud houses about 12 miles long. The Egyptian bands played us through the 10th Soudanese playing us. All the Regiments were formed up in the streets and cheered us heartily as we passed through, most enthusiastic scene. The Soudanese very fine fellows, the 10th excited about us, the men stood our men tea and the English officers all sent their ponies down and fetched us up to breakfast and lunch – they were awfully kind. Marched off at 4 pm and arrived at final bivouac, 11 miles south of Berber, more military bands playing us in. A brigade being bivouacked about a mile south of us. We are now 11 miles N. of actual front. Couldn't get a horse anywhere, so have made arrangements to buy a camel.

Meiklejohn: All the shops in Berber re-opened today, after being shut in anticipation of a siege. Now the moral effect of 2,500 British troops being at hand is great. At the same time we hear that our "forced march" and all the talk of saving Berber was mainly Gatacre's imagination. We were not expected to arrive for another week at least, and our confidence in him is shaken. He has the reputation of wearing out his troops unnecessarily.

4TH MARCH

Teigh: After breakfast we made our first zariba, all round us in case we had an attack. We made it with a lot of thorns. There were a lot of Soudanese in our camp today saying Englishmen very good. We got ½ lb of bread and ½ lb of biscuits and we were very glad of it. Fish is very plentiful here. They gave us a supper of fish. Then we got under our blanket with our rifles by our sides and our equipment on. After I had laid down for a while, I got called up to unload a steamer and two barges.

Cox: Up at 6.30. Brigade built strong zariba enclosing whole force – force at present as follows – one bde (E) at Ralbaca – 1 bde (B) and 1 bde (E) 2 squad Cav (E) 1 batt RA (E), 11 miles

South of Atbara – 1 bde (E) at Berber. Went over to Egyptian camp to see B.M. re signalling between British and Egyptians. Don't think it's practicable but had an interview with some Egyptian signallers and going to experiment tomorrow – rather interesting. Slept in afternoon. Nothing heard of dervishes up to date – not allowed out of zariba without an escort – had to take one this morning. Sun damnably hot. Wasted a 'possible' in the Nile. Rigged up quite a respectable tent with mackintosh sheet. All the villages in ruins, likewise most of Berber. Country once cultivated has run to waste.

Meiklejohn: Rather done up after the long march and sitting up most of the night, but Gatacre still keeps us all on the move. Rumours (possibly Gatacre's) that the Dervish cavalry were near our camp last night, so we had to build a strong zariba of mimosa (camel-thorn) all round the camp, and had orders to fire on anyone trying to break through or remove it.

5TH MARCH

Teigh: Our Company for picquet. I bought a tin of sardines, gave my chum half, fetched up with the stores. They went down well. After dinner I went down to the Nile and washed my shirt, towel and socks and waited for a few minutes till they were dry. I was taken away just before the rum was issued, but when I came back it went down very nice.

Cox: Up at reveille, in fact always up at reveille. G.O.C. sent for me to establish communications throughout the outposts. Not safe to go outside zariba now after dark as sentries have orders to shoot. C. Sgt got a ripping little gazelle, quite young and fairly tame. Hear our tents are coming up, at present my house consists of 4 sticks tied together with rope with mackintosh as a roof.

6TH MARCH

Teigh: On outpost duty. All the company was on it so it was very easy. I got one piastre of tomatoes for dinner. The other troops had church parade service close to us and we could hear very well. After the service, the General gave his usual lecture and said that he did not think the Dervishes would attack us, that being so we would have to go and attack them. After tea some men and me were put on a detached post on the banks of the Nile. I was on fourth relief from 10 to 12 midnight.

Cox: On duty, nothing doing. Had my usual swim in the river in the evening.

7TH MARCH

Teigh: Fatigue duty for the day.

Cox: Up at 5.45, on fatigue all day building and collecting material for shelters. Went out in afternoon with rifle and Barlow with gun, latter got 4 doves and a hare, I didn't get a shot. Bivouac beginning to smell, the space is too contracted. I expect we will have to shift soon.

8TH MARCH

Teigh: Wood cutting till dinner time and unloading boats in the afternoon, carrying sacks of rice and flour off the barges.

Cox: On inlying picquet today. Got a straw hut made, consequently much more comfortable! Got a beastly cold. Am getting beastly sick of this, the discomfort is intense and now hear that our heavy baggage left behind has been looted by stinking natives. As far as I can see our stay here is unlimited. We shall be a sorry sight when we do get back. Have been building shelters for men – lines of long straw huts 11 paces by 3 and 6ft high, a lot of tents have come up but G.O.C. won't allow them to be used; rather a good thing as they are very hot.

9TH MARCH

Teigh: Bathing Parade as usual. Then on fatigue putting up sun shades with blankets.

Cox: Missed a day somewhere! in forced march.

10TH MARCH

Teigh: Greek shops opened and goods were very dear; sardines 4 piastres a tin, small biscuits 8 piastres and cocoa and milk 8 piastres a tin, but I bought a tin of jam, 6 piastres, in our own canteen. Afterwards I was warned for covering party, whilst the company cut some wood and green leaves to make sun shades.

Cox: Outposts.

Meiklejohn: We are quartered in mud huts. I got mine "re-mudded" at once, as it was alive with scorpions living in the chinks in the walls. A dervish army of 16,000 strong under the Emir Mahmud is reported to be advancing on the River Atbara to meet us. This morning Egyptian and Soudanese troops marched through our camp on their way South with bands playing. We formed up and cheered them, were ordered to wear our red serge to impress the natives ("The thin red line").

11TH MARCH

Teigh: We had to pull our shades down that we had put up for shifting three miles further up.

Cox: On outpost duty all yesterday, most infernal dust storm on and came off this morning like a nigger – had a complete change and went down to the river and had a bath off a boat. Hear we shift quarters tomorrow into deserted village 3 miles further south, very good biz. C.Sgt got a small gazelle – don't think it will live.

12TH MARCH

Teigh: Reveille sounded at 4.30. I was on fatigue carrying boxes and laying them out in camel loads. We were finished by 7 and we fell in at 7.30 and started off for another camp. We left the Camerons behind. We had not got far before two bands of the Soudanese met us and there were the Soudanese Regiments formed up in line and as we marched between them they cheered us loudly. We arrived at our camp, Darmali, about 9 am. Here we had a lot of mud huts, where the Dervishes had been driven out. We had to clean them out thoroughly and by the time this was done it was dark. We got two blankets per man here, so we thought we were going to stay a long time.

Cox: Up at 5. Packed and marched off to Darmali, passing through Soudanese brigade who all turned out and cheered us and played us through. Very fair quarters, Boxer and I together in a room, the whole surrounded by a walled in courtyard in which company is quartered, very fair mess, but the best building in the place is the C.O.'s house, of course! Slept outside being too hot; trying to get a native bed but can't raise one anywhere.

13TH MARCH

Teigh: My company was for picquet; Church parade at 6.30 am. I was unable to attend; the Camerons arrived today and we had a Brigade parade at night and formed round the enclosure, in the place where we should go in case of an alarm. Afterwards we received a ration of rum.

Cox: Up early, leave off church, went out with gun and got 4 couple of sand grouse on an island opposite which stinks of doves, never seen so many anywhere – simply thousands. Got to establish signal communications throughout outposts. News reached us that Osman Digna has joined with Mahmud and both are advancing and are at present 15 miles N of Shendi.

14TH MARCH

Teigh: Outpost duty, and very hard to get sticks to make shelters with. It was also very windy. We could scarcely keep our blankets up for shade.

Cox: On duty. Another sandstorm but we didn't feel it so much in this village but it must have been a ripper – very strong wind – played the devil with the zariba – one of our men was out in the desert today attending to the calls of nature when he was caught in a "devil", and a piece of the zariba was caught up and

flung against him. It took 4 men to get him disentangled. I
believe he is in an awful state, the thorns are the very dickens,
they are poisonous and fester. Fellows are shooting lots of sand
grouse. Maxwell got a gazelle today with a shotgun, suddenly
got up in front of him. Berber brigade passes through tomorrow
– things beginning to look more like business, troops concen-
trating.

15TH MARCH

Teigh: The Brigade paraded at 4.45 am and formed in two lines,
and three Regiments of the Soudanese passed through the
ranks. As they went passed our fellows cheered them, and also
gave them tea and biscuits.

After breakfast we got the order to get ready for moving. I was
on fatigue the remainder of the day getting stores ready packed
up. Our blankets were all taken away, so we have to lay on just
what we can at night. We got issued out with a piece of boiled
meat for tomorrow's dinner, and bread and biscuits. So I had
not been laid down long when we heard reveille sounding,
which was 3 am.

Cox: Up at 4 am. The Berber brigade (Soudanese) marched
through the zariba, we all formed up in two lines and cheered
them through. They stopped an hour and we stood them tea
and the officers of the 10th breakfast. The black fellows are
splendid fellows. We have had orders to be ready to shift out
of this in two hours' notice. Things are getting more busi-
nesslike. Mainwaring has got to stop behind, that gives me
command of the Company as well as signalling. I heard the C.
Sgt shout out just now, "Here's a treat for someone. Who
wants a bootlace?" He was surrounded at once – gives you
some idea of the state we are in. We go on tomorrow travelling
light about 6 miles to the place of concentration of whole
force. G.O.C. told me that we shall fight day after tomorrow.
Berber brigade cavalry just passed through, followed by all
the women carrying kits on their heads. The whole show
is most weird – the noise the natives make gives one the
creeps.

Teigh: We marched off again and by daybreak we could see a couple of Egyptian Regiments alongside of us. We only marched about three miles and then we done a hard day's work carrying water and making a zariba around a lot of old mud huts (Kunur). I got a few minutes' rest, so I opened my canteen and the meat we got served out yesterday nearly made me sick. I could not eat it so I threw it away. They were selling some rice at the cookhouse. I bought some and mixed some dates up with it, and this is the way I made my dinner.

I then had to put on my straps and take my rifle and 100 rounds of ammunition to go to the Nile to fetch a camp kettle of water. After that we had to form round the zariba and lay down as we were before. We were issued with the next day's rations, which consisted of bread and biscuits. I was that hungry I ate my bread then. In an hour or two after that reveille sounded and dress for parade was at 3 am.

Cox: Up at 2 am. Nice night in bed! The 79th [Camerons] and 6th [Warwicks] and 2 companies 10th [Lincolns] marched off at 2.30. I had to go with them to establish heliograph communication on arrival at new bivouac. Marched into new bivouac, village called Kunur followed by another Soudanese bde. Three bdes here now with RA and Maxims. Cavalry have lost touch with enemy! The dervishes reported to have seized a ford 12 miles up the Atbara. ½ of the 72nd [Seaforths] and 56 more of our men joined this evening from Cairo, which makes us over a thousand. Much more warlike now, another 50 rounds per man, and sentries with loaded rifles. Correspondents have appeared on the scene. Wretched man in the 6th had his two hands blown off by explosion of packet of ammunition which fell into the fire while he was cooking. Could have shot 3 gazelle yesterday when on the march. They got between us and the river and kept running alongside. Mainwaring has come along after all, much to his delight.

Meiklejohn: Had a nasty experience before breakfast. Private Burrows of my company was warming himself at a fire, and a packet of his ammunition fell into it. He picked it up and was flicking the charred paper off when it exploded. It blew his right hand off at the wrist, and half his left, and he was also hit in the stomach. I was quite close and nearly hit by a piece of his hand. He spun round making a curious moaning sound and then collapsed. I hailed a stretcher at once and was relieved to find the event had not made me feel unduly shaken.

Skinner: An operation was at once performed taking the remains of his right hand off above the wrist joint, they tried to save 3 of the fingers of the left hand but after cutting away the greater part of the palm they had to give it up, as all the bones were all more or less shattered, so it was amputated below the wrist joint; the same evening he was sent back with other sick by boat to Geneinetti where they had established a base hospital.

17TH MARCH

Teigh: I was carrying my stretcher as I always do whenever the Brigade moves anywhere. We had 50 more rounds of ammunition issued out to us. We did a big parade, but we did not see no enemy. There were two more Brigades of Egyptians with us and we got back at 9.30 am. Then we got a small drink of tea. It is getting rough now. As soon as I had that, I took my rifle and 10 rounds of ammunition and went to the Nile to have a wash. We have to take our rifles to protect ourselves. Half a battalion of the Seaforth Highlanders arrived here last night, and the remainder today, with their stores. . . . There are a few deers and foxes about this part.

Cox: Up at 4.30 after sleeping anyhow. The whole force went out under Sirdar and took up a position. They had half an idea that we might come across the dervishes, but no luck, so after a few manoeuvres we returned to bivouack, I mounting outposts. Getting quite used to this rough life but haven't had time to wash for the last 48 hours.

18TH MARCH

Teigh: Parade as usual. Breakfast with biscuits and only one camp kettle of tea, which is only 22 pints for the section, which is about 29 strong, some more. After that I had to go on outpost duty. About 3 pm we got the order to shift again at 4, but that was false. We had 10 men sent back sick. One man of the Warwicks had both hands blown off. He was leaning over the camp fire to get a light for his pipe, when a packet of ammunition fell from his pocket and he tried to pick it up and it went off blowing both his hands and doing him other injuries. Orders were read out to us tonight and said that we were going to do a 48 hours' march across the desert with only a pint and a half of water to drink for the first day and a quart for the next 24 hours, besides what we carried in our water bottles. The Captain told us to get any glass bottles that we had a chance to for the purpose of carrying water.

Cox: Came off outposts at 11 am, relieved late owing to field day, went to sleep afternoon and was awakened at 3 pm to find that everything was to be packed in an hour and the force ready to march, rations for 3 days, no kits, officers and men alike viz one blanket. It appears that Osman Digna has gone up the Atbara and is going towards Berber, getting round us, consequently we have to march out into the desert to intercept him. Later – all prepared, servant, donkey and kit gone down to river to be stored on boats. Marched down and bathed with company in the evening.

19TH MARCH

Teigh: We got relieved off outpost at 10 am and all the stretcher bearers had to undergo a course of instructions in bandaging up wounds.

Cox: No orders to start yet, we went out and manoeuvred. Don't think desert march will come off as it is rumoured that dervish have appeared a few miles south of Atbara and they think they are going for the Dakheila camp. Sorry for them if they do. 4 pm rumoured that dervish force is divided ½ going to Dakala and ½ to ford 7 miles up Atbara – still waiting order with my blanket.

20TH MARCH

Teigh: Church parade at 5.45 am. The General gave us a lecture and said that he expected to be in action in a day or two and said we would fall in at 10.15 ready to start. It was a great sight to see the troops come with glass bottles and jars. Our company had 4 beasty bags. We marched across the desert to the Atbara river about 10 miles distant. When we arrived we had to make a zariba. After that we made a drink of tea and then settled down alongside the native troops.

Cox: If this isn't the height of discomfort, I don't know what is. I've got a beastly cold and spent a miserable night, one blanket, beastly cold and a sandstorm. I do wish we could start somewhere, this waiting is infernal, but I expect we shall have enough of it when it does come, as everything points to a big fight. Orders came and we marched off at 10.15 am, cut across desert and bivouacked 7 miles up Atbara. Many rumours of enemy. River very pretty, back wooded and looking very gamey.

21ST MARCH

Teigh: About 12 at night a sad accident occurred; awful commotion, lots of men fixed bayonets and were running everywhere. One of the Seaforths got stabbed in the arm. The troops got settled down again, but I was not able to get much rest afterwards. We paraded at 7.15 am. The Commanding Officer and the General spoke to us about last night's affair and he was sorry that such a thing should happen in such a good old Regiment. We marched away in the same order. It was very warm and we went another 10 miles to a place called Ras el Hudi to the Atbara River where we could cross quite easy; we got a wash here and we let the sun do for a towel. We made a zariba and then got a rest. The Egyptian Scouts kept bringing in Dervish prisoners. We got a better rest that night but it was very cold towards morning.

Cox: Very cold night. We were awakened in the night by an alarm, I woke up and heard frantic yelling and a shot fired. We thought they were in us, men fell in, fixed bayonets and lined zariba. Nothing happened except that one of our men and one of the 72nd were accidentally bayonetted. Cause of alarm unknown. Paraded at 9.15 am and marched in fighting formation and bivouacked 8 miles further up Atbara, no enemy seen. Osman Digna evidently leading us a dance. G.O.C. cursed us for causing false alarm, it was Wilson's company and all caused by an infernal donkey who galloped over the company when asleep. Man in the 72nd died of his wound.

Meiklejohn: Gatacre had impressed on us that we might now be attacked at any moment, with lurid descriptions of hordes of dervishes suddenly rushing us with sword and spear, and had succeeded in making the men thoroughly jumpy. We all had to sleep EXACTLY in the centre of our Command (Company or Section) with OUR FEET to the zariba, the great idea being that we should then automatically spring up facing the enemy. The men, as usual, had to sleep with their arms through the slings of their rifles, while officers had to have their sword knots round their right wrist, and their revolver at their left hand. (Our swords had all been sharpened.) Half the men had to be awake all night, while subalterns had to take an hour's duty patrolling all sentries. My tour was from 1 till 2 am, so I rolled up in my blanket and went to sleep. About 10.30 pm I woke suddenly hearing the sentry shout, "Stand to everyone. They're on us". Firing began from the Lincolns and Seaforths on our left, facing the desert, which rapidly developed into a roar of musketry. We fell in at once and waited, expecting to be rushed at any moment. Skipwith and a few others unfortunately used the wrong procedure in rising, and hastily rushing forward in the wrong direction to find their men got involved in camel thorn (it was very dark) and their pained remarks added to the general uproar. I jumped up hastily, drawing my sword and revolver, and my company fixed bayonets, the men behaving most coolly, though there was a good deal of noise and shouting going on in other parts. The river showed up indistinctly below the steep banks and we waited breathlessly. Some bird flew off with a raucous cry, and later, a crocodile plunged heavily into a pool, the company wit remarking in a stage whisper, "Blimey! Old Mahmud's fallen in. 'Ope he gets a wetting." Then later, "Pass the word to Mahmud to 'urry up. We're getting tired." "Tell 'im to put it off till tomorrow" etc.

I looked carefully over the bank, but could see nothing, and later Cockburn, my Major, sent me to try and find out what was happening. I made towards the Lincolns' lines, passing the hospital where a man was lying on a stretcher with an ugly wound in his throat. The whole thing was a false alarm. Apparently a donkey had strayed outside the zariba, tried to make its way back, and brayed opposite a young sentry of the Lincolns, who promptly opened magazine fire. The Picquets joined in, and the Seaforth Highlanders charged a small group of Lincolns bayonetting two men. We got well chaffed by the Officers of the Egyptian and Soudanese armies, who, incidentally, as usual, had all turned in in pyjamas, and Gatacre was very angry. Yet the whole affair was entirely due to his continual talk of being attacked at any moment, and the unnecessary strain he puts on all of us. I was on patrol from 11.30 till 12.30 pm.

Skinner: During the excitement a man of the Lincolns was brought to us with a bayonet wound of the left wrist, also a man of the Seaforths with two bayonet wounds in his neck. This man's wounds were rather severe, and it was thought that he would not get over it.

22ND MARCH

Teigh: We had to light fires to keep us warm. Just as we were getting our breakfast we got the order to stand to our arms. We heard plenty of firing and soon found out that we were very close to the Dervishes and the Egyptian cavalry was engaged with them. They killed about 50 as they were crossing the river. We turned out in the usual order and marched for about 3 miles, and then laid down ready for firing at them, but they must have retired for after waiting for an hour in the burning hot sun we marched back to the same camp again and had a rest.

We passed the day strengthening the zariba and making some funny boiling biscuits and grease in a corn beef tin. We had a good night's rest, but before we laid down all the trees and bushes were burnt down to the ground for 1,000 yards in front of us.

Cox: Last night most bitterly cold – not good enough with only one blanket. Got told off by that dear old man for going to warm myself at a cookhouse fire. He was there of course. Our cavalry discovered dervish cavalry 11 miles further up river and lost 8 men killed, 8 wounded, 3 missing. Don't know our movements but wish the deuce we could get it over. Seen some huge fish in the river of all sorts, which are quite uncivilized, take lots of biscuits greedily – wish I had some tackle. River scenery very pretty – palms and other tropical plants. A Soudanese battalion and the cavalry went out about 6 am. At breakfast we heard firing about 5 miles off. We all fell in and marched off in battle array, but old Osman would have none of us and gracefully retired. It's getting very trying. I wish we could finish it. Renissi Ball (B & W artist) says that we are far worse off for comfort than they were on the N.W. frontier.

Meiklejohn: Started at 7 am and marched a few miles to the next ford of the Atbara, Ras el Hudi, or El Gousa. Plenty of rumours – we were led to expect a fight daily. Wonderful scenery along the river, and several birds – parrots, sun birds, etc. Plenty of snakes and of course scorpions. A few hares were put up out of the grass, and officers and men tried a chase after them. The Egyptian and Soudanese troops knocked down the nuts of the Dom palms and ate them. We got some dried dates, which, though hard as stones, are very sustaining. Having no kit we could not even shave and nobody had brought soap or any change of kit. Nights very chilly, but I wrapped a newspaper round my centre which was a help. We again built zariba of mimosa round the camp (the thorns are over 1" long and like skewers), and also put some wire in front. This was tightened up at night about a foot from the ground, to trip the enemy. Actually it was a great success with parties of our men coming back from bathing, a very democratic function, for Officers of all ranks: men: Egyptian soldiers: and Soudanese: all bathe together in the "altogether" with camels, donkeys, horses, etc. Half the battalion bathes while the other half acts as a "Covering party". We wash our clothes and wait for them to dry in the sun.

23RD MARCH

Teigh: I was out in the morning with a covering party getting long grass and leaves to make a bit of shelter. Then we had a wash and I passed the remainder of the day sitting watching the fish in the Atbara River. There is some splendid fish here. We have got a road across the river here and I had to do 2 hours' sentry at night. Each company finds a double sentry at night.

Cox: Up at reveille. Dervish camp fires seen last night. Black brigade went out early this morning to try and get dervishes out of the bush, but with no success. Very uncomfortable and everybody fed up.

24TH MARCH

Teigh: I had dinner of corn beef and biscuits, which I boiled in a corn beef tin, and spent most of the day on the banks of the Atbara River. It is a splendid place here. Our Company had a bathing parade after tea. I had a walk across the other side as the water was not deep enough to swim in. There is still a few prisoners coming in.

Cox: A peaceful day – 2 dervishes (deserters) came in and say that they are hard up for grub and about 20 miles up river. Gyppy battalion gone back to Dakheila thence bound for Shendi to occupy same. A godsend in the shape of a grub store arrived – sardines etc. Tatchell sent back with convoy to get up servants and rest of our kit. Barlow got leave to shoot and came back with 3 geese in about ½ an hour. Much warmer at night – built a palm leaf screen round me and slept on ground for bed. Sun getting very hot.

25TH MARCH

Teigh: Nothing but fatigues and cooking our food and it is terrible hot here every day now. It is hard to get dates now, they are only 10 for a piastre. My chum has bought some and is now boiling them down with biscuits for tea. After tea we got the order to form up, as we were expecting an attack, and we had to keep up till 10 pm before we were allowed to lay down.

Cox: Another peaceful day. Convoy came in but servant didn't turn up with kit till later. Bathed in river in evening but water too hot for enjoyment.

Meiklejohn: Turned in at 10 pm but was kicked up an hour later as the Commanding officer wished to see us all. He said information had just come in that we should probably be attacked at midnight. Little enthusiasm was shown, since Gatacre's panics are now not taken seriously. We all sat up till midnight and a section of each company was on duty all night, but, once again, Mahmud failed to keep his rendezvous. Camels and donkeys make a fearful noise all night, and one donkey with a very shrill voice is universally detested. They used to come out with the Brigade and carried back any men knocked out by the sun, and were known as "Gatacre's Light Horse". We hear that a Dervish crept up and looked over the zariba last night, where the Camerons were, but they did not fire. Presumably they did not want to create another panic! The Sirdar and General are much annoyed.

26TH MARCH

Teigh: It was pretty stiff and when the sun got up it was very hot. There was a Brigade parade but for the Soudanese only and they went out at daybreak. Our troops were glad to get a few moments to get a drink of tea but as there was not much of it, I mostly put a little water with mine to make a larger drink. I then went to the Atbara and sat there looking at different birds and fish. This is where I first saw a crocodile, about the length of myself. It crossed to the other side and disappeared. There is plenty of wild geese, ducks and hares about here, but no signs of the enemy at present.

Cox: Only got 1½ hrs' sleep last night, had to stand to arms as an attack was expected. However, nothing happened. Grub prices abominable – small loaves 1/3, sardines 6 of them 1/-. Few deserters came in today. I saw one of them – fine looking fellow but rather dilapidated. They say they are very hard up for food and must come on soon. Servant heartly ill – alcoholic pressure I think.

27TH MARCH

Teigh: Church parade, after the minister had finished the General told us about General Kitchener and how he captured a lot of Dervishes' cattle and an awful lot of women, who were the Dervishes' wives. He also told us that the enemy was only 15 miles from us and he expected them tonight or tomorrow. He also said that the troops were behaving very well and that we had not had many drunks. But this caused roars of laughter as we had not seen anything to make us drunk since January.

After breakfast our Company went down bathing, so most of us washed our shirts, socks and towels and the sun soon dried them. The Captain marched about half of them back to camp as the others were not ready, so he told a sergeant to bring the remainder on when they got dressed. So we had just got up to the camp, when the word came that Sergeant Mumby was missing. So the officer commanding got four companies and went down and undressed and we all advanced in line up the river, the Commanding Officer in the centre leading us on up and down the river. There were some places we could not bottom it. After a long search we could not find him. The General came down and said we had better come out as the sun was too hot and it might do us harm. Just after that I saw 5 Dervishes prisoners come in. One of them was stabbed in the chest. The Egyptian cavalry brought them in.

There is a Greek shop here with us now. He has got a lot of things but they are too dear, Cheese 12 Piastres a lb., Sardines small tins 3 piastres. Tonight they gave us more rest, one section each company did sentry every two hours. My shoulders and chest are very sore with straps buckled on so long and 120 rounds of ammunition in my pouches.

Cox: Stood at arms again last night. Church parade at 5.45 am. Slept till lunch. In afternoon had to go down with half battalion and dive for the body of Sgt Mumby who had apparently drowned – did not find him.

28TH MARCH

Teigh: Outpost duty. We had not been on very long when we heard Sergeant Mumby's body was found, so 'H' Company came to relieve us, while we buried him. It did not last long. We buried him 200 yards outside the zariba. After that I got a little rest. Then again we had to fall in to escort the Engineers, while they put down two rows of wires to stop the enemy from a rush. We got finished at 10.30 pm. Then again at 2 am until 4 am.

Cox: Standing to arms done away with, consequently had a good night and slept like a top. Mail arrived this morn, I had 6 letters and 5 lots of papers, a great relief after having nothing for a fortnight. Our part of camp quite silent, everybody reading. Sgt Mumby found this morning. Usual bathe in the evening.

29TH MARCH

Teigh: The Brigade paraded at 4.15 am. We did a march of about 7 miles and then we halted just to get a drink of hot tea. Then we started to march back again in the hot sun. There were a lot of men fell out and were carried to the Hospital with sun stroke. We got back to our camp about 12 noon. I was glad to get my straps off. We got a wash after tea, but we have to pay 5 piastres a bar for Sunlight soap. It is my turn tonight for a rest and I am very glad. Two Brigades of the Soudanese went out tonight. I believe they had a fight. We could hear some firing going on.

Cox: Brigade marched out 8 miles up Atbara, starting 4 am, saw nothing. Had breakfast and came back again, very hot. Lovely bath in the evening. Another deserter, this time angular warrior fully armed with camel.

STRATEGY

On 30 March Major General Hunter, in command of the Egyptian Infantry Division, made a reconnaissance in strength, but did not lure Mahmud out. He reported that Mahmud's zariba was very well defended with thick thorn barriers, a stockade, rifle-pits and trenches. While Gatacre was in favour of attack, Hunter advised caution. Kitchener dithered and could not make up his mind. Cairo was consulted:

"I am rather perplexed by the situation here. Mahmud remains stationary, and his army is badly off for supplies, and deserters keep coming in to us, though not in such large numbers as I expected. He is apparently waiting instructions from the Khalifa before advancing or retiring. It seems to be thought by the deserters that, as retirement would be an acknowledgement of fear, he will eventually advance. Here, we are all well off and healthy, with sufficient transport; fresh bread every second day and fresh meat every day.

"Yesterday I discussed the situation with Gatacre and Hunter. The former was inclined to attack Mahmud's present position; the latter to wait here. We should have the great advantage of ground if Mahmud will advance; but if he retires without our attacking him, the opportunity will have been lost of dealing him a blow by which future resistance in the Sudan would probably be considerably affected. I have little doubt of the success of our attack on his present entrenched position, although it would probably entail considerable loss. . . . I should be glad to learn your views on the subject." In turn London was asked their opinion, and later criticized Kitchener for having asked for advice. The Commander-in-Chief of the British Army, Field Marshal Wolseley, who had commanded the relief expedition to Khartoum in 1895, could not understand the Sirdar's inability to make a decision. "You have your thumb on the pulse of the army you command and you can best know what it is capable of."

Hunter was sent out again on 5 April and was attacked by Dervish cavalry, almost cut off, and had to withdraw under pressure. All of this increased the mental pressures in the camp, at least for the officers, who wanted to get on with it. Finally Kitchener decided that he would attack on Good Friday, 8 April. Possibly he thought that Mahmud was aware of the Christian calendar and would not expect an attack on this of all days, or that information had been leaked. On 4 April he moved five miles nearer, to Abadar, and on the 5th made a final reconnaissance.

Then on the 6th the army broke camp yet again and marched to a deserted village, Umdabia, where they bivouacked close to the Atbara and within striking distance, six miles, of Mahmud, Osman Digna and the Dervishes.

Mahmud had formed his zariba at Nakheila just north of the Atbara River in a circular form about half mile in diameter. On both the east and west sides there was thick scrub and the only open ground lay to the north. It was from here that Kitchener chose to make his attack. This could have been a dangerous decision, since over open country the army was more vulnerable. But at the time, and in all exercises during the build-up, the army, and most particularly the British Brigade, had trained in battlefield formations which were not unlike barrack-square drill. They moved, not as individuals, but on the command of an officer or a bugle call. Keeping rank and formation was vital, at least at the start, and Kitchener may have feared that in going through scrub this orderliness would be broken and men become detached from their commanders.

About 5 pm on Thursday, 7 April the British Brigade under Gatacre left Umdabia and moved slowly forward in formation squares. In *The River War* Churchill gives a graphic account. "No operation of war is more critical than a night-march. Over and over again in every country frightful disaster has overtaken the rash or daring force that has attempted it. In the gloom the shape and aspect of the ground are altered. Places well known by daylight appear strange and unrecognisable. The smallest obstacle impedes the column, which can only crawl sluggishly forward with continual checks and halts. The effect of the gloom upon the nerves of the soldiers is not less than on the features of the country. Each man tries to walk quietly, and hence all are listening for the slightest sound. Every eye seeks to pierce the darkness. Every sense in the body is raised to a pitch of expectancy. In such hours doubts and fears come unbidden to the brain, and the marching men wonder anxiously whether all will be well with the army, and whether they themselves will survive the event . . .

"For more than two hours the force advanced, moving across smooth swells of sand broken by rocks and with occasional small bushes. Several small *khors* traversed the road, and these rocky ditches, filled with a strange, sweet-scented grass, delayed the brigades until the pace was hardly two miles an hour. The smell of grass was noticed by the alert senses of many, and will for ever refresh in their minds the strong impression of the night. The breeze which had sprung up at sundown gradually freshened and raised clouds of fine sand, which deepened the darkness with a whiter mist.

"At nine o'clock the army halted in a previously selected space, near the deserted village of Mutrus and about two miles from the river. Nearly half the distance to Mahmud's zariba was accomplished, and barely four miles in the direct line divided the combatants; but since it was not desirable to arrive before dawn, the soldiers, still formed in their squares, lay down upon the ground. Meat and biscuits were served out to the men. The transport animals went by relays to the pools of the Atbara bed to drink and to replenish the tanks. All water-bottles were refilled, pickets being thrown out to cover the business. Then, after sufficient sentries had been posted, the army slept, still in array.

"During the halt the moon had risen, and when at one o'clock the advance was resumed, the white beams revealed a wider prospect and, glinting on the fixed bayonets, crowned the squares with a sinister glitter. For three hours the army toiled onwards at the same slow and interrupted crawl. Strict silence was now enforced, and all smoking was forbidden. The cavalry, the Camel Corps, and the five batteries had overtaken the infantry, so that the whole attacking force was concentrated. Meanwhile the Dervishes slept.

"At three o'clock the glare of fires became visible to the south, and, thus arrived before the Dervish position, the squares, with the exception of the reserve brigade, were unlocked, and the whole force, assuming formation of attack, now advanced in one long line through the scattered bush and scrub, presently to emerge upon a large plateau which overlooked Mahmud's zariba from a distance of about 900 yards."

This was the experience of Private Teigh, Lieutenant Cox and others in the British Brigade.

The Sirdar's Army was deployed along a curved front of about 1,500 yards facing south. The British Brigade under Gatacre was on the left or east of the line, with the Egyptian cavalry further east, and the Egyptian and Soudanese Brigades further to the west. Batteries of artillery were in strategic positions. A Rocket Battery under Lieutenant Beatty, RN. was available, proving very effective, and Maxims were placed behind with the cavalry.

At 6.15 am an artillery barrage opened up and the Maxims stopped any attempt by the Dervishes to advance. This barrage lasted for an hour and a half, before the infantry advanced towards the zariba. Gatacre placed himself at the head of his brigade and led them on foot into battle with drawn sword. Beside him was Brooke, his ADC, his chief clerk, Lance-Corporal Wyeth, carrying a large and conspicuous Union Jack, and his orderly, Private Cross. Behind this group were the Camerons in line abreast and behind them the Lincolns, the Seaforths and the Warwicks, from right to left, drawn up in column of companies.

When, at 7.45 am, the "Advance" sounded the long curved line of troops moved forward with beating drums, skirling pipes, flashing bayonets and shouts of "Remember Gordon". There was no immediate response from the Dervishes, who held their fire, doubting their own marksmanship and having inferior Remingtons, some without sights. The many months of practice on the desert allowed the British Brigade to move forward with parade-ground precision, "as slow as a funeral" in General Hunter's opinion. The Sirdar and his staff were almost immediately behind the Lincolns, which for Lieutenant Cox was helpful, as much signalling was required. As they advanced the officers assumed an air of nonchalance, while the NCOs checked the dressing in the ranks and ordered adjustments. Occasionally they halted to allow the Camerons at the front to fire, but Gatacre, in positioning his three other battalions behind them, reduced the firepower of his brigade.

At about 300 yards the Dervishes opened fire, having already suffered considerable losses. On reaching the zariba the troops found it to be much less of an obstacle than originally reported. Gatacre was the first to reach it and was attacked by a whirling Dervish with a huge spear as he tugged at the thorn branches. "Give him the bayonet, lad!" he growled at his orderly. Meanwhile the bearer of the Union Jack had been seriously wounded by a bullet in the leg, from which he later died, bringing criticism on Gatacre for unnecessarily exposing him as a target. The Dervishes fought with desperate ferocity but were soon overcome, and in half an hour the zariba was taken.

Henry Keown-Boyd in *A Good Dusting* writes: "'The Blacks went through the zariba like paper,' wrote Walter Kitchener, (the Sirdar's brother) and, as a result, suffered fewer casualties at this stage than did their British comrades, whose stately progress up to the defences had cost them the majority of their one hundred and twenty-five killed and wounded. The mayhem and carnage within the zariba was a nightmare of horror. Men, women, children and animals, shattered and disembowelled by shell-fire, littered the ground and filled the entrenchments. Both British and Egyptian Army officers temporarily lost control of their men who rampaged through the Mahdist camp venting their blood-lust indiscriminately. Even Dervishes holding out the traditional mimosa sprig of submission were ruthlessly shot, bayoneted or clubbed. 'Tommy was as bad as the Blacks,' observed Walter Kitchener, and remembered Brooke remonstrating furiously with a British private: 'Hey, you, what did you shoot that man for?' and getting the indignant reply, 'Well, sir, I didn't think he was quite dead!' . . . Despite the inhibiting formation adopted by Gatacre, the four British battalions managed to loose off some 56,000 rounds of ammunition, probably about half during the advance and the remainder inside the zariba."

The British Brigade continued its advance right through the zariba until the river was reached, with Dervishes fleeing in front over the soft sand of the river bed, and because their progress was slow many more were killed. The water,which many foolishly drank, was reddish with blood.

Osman Digna, who took little part, moved away early and escaped capture, as he had done before. The Soudanese found Mahmud crouching wounded in a dugout, and he was rescued from the bayonets of the soldiers to be dragged before the Sirdar. An interesting conversation took place:

"Are you the man Mahmud?" Kitchener asked in Arabic.

"Yes. I am Mahmud. And I am your equal in rank."

"Why did you come here to burn and kill?"

"I obeyed my orders, as you obey yours."

A few days later he was paraded through Berber dragging chains which were riveted round his ankles and wearing a halter round his neck. His hands were bound behind his back, and he was driven forward by Soudanese guards who lashed him with whips when he stumbled, while crowds pelted and reviled him. Kitchener rode on a white horse in triumph. Mahmud was then imprisoned.

The Anglo-Egyptian casualties were heavy: 570 killed and wounded, including five British officers. Of the Lincolns Sergeant Malone was killed, and the Commanding Officer, Colonel T. E. Verner, was badly wounded in the face and invalided home. Major Simpson temporarily took command. Lieutenant Boxer, who shared a tent with Cox, was wounded. It was estimated that three thousand Dervishes died in the zariba, and more as they tried to escape. Few were prepared to be taken prisoner.

A small First-Aid Post had been set up nearby, but proved wholly inadequate and very badly equipped. Wounded lay on stretchers for hours in the hot sun before being taken to the hospital at Umdabia, eight miles away. Some of the wounded died before receiving proper attention.

The result of the Battle of the Atbara was enthusiastically received in London. The Sirdar's achievement lay not so much in his strategy in the battle itself – and Gatacre's positioning of the British Brigade was questionable – as in having brought an army of this size to such an extremely inhospitable place, and fed and watered it. That was indeed worthy of congratulation.

Colonel Verner made a formal report to General Gatacre:-

"British Infantry Brigade,
"Sudan, 9th April, 1898.

"Sir

"I have the honour to submit a report of the part taken by the Battalion in the action against the Dervishes, fought yesterday. At the conclusion of the bombardment of the Dervish entrenched camp by our Artillery, the Battalion under my command advanced in column in rear of the right of the 'Queen's Own' Cameron Highlanders. When the 'Queen's Own' Cameron Highlanders halted, about 50 yards from the zariba on a slight rise, I ordered 'B' Company [Cox's] of my Battalion to prolong the line on the Cameron's right, and assist with fire. The advance was resumed in about a minute and a half and continued up to the zariba, 'B' Company 1st Lincoln Regiment falling into its old position. The Camerons' right Company pulled away about 30 yards of the zariba. 'A' Company, followed by 'B' Company, which deployed to the right, came to the first serious obstacle, a palisade with trench beyond. No more Companies could deploy, as the 11th Soudanese were in touch with my right. The men followed their officers quickly over this obstacle, and all advancing together, firing at men in the pits. The casualties amounted to one sergeant killed, and three officers and fourteen men wounded. All of these, except the sergeant killed and one man wounded, occurred inside the zariba. Two out of the three officers wounded, including the sergeant killed, belonged to the two leading Companies of the Battalion.

"Owing to the restricted front available, I was never able to deploy more than these two Companies, but the Officers commanding the rear Companies led them independently through the zariba, and assisted wherever required. The enemy was pursued down to the bank of the river and then fired upon.

"'G' Company, under Lieutentant Wilson, assisted Captain de Rougemont's Battery to drag their guns and carry ammunition through the Dervish camp."

Here Private Teigh and Lieutenant Cox fought their first battle.

4

THE BATTLE OF THE ATBARA

<u>30TH MARCH</u>

Teigh: Just as our water was boiling for breakfast the order came to shift. So we had to throw the water away to pack up the kettles, and after all our troubles we did not shift. So I had a sit down in the shade and wrote a letter home. We had another man die with fever. His name was Bailey. This is 3 of my great friends, as they all enlisted when I did, and have been in my company all the time. I have to do duty again tonight.

Cox: Up at 4.15 am. On patrol last night 12 to 2, heard firing in the distance. Our cavalry and a black brigade were out. Hunter made reconnaissance and discovered dervish position. They have strongly entrenched themselves in a position 3 miles long, which I've no doubt we shall know more of later. Had usual wash and swim in river in the evening.

<u>31ST MARCH</u>

Teigh: We paraded at 5 am and did a few movements on the desert till 9. When we returned there was an awful lot of whirl-winds and they had our shades all down. As General Kitchener was coming into our camp he had a fall over the wire, but did not hurt himself.

Cox: Up at 4.15. Mounted outposts at daylight 5 am. Began letter home. Quite missed my bath. Mainwaring, Forrest and Wilson gone back to Kunur and Darmali with convoys to fetch men's kits.

1ST APRIL

Teigh: Paraded again doubling over the desert. Lots of our men still keep going into hospital everyday. I have to go about 2 miles with my blanket to cut some grass and bring it into camp for the Mule Battery. I have to cut it with my pocket knife which we all had one each issued out to us before leaving Cairo. I was on sentry and it was something awful for the pi dogs were barking all night and wandering about in search of dead animals. They created a great noise fighting for pieces of meat and in the daytime we could see a lot of great birds feeding on the same food.

Cox: Up at reveille and on parade at 5.30, brigade manoeuvres. Another mail in today. Heard that Barter comes back, that just upsets my promotion. Bathed in the evening. On patrol from 8 to 10 pm.

Meiklejohn: The April "fooling" today took the form of "reliable information" (started by Skipwith and Co.) that Mahmud's force had retired on Khartoum, and that the British Brigade were returning to Cairo. This created such alarm and despondency that it was not persisted in. Actually the Sirdar has sent an Egyptian Brigade down the river, and they have attacked and captured Shendi, where Mahmud had left his women. Our booty consisted of 8 war drums: and 160 women! Over 150 dervishes were killed. We imagine this must result in "drawing" Mahmud.

2ND APRIL

Teigh: We had our morning parade as usual and had a little meat for dinner, the first that we could eat up to now, as they used to cook it at nightime and by the time we wanted to eat it the next day, it was bad. We had to throw it away and eat biscuits. The Cavalry has just brought 7 more Dervishes in.

Cox: Up at reveille and on parade at 5.30, Brigade manoeuvres. This appears quite true about Barter, such a damned nuisance just when I had mapped out such a ripping future for myself. Goodness knows when I shall get my company now. On foraging fatigue t'other side of river in morning and read all afternoon, bathed in the evening, I don't know what we should do without our daily tub. Adamson gone back to take charge of hospital at Darmali – very sorry – don't know who we shall have now.

3RD APRIL

Teigh: It is our Company's turn for outpost today. I cooked some dates and biscuits for breakfast and me and my chum made a shade and sat down and ate them, but we could not sit down in peace as there were so many flies. After we had finished, I got a paper and read a little to my chum, as he is unable to read. Next morning when we got into camp the first thing we heard that the order was to advance at 5 am.

Cox: Up at reveille, rather a head on owing to dining last night with the correspondents who did me very proud – phiz! cut whisky and soda tumblers. Church parade at 6.45. We move on tomorrow.

Meiklejohn: Church parade in the morning. We had the hymn "Soldiers of Christ arise" which was sung enthusiastically, and after the sermon General Gatacre made a speech in which he surpassed all previous efforts. He described the zariba as 8 to 10 ft. high and enormously thick and strong held by thousands of terrible warriors, who, we gathered, were certain to get in amongst us. He ended by saying that some of us might think we had an easy task: others might picture wading ankle-deep in blood: actually we were more likely to find ourselves knee-deep in it before next Sunday. To anyone who did not know Gatacre it might have had a most depressing effect, and not calculated to cheer the spirits of troops or improve their morale. Actually nobody took it very seriously and we were all rather amused.

4TH APRIL

Teigh: We started on the march again from Ras el Hudi and marched about 6 miles, when we reached our new camp called Abadar. Here we settled for about 2 days, but as soon as we arrived we had to make a zariba again. But everyone had to help with it, so it did not take too long to get it together. We rested for the remainder of the day.

Cox: Paraded at 4 and up at 3.30 am. We marched on to a new bivouac about 5 miles further. A ripping stop, beautifully shady bush and palm trees with all sorts of birds, all colours and including parrots, some of them sing beautifully. Killed 9 scorpions making a pathway through the bush, and saw a gigantic lizard about 2½ feet long. Been trying to fish again but didn't succeed, Woodcock caught 2. Had the whole plan of attack given us, but don't believe it until it comes off. Very hot in the day, reporters not allowed to send temperature home to papers, yesterday it was 115° in the shade.

5TH APRIL

Teigh: The General came round this morning and gave us a lecture about the Dervishes' position and told us to have some gloves made of skin on purpose to pull away the zariba. So we had some made. There was a lot of men told off to make these gloves at 1 pm and did not get finished till 8 pm. You should have heard how they grumbled when they got back.

Cox: Up at 4.15 – I always begin like that somehow – stood to until daylight, when we collected stuff to make "Tables" and accoutrement racks. Had rather a fine breakfast, kedgeree made of potted salmon and rice followed by bullock's heart and bacon! At 9 am heard very heavy firing and the usual panic ensued, viz the whole brigade rushed across and dressed. However, firing ceased, the reconnaissance going on I suppose. We shall hear later. Later – It appears that the guns and cavalry were nearly cut off this morning – Pearce shot through the arm and 6 Egyptian cavalry killed – dervish's losses unknown. We got close to the position and dervish cavalry came out both sides and surrounded us. Consequently we had to cut our way back.

6TH APRIL

Teigh: Today Colonel McDonald's Egyptian Brigade joined us and also the Rocket Machine Battery under a naval Officer[1]. They soon started to prepare for action. They got the Machines in splendid condition and everything was ready for use.

Cox: Reveille this morning at 2.15. We marched off at 3, went 6 miles and zaribered (Umdabia). We passed a deserted village of straw on the way with all the beds and native furniture strewn about the place, also some exploded shell used yesterday. My servant collared a native bed on which I have ensconced myself and had a beautiful rest during the day. Plenty of evidence as to dervishes having been here, all the palm trees stripped of nuts. We are only 6 miles off the dervish position now and ought to be at them soon. This is not a good bivouac, no decent shade and very poor water.

7TH APRIL

Teigh: The morning came and the news soon went round the camp that we were going to start on the march tonight, ready to get in position for the 8th. The time kept passing by and by 2 pm we got the order to get ready and everything was soon put together ready for starting and about 5.30 pm we marched in squares for about 5 miles. Then we halted for the night. Here we had our next day's rations issued out to us, which consisted of corned beef and biscuits, and then we had a lay down on the desert.

Cox: Had a most disgusting night. We slept on ground which has once been cultivated, which gives out a fine sandy soil, almost as fine as smoke, and of course as luck would have it we had a most terrific sandstorm, and everybody appeared this morning like sweeps. The fight is going to come off at last, orders have come and we march 5 miles into the desert parading at 5 pm this evening taking nothing but ammunition – cooking pots. At 2 am tomorrow morn we advance on the position. The fight is to be preceded by ¾ of an hour Artillery fire, after which the infantry assault. We are in the assaulting line consisting of 3 brigades. I hope all may go well

---

[1]   Lieutenant David Beatty, RN. later Admiral of the Fleet the Earl Beatty.

and the men behave like Britishers. The Sirdar has chosen a good day.

Meiklejohn: At 10 am we got orders that we were to parade at 5 pm and attack Mahmud at dawn tomorrow. The Sirdar ended his order with the words, "The Sirdar feels absolutely certain that every man will do his duty. He has only these words to say: 'Remember Gordon. The men before you are murderers'." We got verbal orders to be careful of passing any enemy wounded, as their trick was to feign death and then stab from behind. Even the genuinely wounded might do this. If a man held up his hands he was to be spared. I was on fatigue most of the morning. Then wrote some letters in case of accidents and made a short Will. We are told that the enemy zariba is very high and thick. The orders are that the Camerons will advance in line, keeping up a heavy fire, and will tear away gaps in the zariba. Then the Lincolns on the right, the Seaforths in the centre and ourselves on the left will go through these gaps and clear the inside. We are also to guard the left flank against attack, specially the Cavalry.

Everybody very excited and discussing things when we have a chance. The Camerons have made straw ropes to cross the zariba, while we are going to try and carry some blankets to throw on top, as the very long, sharp mimosa thorns may prove a difficulty. As Major Quayle-Jones is in Command, and Major Cockburn 2nd in Command, I am the only officer with 'F' company, but, though the junior 2nd. Lt. it has been decided that I shall remain in command, and nobody be brought in. Cockburn tells me this is a great compliment, to be allowed to command a company in action while so young. It has been decided that 'G' company, under Caldecott, is to lead. Mine was suggested but somebody remarked that I was the only officer, and if I got shot there would be no other available. I retorted that I did not mean to get shot, and thanked Skipwith for his kind suggestion. He retorted that you never knew your luck. We are told that the Dervishes have every kind of quaint guns, and fire even stones and glass from their rifles. Somebody remarked that it would be a fitting end to Sergeant – to get half a beer bottle into him! We have kept 6 bottles of champagne and have agreed to take these on the mess camel at all costs to commemorate our victory. Later General Gatacre came round and spoke to each battalion. The conversation was typical and went something as follows:

General G: "Now they all understand that they have to go straight through everything?"

Major Quayle-Jones: "Oh yes. Sir."

General G: "If they come to a stone wall 10ft. high, the first company will go through it and the others follow."

Major Q-J: "Yes, Sir. We'll do it."

Gen.G: "There must be no firing in the zariba. Only bayonets."

Major Q-J: "Yes. Sir."

Gen.G: "And they are not to stop for anything till they reach the river."

Major Q-J: "All right, Sir. I'll stop them there." Etc. Etc.

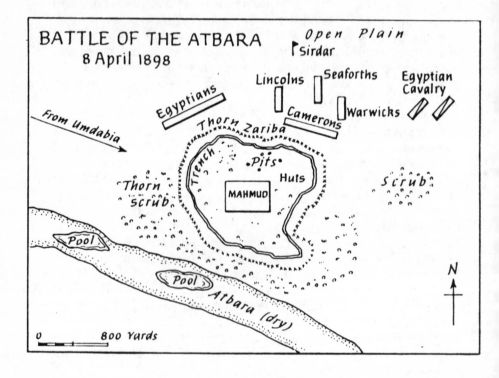

The 21st Lancers preparing to march.

0. The Warwickshire Regiment and the Seaforth Highlanders in action in 1898.

11. The Sirdar directing the Battle of Omdurman.

12. In front of the zariba at Omdurman: guns sited between the British and Egyptian Brigad

3. The Rifle Brigade entering the city.

4. The Guards entering the city.

15. The Mahdi's tomb.

16. Débris in the courtyard of General Gordon's palace.

It struck us as curiously reminiscent of a "Punch and Judy" show. Rene Bull had already drawn and sent off a picture of our storming the zariba for "Black and White". British troops in a terrifically high zariba, being charged by dervishes led by one clearly meant to represent Bennet Burleigh[1] whom he detests.

8TH APRIL: GOOD FRIDAY

Teigh: About 2.30 am this morning we started marching again and we had a very long course to take before we reached the Dervishes' position. I should think it was about 12 miles before we reached our destination, but we were soon in position. When we got there and the Egyptian Artillery opened fire upon the Dervishes, which lasted for about an hour, and then we started to advance and did some very brave deeds, especially the Lincolns. They very soon got the zariba away, and were soon inside amongst the Dervishes, slaughtering them. Everyone they saw they had a shot at or stabbed them with our bayonets, whether he was dead or alive, for we thought of the hardships they had put us to, and also the long dreary marches across the desert before we came to them. When we were on the march I could hear the troops saying that they would make sure that every Dervisher they passed, they would make sure that he was dead before leaving them, and they kept their word. But it was a horrible sight to see the dead women, men and children. It made my blood run cold for a short time, but I soon got warmed up. The battle lasted about 2 hours and a few troops gave a ringing cheer. Shortly after, they called the roll to see who was absent or killed. Just as they were doing this our Colonel came past and we gave him 3 cheers for he led the Lincolns into the zariba but he got wounded and had to go to the Hospital. We also gave the Sirdar 3 ringing cheers. After the Roll was called in our Battalion, it was found that only one was killed, which was Sergeant Malone, and about 17 wounded. The Brigade was formed up and piled arms and men were told off to go to the river to fill the camel tanks with water, but the water was so dirty scarcely anyone drank it. In the river there were a lot of

[1] A *Times* correspondent.

dead Dervishes that fell during the fight and this is the water that we had to drink. Soon after that the men started to patrol around the side of the zariba, where we had just been fighting to find curios such as spears, swords, rifles and daggers or any mortal thing they could find. There was a great lot of spears and rifles found and also some of Mahmud's flags and etc.

After that we had to get ready to march back. We started at 5.30 pm and did a march of about 14 miles across the desert, when we rested for the night ready for our next march.

Cox: Last night we paraded at 5 pm, marched in brigade squares 4 miles up Atbara, lay down and slept till one. At one we marched on out into the desert, making a detour of dervish position and attacked them at 6.15 am. Details of fight see Appendix I. Shan't forget this Good Friday in a hurry, had a splitting headache all day and had been in the sun until 4 pm when we marched back to former bivouac. We were very glad to get away from the battlefield as it was beginning to smell 'orrid, dead bodies and wounded dervishes all along the route. After my experience today I have come to the conclusion that a married civilian is the life for me. Of course – the dressing station had no chloroform!

Cox – Appendix to Diary:
ATBARA – 8.4.97 [sic]
Fought 30 miles up the At^r ara on the right bank. After frequent reconnaissances by Egyptia 1 troops under General Hunter the dervish army under Mahmud was discovered entrenched. The front of his position was protected by a mimosa bush zariba in rear of which had been dug rifle pits capable of holding 2 or 3 men each, and so arranged as to afford 3 tiers of fire; they also afforded an obstacle to assault in that they were about 3½ feet deep and irregularly arranged. Immediately in rear of zariba a palm tree palisade was constructed about 3½ feet high with trench in rear. The position extended along a front of 1½ miles and 600 yards from front to rear. The rear of the position was protected by the river and bank, the latter being thickly wooded with palm trees. On the 7th inst. the situation of the British bivouac was situated on the Atbara 6 miles west of the dervish force. At 5 pm the British and Egyptian force paraded and marched in column of brigade squares along river for 3 miles, halted and lay down. At 1 am on the 8th inst. the force resumed

its march, marching east into the desert, changing direction to the right, and arriving 800 yds in front of the dervish position at dawn. The infantry formed up in line, the British brigade on the left, 3 Soudanese brigades, and one Egyptian brigade in reserve. All cavalry were on the left flank. Guns were massed in front of the centre of the line.

The Artillery opened fire with shrapnel at 6.15 am.

On arrival in front of the position dervishes were seen to be retiring irregularly into the zariba – and white flags were hoisted at different intervals along the line. The guns continued firing with great precision for an hour and a half – every shell appeared to burst in the position – and numerous straw houses and palm trees were set on fire. The rockets appeared to be a failure. During this cannonade no dervishes could be seen moving about. At 7.45 am the order was passed round: "The infantry will prepare to assault". At 7.50 the infantry moved forward in quick time – bands playing – fixed bayonets at the slope. There was no sign of dervishes until the infantry had reached a point 300 yards from the zariba, when a very heavy fire was opened from the palisade and rifle pits. My company was at once ordered up on the right of the 79th to fill the gap between them and the Soudanese brigade. The enemy's fire was very heavy but inaccurate, most of the bullets were heard whizzing overhead – explosive bullets were also heard bursting. About 150 yds from the zariba a man in front of me was hit near the eye and turned round and spoke to me. He went on when I told him. At that moment a bullet went through my helmet. I then spoke to Sgt Malone on my left who fell shot in the mouth. We continued to advance. I heard after that Sgt Malone was killed. On arrival at the zariba there was a momentary check while we pulled away the bushes, the enemy's fire still being heavy from the rifle pits. Entrances being made in the zariba we went over the palisade wall into the middle of them firing and using the bayonet. Dead dervishes, donkeys, ponies, camels and in places women and children lay dead and wounded in indescribable confusion – the smell was a bit like a slaughter house. The disgusting sanitary arrangements were much in evidence, likewise the so-called humane conduct of the Englishman, who except in a very few occasions, where officers were on the spot to prevent it, spared nothing except the animals. Funny that the animals should be spared, perhaps it was animal instinct. However, not a man got off. Wounded or no, bayonets were shoved through anything human in the most brutal and cold-blooded fashion. Instance – a man (dervish) dropped his weapons and threw up his arms for mercy in front of one of the 79th who turned round and appealed to a sergeant who said, "Put him out of misery, Sandy. We don't want none of these buggers 'ere." The private turned round and bayoneted him through the neck and again through the back as he fell. However, there is only one thing to be said that one must remember what perfect devils these dervishes are – their frightful cruel habits – Gordon's murder – and their treatment of the Jaalins.

However, to continue, the advance was continued steadily until about half-way through the position when the dervish fire lessened and ultimately ceased as they broke and fled across the dry river bank where many were shot. As we reached the river the "cease fire" sounded followed by the assembly, and we formed up by battalions outside the position. Directly the "cease fire" sounded every regiment broke into tremendous cheers. We then marched about ½ mile and piled arms and fell out. I collapsed with a headache and consequently didn't go over the field after, but I think the sight of those rifle pits full of writhing bodies and frightful wounded as we passed over them didn't invite a second visit. The Regt. captured a Krupp gun and numerous flags and of course individuals got numerous weapons. The dervish firearms consisted mostly of Remingtons; a few modern Italian magazine rifles were found. In the evening we marched back to bivouack and were allowed to sleep without our equipment and boots on, the first time for weeks – such a rest to the feet. Total loss on our side 510 men killed and wounded. Dervish forces 3000 killed, 4000 prisoners and a large number of camels, donkeys and horses. All their Emirs were shot and Mahmud captured, Osman Digna escaping.

NARROW SHAVES IN THE REGT.

My helmet shot through, Maxwell hit with spent bullet on knee, Plunkett carrying a sack under his arm to put over the zariba – sack shot. Marsh – shot through the seat of his breeches.

Findlay in the 79th speared from behind by shamming dervish – poor chap only been married 3 months. A man in the

79th helped a woman out of a pit and told her to go off to the rear, when he turned his back she snatched up a rifle and shot him – she had 7 bayonets into her simultaneously!

Meiklejohn: After filling our water bottles we started off again. The ground was hard and having all our kit on we could only sleep on our faces. It was cold and we all woke up rather stiff. We moved on slowly till 5 am. In places there was a wonderful aromatic scent from some desert vegetation. The night was brilliantly star-lit, and one could distinguish the masses of men moving slowly through the darkness. We speculated on what was before us. Some feared Mahmud might retire without fighting; others maintained we had a very stiff job to carry out. About 5 am we halted for an hour about 1 mile from the enemy. Day and I lay down together to keep warm, and tried to sleep. But we soon woke feeling very cold and walked up and down to get warm. Gradually dawn came and the order to rise was whispered along. No lights were allowed and words of command had to be given in a whisper. Then we moved off, getting into our fighting formation. The Camerons led in line. We were in Company column on their left, my company being in rear. The Seaforths and Lincolns were also in company column behind the Camerons. Soon we saw large fires in the valley beneath, and realised that the enemy were still there! A huge flock of vultures, about 200, rose just on our left. They had doubtless gathered for the offal from the dervish camp, but it looked as if they realised they would soon have a feast. Then we saw Dervish cavalry scouts appear in front, scan us for a moment, then dash back to report. Almost immediately the fires in front of us began to die out, though there was no sign of life from the zariba. We could make out the zariba itself, and many huts, tukkles, etc. inside it. When we were about 800 yards from it we got the order to halt. My regiment (only 6 companies as two were at Korti) at once faced left (outwards) to watch the flank, while the Egyptian cavalry moved up to our left rear, and the artillery came up on the right, between Maxwell's and Macdonald's brigades. Then, so suddenly as almost to startle us, there was a "Bang, Bang" on our right, followed by two smaller reports, and two shrapnel shell burst beautifully over the zariba, sending up clouds of dust, while two small puffs of smoke hung in the air. Our artillery consisted of twenty-four 12 pr. guns throwing a 25 lb. shell (double weight). These were under Colonel Long, and manned by Egyptian gunners. He had also 6 Maxims. Major Hunter-Blair, who was with us had also 6 Maxims, three on the right of the Camerons, and three just in front of us.

Shell after shell landed in the zariba, or burst with a white cloud just over it, the shrapnel raising a cloud of dust. Then rockets curved over from our battery, landing in the zariba with a crackle and firework display, and soon some of the tukkles caught fire, as well as straw huts. For a while there was no reply from the enemy, then suddenly I saw a flash in the zariba nearly opposite me, a shell whined and screeched over our heads and burst nearly ½ mile in rear. The men all laughed. Now and then we saw one or two dervishes walking unconcernedly about in the zariba, despite the hail of shells, and sometime shrapnel caught them and they sank down. A camel broke loose and hobbled about. Then a shell caught it and it vanished. Once I saw a body thrown a short distance into the air by a percussion shell. Then, suddenly, a quantity of white and coloured flags appeared in the zariba. Instantly a storm of shrapnel was poured into them and most collapsed. This was followed by a yell of defiance, which sounded rather weird. Then we suddenly saw the Dervish cavalry under Osman Digna coming slowly through the scrub on our left flank. They were in chain armour and helmets, looking like the Crusader knights of old may have appeared. We got ready to meet the charge. Then all the bugles sounded "Advance" and our force rose and moved slowly forward. Our artillery, who had now been firing for some 1½ hours, limbered up, and there was an ominous silence. As we moved silently on the zariba the Camerons edged off slightly to the right, so my Company got orders to fill the gap between them and 'G' company, and I took them at the double into the front line. Silently and slowly we moved forward, wondering when the enemy would open fire, but still ominous silence reigned. Then we moved up a gentle rise, at the top of which we found ourselves looking down on the zariba some 300 yards from us. Still no sound. The Union Jack was flying gaily in the centre of the Camerons, also the centre of our brigade. Then, on the top of the rise the "Halt" sounded, and we opened fire, the front rank kneeling and the rear standing. There was a terrific roar of musketry as 12,000 rifles and 12 Maxims swept the enemy position, and almost immediately the dervishes replied. I suddenly heard shrill notes which for a couple of seconds I imagined might be birds calling: then an angry buzz passed me rather like some huge infuriated bee. Yet I was so taken up directing the fire of my company that I did not grasp its significance. But a few seconds later there was a clatter, and I saw one of my company roll over on the ground, while shouts for stretcher bearers came from different parts of the line. Then, in a flash I realised that the sounds were dervish bullets, and it was not too pleasant! One or two men collapsed suddenly. Then Hunter-Blair moved forward some 50 yards with his 3 Maxims to a small rise, his gunners seizing their mules' heads and dragging them forward. One mule was hit just as they got there and fell kicking, but in two or three seconds they wheeled the guns round and opened fire again. I got orders to cover the Maxims, so sent ½ company on their left and took the other on the right. The dervishes concentrated fire on us, but most flew overhead. But as we moved up I heard another grim clatter behind me and saw Private Power lying on his face. I halted my men at the guns and gave the order for section volleys, then went for a second to Power and told him a stretcher was coming, and he would be all right. A red patch was slowly spreading on the front of his tunic and his face was dead white. He only said, "They've done for me, Sir". An awful tragedy, as he had been reduced to the ranks from Sergeant only a few days previously for "sleeping on his post" and transferred to my company. An excellent man, and cruel luck, as at the time we were all dead beat from long marches and unnecessarily long outpost duty! However, his fiance never knew he had been "reduced" and we got him in the casualty list as "Sergeant Power".

Now the dervish cavalry again advanced, but hesitated some 1,500 yards from us. 'G' and 'D' companies gave them a few volleys, and the Egyptian Maxim treated them to a short burst. They fell back into the bush. 12 men and 5 horses were found dead afterwards. We saw Osman Digna's white banner in their centre.

My company was now under heavy fire, as we were in front of the rest of the force, but it was nearly all over us, and bullets, slugs, etc flew in a continuous stream over our heads. Private Southall got a large bullet in the shoulder, which knocked him over backwards. After one or two attempts he got up, came to me and saluted with his left hand and asked if he might fall out. A fine example of discipline. Another man was hit in the stomach, and Dixon, our Quartermaster, came and took him off on a stretcher. A bullet hit the ground close to my feet, kicking up a bit of stone against my calf. Another of my men had his rifle smashed by a bullet, but was not damaged himself. The Maxims were hit in several places.

Suddenly some dervishes began emerging from cover in the zariba and collecting in front of us, as if to charge. When there were about 30, Hunter-Blair and I poured in a heavy fire, and they were mown down, but the one or two survivors disdainfully turned round and strolled unconcernedly away. They are gallant fellows! One was in a very gorgeous jibah and Hunter-Blair shouted out "There goes Zaccariah!" (The Emir of Isa Zakenal). A Maxim was turned on him and dust flew up all round him. He began to run, but a second later went over like a shot rabbit and lay quite still. Then Dixon, who had stayed with me, saw another walking off and took a shot. He missed, whereupon I laughed and Dixon was quite annoyed. He took another steady aim and the man staggered a few paces then sank down. Meanwhile our casualties were mounting up and the order came to prepare to advance. As my company was escort to the Maxims I was in some doubt as to whether I could leave them, so doubled back to Major Jones to ask leave to go with the Camerons. He said I must use my own judgement. I just got back when the bugles sounded "Advance". The whole force rose with the Union Jack raised high in the air and moved slowly forward. The Camerons and other battalions in line fired as they moved, while the "assaulting columns" moved behind them in mass companies in line. The Soudanese Brigades moved forward by short rushes. The bagpipes struck up, and our fifes and drums played us on. Caldecott, on my left, stood fast, as ordered, as I had to wait also, but my men were all "straining at the leash". When the Camerons were about half way Hunter-Blair said he did not want my escort any more, so we moved forward. I tried to hold back my men but our pace was fairly quick. We saw some of the enemy off to the river, but most stayed and faced us. A drummer boy was shot, but the others played on.

Just as we reached the zariba the dervish cavalry again appeared. Four Companies of my regiment halted and faced outwards, but Caldecott moved on. I ordered Colour Sergeant Brackpool to support our flank with half the company, and took the other half. Caldecott's men were at the zariba, so we went at a double. The much vaunted zariba, which Gatacre had led us to esteem such a terrific obstacle, was a miserable affair. A few branches of tangled camel thorn only 4ft. high and a few feet thick. I had my sword in my right hand and my revolver in my left, and had stuck my sword scabbard through my Sam Browne belt to keep it from dangling about my legs. I took a flying leap at the zariba, but something caught the top, and I fell sprawling inside. I heard a voice from my company just behind say, "Blimey! He's copped it." A bullet whacked into the ground unpleasantly close to my head and I was up in a moment. I saw two Camerons bending over an officer just on my left. This was Captain Findlay who was mortally wounded just after getting into the zariba.

Close by me was a dervish gun, with several dead gunners beside it. About 6 yards beyond the zariba was a ditch and straggling stockade and here we met some of the enemy. My men gave a cheer and somebody shouted, "Now you're into them Warwickshire lads. Stick every mother's son." There was some angry work with bayonets and rifles. Everyone went mad and I have a rather hazy idea of events. The dervishes were few and outnumbered, but fought bravely. I glimpsed one man in the ditch raise his rifle at me. I spun round and fired at him with my revolver at about 10 yards, and saw a spirt of dust fly up just beside his shoulder. Simultaneously a flash came from his rifle, which seemed to pass just by my head with a loud whizz. I was just going to fire again when two of my men were on him, their bayonets flashed and went in up to the hilt, and he sank down in the ditch. Then one of my men and a dervish had an exciting struggle. The latter was grasping the bayonet in one hand, while trying to draw his knife, and the two were going round in a circle. I was going to the rescue but the Tommy recollected that his rifle was loaded and managed to pull the trigger, with the result that the dervish was blown away a foot or so. Another of my men and a dervish got too close to use their weapons, so grappled at each other's throats and fell to the ground. Another of my men ended the struggle by bayoneting the enemy.

I had no more personal encounters till we were inside the zariba. Then, skirting a large tukkle, I came on a dervish with a huge long spear looking round the other side and waiting for my men. He saw me and his spear flashed upward, but I was just in time. The point of my sword caught him full in the chest, and I felt nothing till the hilt came against his ribs. Letting my revolver loose I caught his hand, for he made one supreme effort, which nearly brought us both to the ground, then crumpled up. I took his spear as a trophy, but the point was almost off it, and as it had fresh blood on the blade, he had evidently used it. The sight inside the zariba was really appalling. The trenches were piled up in places with dead or dying, while men, camels, donkeys, and horses, dead or badly wounded, lay thick on the ground, or struggled to get up. To make things more ghastly, several of the straw tukkles were on fire, and dense clouds of black smoke made a pall over parts of the ground. Many bodies were burning, and there was a horrible smell of roasting flesh. Unfortunately some women and children had been involved in the carnage. One poor wretch lay dying on the ground with a very young baby beside her. But, as they fought also, it was very difficult to distinguish them from the men in the dust and smoke. One Amazon, stripped to the waist, came for me, and realising it was a woman, I gave ground, keeping her off from knifing me with my sword, which she tried to grasp. Luckily two of my men managed to pinion her from behind, but she fought and bit like a wild cat. They found her young baby just behind, and that evening I saw her sitting very happily with our lads, eating some of their rations, while one had her baby on his lap!

Meanwhile the zariba was distinctly unhealthy. The black troops especially had, in their excitement, forgotten the order not to fire, but to use the bayonet only, and their bullets, as well as the enemy's were whistling past pretty thickly, smashing through huts, or thudding into the ground, which in places was quite slippery with blood. Finally I found myself at the river bank, looking down at the Atbara, which was little more than a succession of muddy pools. Everywhere there were bodies, and some pools were literally reddish. The Camerons and others were lining the banks firing on the fugitives. Then, by degrees, the firing died down. The Egyptian cavalry started off in pursuit and our bugles sounded "Assembly". I had lost most of my company in the general confusion, but men of different regiments followed me as we made our way back to the entrance of the zariba and formed up in a general crowd. It was then, I think, that the realisation of victory came to us, and cheer after cheer went up. We were not a pretty sight. Officers and men smoke-begrimed, and covered with dust and blood. Incidentally, on reaching the river, we had all dashed in and drunk, for the heat, smoke and dust made us terribly thirsty. I drank through a very dirty handkerchief, but it was foolish as the river was highly contaminated, and many of us suffered.

Then the Sirdar came riding up and we all formed round him, cheering wildly for some 5 minutes. He looked deeply affected! Then we began to fall in by companies and battalions, and it was a great relief seeing various pals once again and finding they were safe, while it seemed strange to realise one had come safely through oneself.

Mahmud, the Dervish Emir, had been captured, hiding under a bed, but the Soudanese, with some of the Lincolns and Seaforths had suffered in rushing his special stockade, while the leading company of the 11th Soudanese had been almost wiped out. We were, however, relieved to find our losses had been, comparatively, very slight. My regiment had only Lt. Greer wounded in the thigh: 3 men killed: and about 15 wounded, nearly all from my company and Caldecott's, the only two that were really in it. The Camerons had lost Captains Findlay and Urquhart killed, and Major Napier and another Officer wounded, the former dying a few days later. The Seaforths had lost Lt. Gore killed, and about 6 officers wounded. The Lincolns had 3 officers killed or wounded. The proportion of officers was high, as they led their companies in. The losses of the black troops were 400 or 500. The enemy's losses are estimated at 8000 to 9000, mostly killed, as they asked no quarter, and few prisoners were taken. Their religion teaches that any man who kills an infidel goes straight to Paradise, where he is attended by a bevy of lovely houris. Our Union Jack had several bullets through it, and two men fell while carrying it.

By degrees one heard many incidents of the battle. Pioneer-Corporal Jones of my regiment, a mighty giant well over 6ft, unofficially joined my company armed only with an axe, which he had carefully sharpened. A dervish met him and thrust at him with a spear. This he dodged, then, swinging his axe over his head, brought it down on his enemy's head, almost severing half his head and shoulder. Captain Findlay led his company into the zariba. On reaching the stockade he killed a dervish on his right with his revolver, but another on his left shot him through the body at short range. He gasped out, "Go on my Company. Never mind me," and died very shortly after. The 13th Soudanese advanced on the zariba with their band playing their regimental march ("Scotland for ever"). On nearing the enemy they all got wildly excited, and wandered off in different directions, each man playing his own instrument and tune. The big drummer and his assistant went on together, the latter seizing one of the sticks and hitting wildly at the drum, while the big drummer himself did a sort of war dance. After crossing the zariba both fell headlong onto the first ditch, and the latter got wedged in with his drum, and was, I believe, speared. His assistant ran amok amongst the dervishes with his drum stick.

Our mess camel was unfortunately hit. After making more than usually unpleasant noises, it settled down quietly and chewed the cud, raising hopes that its wound was not serious. Suddenly it is said to have put on a most indignant expression and rolled over dead.

When we had formed up we had some bully beef, biscuit, and water. The dead were buried at 3 pm. They were rolled in blankets and buried together in a trench, the three officers on the right. I went through the zariba again, but it was a ghastly sight. We all picked up some trophies and studied the effect of our bullets with the tips filed off. The hospitals were an unpleasant sight. About 60 dead were lying outside the Soudanese hospital, in two rows, and many had not even their faces covered.

At 4 pm we marched back to Umdabia, a weary trek since we were all very fagged having done two hard days' work with practically no sleep and scanty rations. The wounded were carried on stretchers by the Soudanese. We got in at 10.30 pm sleeping in our full kit round the zariba as usual.

Skinner: In the rifle pits which had been dug all over the encampment were hundreds of the enemy chained to their places to great stakes of wood driven in the ground. These poor creatures, both men and women, were those whom the Dervishes had forced to fight. Not many of these poor devils were left alive. The few that managed to come through were taken prisoners of war, quite overjoyed at being freed from their yoke, and when they heard that Mahmud was a prisoner in our hands they did not know how to show their joy.

THE RAILWAY

Though victory at the Battle of the Atbara had been achieved quite early in the morning, the troops did not leave the field till later that night, returning first to Umdabia, and then by stages to near Berber, where they soon became encamped close by at Darmali and El Selim. Here they were to remain for nearly four months. There was no question of going further south until the railway had reached south of Berber, until the Nile had risen to make it more navigable for barges to help the transport of both men and equipment, and to push up the gunboats, and until reinforcements had arrived to increase the size of the army which would attack the Khalifa in his stronghold, Omdurman, close to Khartoum, in all 1,260 miles from Cairo.

For all concerned it was to be a most uncomfortable period. First, everyone was exceptionally tired after the marches to and from Atbara, not to mention the experience of the battle itself. Secondly, sickness broke out in the form of enteric fever to which many succumbed. Thirdly, there was the utter boredom to contend with, being camped out in the harshest of desert conditions with little to do. Some of the officers went on leave, either to Cairo or Constantinople, some even to London. But for the men it was a question of sitting and waiting. Some attempt was made to organize concerts and sports, but at the same time, once the period of rest was over, the troops had to be kept in a state of fitness for the final push south, so parades and exercises could not be abandoned.

It is possible that Lieutenant Cox went on leave, but he gives no indication of this. Instead, he hints that there is nothing to record, and stops all entries for two months. Private Teigh continues his daily description and clearly shows how repetitive the daily routine became. Gatacre had at the start ordered that the men should not have alcohol. This did not include the daily ration of rum, which was as much a part of army as navy tradition. Wellington had believed that all his soldiers enlisted for drink and it remained a welcome addition to the soldiers' diet in the trenches of Flanders a hundred years later. In 1884 General Wolseley, on his unsuccessful campaign to relieve Gordon, had replaced it with an issue of jam and marmalade! Queen Victoria approved, but his campaign was a failure. At least Gatacre did not make the same mistake, and Teigh records the issue for nearly four months on a daily basis.

Meanwhile the Sirdar was planning. One of his first priorities was to bring the railway further south, the railway being one of the most important reasons for Kitchener's success.

For a number of years there had been a line from Cairo to Nagh Hamadi, a distance of 340 miles. The next 205 miles from the railhead to Assouan could be travelled by boat up the Nile. At that point the Nile continued south to Korti, where it turned north-east to Abu Hamed, before continuing south again to Berber, then to the confluence with the Atbara River, and on to Omdurman and Khartoum.

During the Dongola campaign in 1896 the Nile had been the main supply route, though some additional miles of rail had been laid close to the Nile where navigation was difficult. But when it became clear that it was impossible to regard the occupation of Dongola as anything other than a step on the way to the reconquest of the Sudan, the whole question of supply routes became a major issue. While the Nile was navigable in certain stretches, the lack of water during the dry season and the existence of a number of cataracts along its way made for difficulties. A railway also presented considerable difficulties. If it was routed along the Nile south of Assouan it would at some stage have to cross the river in order to strike south. A bridge had a strategic disadvantage, while the area immediately to the south of Assouan was more open to marauding attack from the Dervishes and would require constant protection.

Previously there had been a plan to build a railway directly across the Nubian Desert from Wadi Halfa to Abu Hamed, nearly 250 miles. Because of the apparent lack of water, marauding Dervishes would find this a less inviting area, though this applied equally to those building the railway. However, on the assumption that as soon as the line was laid, supplies could be carried, this was not regarded as an insuperable problem. Kitchener had to make the key decision.

"The plan was perfect, and the argument in its favour conclusive. It turned, however, on one point: Was the Desert Railway a possibility? With this question the General was now confronted. He appealed to expert opinion. Eminent railway engineers in England were consulted. They replied with unanimity that, having regard to the circumstances, and remembering the conditions of war under which the work must be executed, it was impossible to construct such a line. Distinguished soldiers were approached on the subject. They replied that the scheme was not only impossible, but absurd. Many other persons who were not consulted volunteered the opinion that the whole idea was that of a lunatic, and predicted ruin and disaster to the expedition. Having received this advice, and reflected on it duly, the Sirdar ordered the railway to be constructed without more delay."[1]

[1]   Churchill, *The River War*.

98

The first spike was driven on New Year's Day, 1897. Although Kitchener was an engineer, he did not want to be told how to build the railway by anyone approaching his own rank. So Lieutenant Edouard Percy Girouard, a French Canadian, and a brilliant railway engineer, who had worked on the Canadian Pacific Railway, was sent for by the Sirdar and entrusted with the task. Neither Teigh nor Cox were in Egypt at the time the Desert Railway was started, but both have descriptions of it creeping forward daily during the 'Long Hot Summer' of 1898, when it was extended south of Abu Hamed. Girouard was a perfectionist and his success was mainly due to his most detailed preparations. Five considerations had to be taken into account. First the military precautions; second the apparent lack of water along the route; next the feeding of 2,000 platelayers in a barren desert; fourth the necessity to complete before winter, and finally that it must be built within cost. One piece of luck helped greatly. A well was sunk at a likely spot some seventy-seven miles from Wadi Halfa and a continual supply of water found. A second well was found some distance further on. These two wells, apparently the only two to be discovered, increased the carrying capacity of the railway after its completion since less water had to be hauled to keep the engines moving.

Churchill gives a graphic description of the progress of the line, which is echoed in Private Teigh's comment that "the metals are getting near us".

"It is scarcely within the power of words to describe the savage desolation of the regions into which the line and its constructors plunged. A smooth ocean of bright-coloured sand spread far and wide to the distant horizons. The tropical sun beat with senseless perseverance upon the level surface until it could scarcely be touched with a naked hand, and the filmy air glittered and shimmered as over a furnace. Here and there huge masses of crumbling rock rose from the plain, like islands of cinders in a sea of fire. Alone in this vast expanse stood Railhead – a canvas town of 2,500 inhabitants, complete with station, stores, post-office, telegraph-office, and canteen, and only connected with the living world of men and ideas by two parallel streaks, three foot six inches apart, growing dim and narrower in long perspective until they were twisted and blurred by the mirage and vanished in the indefinite distance.

"Every morning in the remote nothingness there appeared a black speck growing larger and clearer, until with a whistle and a welcome clatter, amid the aching silence of ages, the 'material' train arrived, carrying its own water and 2,500 yards of rails, sleepers, and accessories. At noon came another speck, developing in a similar manner into a supply train, also carrying its own water, food and water for the half-battalion of the escort and the 2,000 artificers and platelayers, and the letters, newspapers, sausages, jam, whisky, soda-water, and cigarettes which enable the Briton to conquer the world without discomfort. And presently the empty trains would depart, reversing the process of their arrival, and vanishing into the air and run at a tangent into an unreal world.

"The life of the strange and lonely town was characterised by a machine-like regularity, born perhaps of the iron road from which it derived its nourishment. Daily at three o'clock in the morning the 'camp-engine' started with the 'bank parties'. With the dawn the 'material' train arrived, the platelaying gangs swarmed over it like clusters of flies, and were carried to the extreme limit of the track. Every man knew his task, and knew, too, that he would return to camp when it was finished, and not before. Forthwith they set busily to work without the necessity of an order. A hundred yards of material was unloaded. The sleepers were arranged in a long succession. The rails were spiked to every alternate sleeper, and then the 80-ton engine moved cautiously forward along the unballasted track, like an elephant trying a doubtful bridge. The operation was repeated continually through the hours of the burning day. Behind the train there followed other gangs of platelayers, who completed the spiking and ballasting process; and when the sun sank beneath the sands of the western horizon, and the engine pushed the empty trucks and the weary men home to Railhead camp, it came back over a finished and permanent line. There was a brief interval while the camp-fires twinkled in the waste, like the lights of a liner in mid-ocean, and then the darkness and silence of the desert was unbroken till morning brought the glare and toil of another long day".[1]

When the line had reached 130 miles from Wadi Halfa action was required to secure Abu Hamed then in the hands of Dervish forces. This General Hunter did without too much difficulty, and the way forward for the line was secured. The speed of construction was remarkable. As the result of Girouard's preparation nearly two miles was laid in one day. Now, in 1898, the line was being extended further south to Atbara at the confluence of the Nile and Atbara Rivers.

The telegraph wire had accompanied the course of the railway, and this in time was to be important, since it allowed Kitchener to consult, even to London, when deciding his strategy. This he had done before the Battle of the Atbara.

This was the origin of the railway line, which the British Brigade waited to arrive at their camps at Darmalia and El Selim. The waiting was a period of great boredom and difficulty, particularly for the men.

---

[1]   Churchill, *The River War*.

100

5

THE WAITING BEGINS

9TH APRIL

Teigh: Resting all day and started to march in the evening at 5.30 pm and we reached our new camp, Darmali, and there we stopped for a short time. We heard that we had to stop for 3 months until the rise of the Nile.

Cox: Such a ripping night's rest after yesterday's fatigue, slept without my boots for the first time for 7 weeks. Have been collecting loot all day, got 3 jibbers and a suit of tunic armour and spears, costume, not a single one of those circular shells to be had anywhere. Paraded at 4.30 and marched back to the Parrot bivouac, very tiresome march over rough ground in the dark. Bringing along all the prisoners and deserters with us. Went to Hospital – some poor chaps very bad, very much under-strength in doctors. Sick convoy gone to Dakheila. Boxer very down.

Skinner: Our party for this engagement consisted of 1 Staff Sergt. 1 Sergt. 2 Cpls. and 13 men with 5 Medical Officers, and we found that we had plenty of work to do, but we all went about it with a good will, and it was wonderful how we all stuck it, considering that we had had nothing to eat and drink with the exception of 2 biscuits and our water, since 8.30 pm the 7th (Thursday) until 8 am on Saturday the 9th. . . . As soon as we reached camp we prepared hot milk (tinned) and Bovril for the sick.

10TH APRIL

Teigh: We had a church parade, but it was a very short service. I suppose the Chaplain thought that we were all tired. We had just got back from church when the assembly sounded and the

Sirdar read out several telegrams to us from the Queen and one from the Khedive and other big men. As soon as he had read them there were 3 cheers given for the Queen. We had a man of our Regiment die today that was wounded on the 8th (Good Friday). I think there will be a lot more die, for there is no shelter or rest for them. We are moving to the Nile so quick, in fact it is nearly killing some of us to march; no sleep and very little to eat. Before going to bed tonight we had 2 spoonfuls of rum issued to us to make us sleep, but they did not let us sleep for long for reveille sounded at 1 am and we paraded at 2 am.

Cox: Reveille at 6 am. Church parade 7, marched 7 miles last night to Abadia on our way back, congratulatory telegrams from Queen etc. read out to us, followed by much cheering. Taylor of 'A' Comp. succumbed to his wounds.

Meiklejohn: Church Parade in the morning, and we had "Soldiers of Christ arise" and "Alleluia. The strife is o'er", both of which were sung with much feeling.

11TH APRIL

Teigh: I got one of my boots changed with one of the sick, for one of mine had fallen to pieces but I did not march far, for this fresh boot that I had got from the sick hurt my toes, and at 7 am we halted and had a drink of coffee and some of us got a wash. We paraded again at 5 pm and Major Simpson who is in charge of the Battalion owing to the Commanding Officer being wounded read a telegram from the Queen and congratulated us on the gallant way we fought and said she was sorry for losing some of Her Officers and men during the fight. Major Simpson also told us that we had to do a long march, but it would be the last for some time, as we were going to our rest camp.

Before starting we got an extra biscuit. I was very bad on this march with cramp in the stomach. We marched on till 11 pm, when we laid down on the desert and fell asleep until twelve midnight, when we got a drink of rum and water, and on again we went until about 10 am when we got to our rest camp.

Cox: Reveille went this morn at 12 midnight. Marched off and reached Hudi at 7.30 am. A lot of bush here. We leave for

Darmali at 5 pm sleeping in the desert to clear the bush. Thank "Gaude" but I believe we have seen the last of the Colonel. He is on his way to Cairo; the atmosphere already is quite different without him.

12TH APRIL

Teigh: I had a rest until 6 am when we got into our old places in the huts and I laid down all the day for I did not feel very well. Night came and I had to get up several times.

Cox: We paraded and marched off last evening at 5 pm and marched all night arriving at Darmali at 5.45 am – about 17 miles. We halted halfway for 1½ hrs for rest and issue of rum to the men – good road and cool night so we didn't feel it much. We are in our old quarters, Hollins taking Boxer's place and sharing my hut. Now for some complete rest I hope. Packed up my loot and hope to get it off at the first opportunity. Egyptian troops with exception from brigade all gone to Berber, where the Sirdar has a big review tomorrow to try and pacify the natives. Lots more literature in today and two letters from home. Quite forgetting about the fight, seems like a bad dream. All wounded doing well and at Dakheila awaiting to be shipped down to Geneinetti to railhead.

13TH APRIL

Teigh: A Brigade of Soudanese passed by our camp to go to Berber. They looked very tired through the hard marching. They had a lot of Dervishes with them that were taken prisoners on the 8th. We have put canvas over the top of the mud huts to shade the sun off us.

Cox: Reveille at 6 am. Another peaceful day – a dervish came in with a frightful gaping sword cut on the back of his neck, they take a lot of killing these fellows, I believe heaps of them are coming into Darmali. Barlow has got orders to go home, lucky dog, and I wish I was him.

14TH APRIL

Teigh: We had a parade at 6.30 am for exercising the troops, but I think we have had enough of it lately. We were out for an hour. After breakfast we had a job making tables for the use of making out our meals. Then we had to make beds of the same material. That kept us busy all day.

Cox: Up at reveille. Nothing on much. G.O.C. has ordered no parades for 10 days. Finished fixing up compound. Mounted outposts at 5 pm, but we only have night outposts now.

15TH APRIL

Teigh: I was on Quartermaster's fatigue cleaning up the lines and digging holes to put all the rubbish in. This kept us busy until dinner time. It was close to the Nile and a good job too, for I had to keep drinking a lot of water. Then after dinner, I got a rest.

Cox: Day missing.

16TH APRIL

Teigh: I done my washing and changed everything. I also had a clean shave. It was the first for a month, and my hair cut. It came out in our Regimental Orders at night that the Khedive had approved us a Medal and clasp.

Cox: Came off outposts at reveille. Loafed and read all day. Had rumours of our leave, do a lot of good. 9th Soudanese passed going to Berber. They had a lot of dervish prisoners with them. Dysenteric diarrhoea very bad in brigade, must be owing to bad water on the Atbara. Not much effected myself, thanks to filter and typhoid. Lucky Barlow left for England, d— him!

Skinner: Sergt. Wyeth the brigade clerk, who carried the Union Jack in the battle had his leg amputated, but did not survive long after, dying at 6 pm the same evening.

17TH APRIL

Teigh: We had a church parade at 6.15 am. We had no sermon this morning only sang a couple of hymns and after singing the Queen, our General gave us our usual lecture and said he was not able to be with us on Sunday owing to visiting the sick and wounded in the hospital. He also spoke about the battle and said that he was not satisfied with both Officers and men of his Brigade for no heed was taken, when the cease fire sounded, causing the death of some of our own men with our own bullets. He said that the men were a little excited, but the General is a man that is never satisfied and he is not afraid to tell you so. Then he told us that we were likely to stop here 3 or 4 months till the Nile rises and he expected some more English troops up here. The troops all reckoned that he was mad and are very angry about him not being satisfied with the battle after General Kitchener, the Sirdar, being so well pleased with us.

I went to church again at night and the Rev. Watson gave us a very good sermon.

Cox: Up at reveille – on bathing picquet most of the day. Soudan + Medal and clasp granted for Battle of Atbara. Rather a lot of fever and disenteric diarrhoea about.

18TH APRIL

Teigh: Our Company is on wood cutting today for the bakery. We had to go a long way for it, but got finished shortly after breakfast. Some of them went out to kick the football but I took a walk round the market. There is about 50 Greeks' shops, and the troops are delighted in walking round them. There is a great sale of pancakes, 3 for 2 piastres. I had 3 and a drink of lemonade. Just as I got back to my hut the bugler sounded, letters from home and there was a lot of cheering as this was the first mail for 6 weeks.

Cox: Up at 4 am and went after gazelle. I ought to have got a couple – difficult stalking – hit one badly but when following up he gave me the slip. Bathed in the evening. Orders out that we move tomorrow to El Selim, a village 1½ miles N. of this. Give everybody more room. Sick getting rather a nuisance. 13

serious enterics in Hospital and numerous dysentries. Hill, Hollins, Maxwell, Wilson officers ill and 3 wounded makes us short-handed. Mail in, two letters from Mother and one from America.

19TH APRIL

Teigh: We changed camps. Our Regiment and the Warwicks had to shift about 1½ miles down the river to a fresh lot of huts. We are a little further from the Nile. It took us a little time to get settled down. I think this is our standing camp for a while. I am in a nice little hut, but it is too hot to sleep in at night.

Cox: Battalion paraded at 6 am and marched to El Selim, a village 1½ miles north of Darmali, where we settle down for the summer. Personally I am not so well off, not having such a good hut. Am doubled up with Mainwaring. I stopped behind this morning to establish permanent signal stations between the villages. That brute Ed Fowey hasn't come back from Berber yet. I shan't let him go again. Man of 'D' Co. died of enteric this morning – it's pretty bad I believe in hospital, but this move will open out the place a bit, and give more air.

Meiklejohn: The last few days have been peaceful, but Caldecott and several men are in hospital with fever, while others, like myself, have dysentery. This is another mud village and as I am still pretty seedy I have been given a good hut. My native servant has remudded the walls and I have an angoreeb. But it swarms with scorpions.

20TH APRIL

Teigh: The Battalion paraded at 6 am. Every Company was taken for different fatigues. Our Company had to go to Darmalia to look for some great coats that were missing. We found 7 and we got back about 8 am. Then we got a rest in the hut all day. Major Simpson had a concert at night. He had a stage put up and we enjoyed a good hour's enjoyment. A lot of songs was sung by Officers, N.C.Os. and men of the Battalion. We finished up by singing the Queen but before turning into bed, we had another issue of rum, which is very good and strong.

Cox: Very hot day, sweltering simply. Bathed in the evening, regiment concert on but I didn't go, don't believe in them, damn sight too much familiarity with the men. ½ tots of rum issued. Adamson came back from Darmali.

21ST APRIL

Teigh: I was on fatigue cleaning up the huts for the hospital and making extra windows for ventilation. We are having a lot of sickness here now in the Brigade. We had another man die yesterday. His name was Holland.

Cox: Paraded with company at 5.30 am, wood-cutting for bakery, breakfast, out and back at 10 to signal station where I stopped an hour or so. Read in the afternoon and went out with my rifle at 5 to prospect the country about here for gazelle – had one long shot – not so good as last place. Hodgson somewhere about with 17 men.

22ND APRIL

Teigh: I had a nice swim in the Nile. The friendlies here are working the land very well. We rest all day, as the sun is too hot to let us do anything out in it. We have to finish all our fatigues before breakfast and after tea I was making steps down to the Nile for the use of the hospital tonight.

Cox: Fatigue parade at 5.30 am. Rode over to Darmali to see signal station and the invalids – the latter progressing favourably. Hodgson and draft arrived in the morning. They have joined signal station, so useful that they have ordered lamps. Mail in today, but our bag has been lost. All our heavy kit from Halfa arrived. Quite a treat to put on a flannel suit and to have a basin!

23RD APRIL

Teigh: The Commanding Officer inspected our Company's straps and clothing. I have no boots, so I have to parade in my slippers and several of the Regiment have got no boots. We are getting some good bread now, and jam once a week. We had half a ration of rum at tea time. After that we had a concert and some very good songs being sung. The Warwicks who lay close to us had one also and it lasted a little longer than ours for just as I got laid down I heard them singing the Queen. Every man got 1lb of tobacco today by paying 5 piastres. That is to pay for the duty.

Cox: Went over to Darmali on business before breakfast, also saw invalids and found them much the same. Mainwaring got hold of a wonderful soda-water machine. I have written for one. Since arrival of kit have stopped bathing in the river and use M's bath. Doesn't make one feel so slack. Wrote home. Gorst – arm amputated, Dale – leg.

Meiklejohn: Have been put on the "Sick List" as I am still pretty bad and weak, and can't carry on with normal duties.

24TH APRIL

Teigh: Our Company was ordered for wood-cutting, but that was cancelled, so we did not get to church. I bought 2 packets of dates and made some jam of them and put them in a tin to use through the week. For the small tins that we buy in the market are 7 piastres a tin. I went to evening church and Mr Watson gave a splendid sermon: "On this rock I built my church". He told us a lot about the Dervishes and how they were taught in olden times to patch their clothes with anything that they could get hold of. They have still kept it up only now they put them in square patches of any colour they can get.

Cox: Paraded at 5.15 am and had to march to other village for church. Why they make two English regiments march all that way to suit a few Highlanders, I don't know. . . . Leave been granted to 25% officers to Cairo. Small mail in but nothing for me. Pte Dale, 'C' Comp. died of wounds after amputation.

Stopped for communion this morn, most weird performance in a back yard.

25TH APRIL

Teigh: We did our wood cutting today. We only had to cut it down and then the camels carried it to the bakery. We got finished about 9 am. There is a lot of men dying through bullet wounds and fever. The Nile has started to rise and the water is getting very bad, but here is one thing, they give us plenty of tea. We get it 4 times a day, and we get tea and sugar issued out to us to make a drink when we like.

Cox: Mainwaring and 5 others gone on a month's leave today, which leaves me alone in my tent. Rode over to Darmali to see Bde Major. Got off the annual inspection for the brigade and got an urgent acquisition for signalling stores through. Forrest made PMC with Peters and King committee. They are bucking up and are going to make a comfortable mess. Pte Dale died dysentery. Clouds beginning to work up – rains coming, I suppose.

Meiklejohn: Hear I have been promoted Lieutenant, much earlier than I expected. The Doctors want me to go to Alexandria for a month's convalescence, but I have refused as I fear they might keep me there and I might miss the next show. I am told I must take all risks if I stay as they won't be responsible.

26TH APRIL

Teigh: We are making guard beds to pass the time away, and it is awful. The sweat rolls off us, even in our tea as we are drinking it. I saw 2 alligators when I went for a walk. I believe they have been here several days for I think they are living on the dead Dervishes that come down the Nile.

Cox: Went over last night and slept at Darmali in Cumberland's place. Up at 3.30 and after gazelle. Got to the place which I knew of and just as I was going to have a shot – bang and whiz came a bullet. I got up and found a damn native had just shot at a runaway bull. I kicked him first, then ran after and shot his bull! Carried away the liver, heart and kidneys as 'backsheesh', which proved excellent eating in the mess. Corp. Shulock died of combined dysentery and enteric, Ptes Ellis and Burnham of dysentery.

27TH APRIL

Teigh: I had to go to the other camp this morning for our rations. There are 10 men who go every morning to load the camels. We had the usual concert tonight and rum.

Cox: Had another window made in house and straw-mat awning made over door to try and make things cooler. Still rain-proof mad, I wish they would chuck it. Steady drill is what they want now and nothing else. Rumours afloat that we don't go on till October. Adamson prepared to bet that we lose 200 men if we stop here for the summer. Rather a cheerful outlook. Gamble dined and stopped the night.

28TH APRIL

Teigh: The General came round our huts to see us making beds and cleaning. Lots of our men go fishing every day and catch some very fine fish.

Cox: Nothing doing. Got orders to go down to see sick and wounded tomorrow.

29TH APRIL

Teigh: Fatigues as usual. Still getting news about wounded and dying. They have called for a few men in hospital to help the orderlies with the sick.

Cox: Started for Field Hospital at 10 am, arriving at 5 pm. Saw Boxer, very down in the mouth and makes himself out worse than he is – 6 wounded officers and 140 men and a lot of enteric and dysentery cases – only one of our wounded men doing badly. The whole scene really depressing, most cheerful of the lot is Baillie of the 72nd with his leg off. Had an excellent dinner off the operating table! G.O.C. who came down with me been pitching into the doctors for not looking after the food. Heat intense – there are about six chickens belonging to Bainbridge gasping on the floor of my hut, into which they have strayed for shade. They don't mind me a damn.

30TH APRIL

Teigh: We made a line all round our huts with pieces of mud. My section and another were on outpost duty at night and just before going we had a tot of rum. There was a concert tonight. We could just hear the chorus of a song now and again.

Cox: Went round all the men today, paid them and dished out baccy, soap, paper and Ally Slopers! Seemed pleased to see me. Gorst with his arm off very cheerful, some of the tents filthy from sandstorm. Go up to railhead tomorrow with sick convoy steamer and then back to El Selim by first boat. Heat damnable and short of water – filter broken.

1ST MAY

Teigh: We came off outpost at reveille and missed Church again. I went and did my washing before it got too hot, but I went to church at night and Mr Watson gave a splendid sermon again on Pilgrimage. He explained to us that how we were all pilgrims in a foreign land and it was very interesting.

Cox: Left at 3 am on the *Tamai* with 6 wounded officers. It was rather off when we got to railhead getting them on to the train. They couldn't get the beds into carriage and had to lay them out on stretchers on the ground naked with amputated stumps sticking in the air. However, we got them off all right without accident. Dined with Sitwell and the 4th Battalion, slept at Abadia on land and fairly eaten by mosquitoes.

2ND MAY

Teigh: We started parades. The Battalion fell in at 5.30 am and went on the desert and did a few movements till 7, but I was put on Officers' Mess fatigue because I had no boots. I got plenty to do there carrying water and washing dishes. Today we got a bit of meat for dinner. The soup with it was like dirty water. In fact I washed my canteen in it. Then I went back on fatigue washing up the Officers' dishes. The Officers live as well here as they do in barracks. The hut I was washing up in was filled with bottles of liquor.

Cox: Left at 9 am for Berber arriving at 12 noon. Went on shore in the evening, rode up to and dined with Gamble and the 13th Soudanese. Big native festival on to celebrate delivery of Berber from dervishes, most fiendish row. All the natives have been allowed have their women up.

3RD MAY

Teigh: I was on Quartermaster fatigue and I spent most of my time in his stores. The Sirdar came round and inspected the camp of different kinds of liquors, but I could not touch them.

Cox: Returned to Regiment today. Sirdar and staff on hand coming to inspect Darmali and El Selim. Mother's letter in first after battle. No papers, absolutely the first mail which has arrived without papers from home.

Meiklejohn: Came off the "Sick List" today. The General inspected our huts. I was strolling round when Kitchener suddenly rode past. He stopped and called me by name and asked how I was. I was amazed at being recognised and at discovering that he knew about my having dysentery. The daily "fatigues" are very arduous and the heat intense. One subaltern has to superintend the filling of the fantasses and loading them which takes two hours every morning and evening. Frequently the unfortunate men fill up the fantasses, carry them up the bank, load them on the camel, one on each side, and then the brute gives a violent heave, the saddle ties give, the fantasses fall off and frequently much of the water is spilt. An exasperating

112

job in the heat, and one simply can't go for the men if their remarks are violent. Then we have to unload supplies from the steamers, cut grass and wood each day, build grass huts, do outpost duty, etc. It is now 128 degrees in the shade, and the thermometers in the hospital won't function. It is not possible to touch one's sword or any metal if left a few minutes in the sun.

4TH MAY

Teigh: We had a bathing parade after breakfast. I got issued with a pair of boots. We had sports today, a little donkey riding, and a few other things. Afterwards we had another issue of rum. Then the concert started, which passed a very nice evening away.

Cox: Up at reveille – went around Company compound and rode over to Darmali to inspect signal stations after breakfast, also put in a drink with the 72nd. Loafed the remainder of the day and mounted outposts at Retreat. Dysentery and enteric still going ahead and river getting dirty. However, they have issued a large Berkfeld filter to each battalion, which is decidedly good biz!

5TH MAY

Teigh: I was on water guard and it was rather dusty and windy and not much shade. They make us clean our straps and buckles now. We clean our straps with sand to make it the same colour as our khaki. There were 8 men mounted and 6 of them got paraded over for not being clean enough. They have got a machine here for filtering the water. It pumps it very well. There is another pump here. I had to laugh at the natives trying to work the pump, after it had been still for a while. They could not get it to work till I showed them the way. Then they stood with their mouths open looking at each other.

6TH MAY

Teigh: I came off guard and had a rest in the old hut till tea time, when I was wanted for a fatigue to go up to the other camp for a lot of blankets. We had to load them on camels. While there I saw they had about 20 Dervishes operating on them, some with arms off and others with legs off, but they are very happy and say that English very good.

Cox: Parade at 5.30 am, drill. Forded river with Greatwood and went over to see if we could get a shot at a crocodile. I spotted one on a sand bank and hit him. He stood up and fell. I thought I'd got him but the brute just managed to crawl into the river. Also had a shot at a pelican but missed him. Guest night but no guests, but first time band played since start.

7TH MAY

Teigh: I am orderly man today, and plenty of work carrying water from the Nile. We had our usual concert tonight again, opened by the band playing a dance. This amused the troops.

Cox: On duty. Feeling rather off colour today. 72nd got a gymkhana on. Weather much cooler the last few days.

8TH MAY

Teigh: I got on Church parade today, but we had no sermon. Mr Watson read a letter from the Bishop of Lincoln sending his love to the Old County Regiment and said he always remembers the Regiment in his Daily Prayers. We also had a letter from our Colonel (Verner) and he said he was proud of the way in which the Regiment fought at the battle. He said that it was our good shooting that caused us to have so few casualties. I went to church again at night and Mr Watson gave a nice sermon as usual. This time he spoke about men should always hear more than they say. He said there was one man on the Expedition who done that and it was Sir Herbert Kitchener and I believed him too.

Cox: Paraded at 5 am. Woodcutting fatigue. Strolled out with my rifle in the morning along the river, saw nothing but made a marvellous shot at a dove. C. Sgt. going on leave tomorrow.

9TH MAY

Teigh: I was on wood fatigue before breakfast and then again after tea, as we had a lot of wood to chop. I did not get finished until after 7 pm and then I had to get ready for next morning's parade.

Cox: Strolled out before breakfast with rifle after gazelle, but didn't get a shot and again in the evening. Shot a large vulture, awful brute with a large bald head and beak.

10TH MAY

Teigh: We paraded at 5.30 and went on a route march. We are to have one every Tuesday and Saturday. We formed up and marched a couple of miles over the desert and then the alert sounded and we formed into line and fixed bayonets and then we got the order to fire 2 rounds of ball ammunition. After we had done that the General said we could fire all the old ammunition, so we are going to use it up every route march. I think it will be good practice for us. He said we get the new Dum-Dum Bullets up now. Each Regiment has got a flag the same colour as the pieces of linen in our helmets and they are fastened on Dervishers' spears. They look well. Ours is the white one with a red 'X' in the centre of it. This is the number of our Regiment. We got back to camp about 9 am.

Cox: Paraded at 5 am, brigade route march – first parade since the battle. On duty. don't think I shall keep this diary up – nothing to share in it these slow times. Gazelle are practically off. The whole brigade opened fire in line this morning with ball ammunition, enough to frighten all the gazelle within miles.

11TH MAY

Teigh: I was on Hospital fatigue cleaning up and shifting the zariba back a little to make more room to pitch canvas for the sick. I was not on fatigue at night.

Cox: Went out early with rifle but saw nothing. Rode over to Darmali in afternoon to play in cricket match against them. Seaforths stood free drinks and smokes.

12TH MAY

Teigh: I was on company fatigue cleaning up the huts and etc. and the same at night again. Just finished before our 2nd tea came up at 6 pm.

13TH MAY

Teigh: I was out wood cutting again, cutting stakes to build a stable roof with, and then I went and had a swim in the Nile. We have got a camp kettle in our hut and we often make it full of tea to drink during the day.

14TH MAY

Teigh: We had our route march as usual and we fired a few more rounds of ammunition and we also had our concert at night. There was a good turn out by some men of the Cameron Highlanders. They sang some very good songs. After the concert we had our usual tot of rum issued to us.

Cox: Route march – two a week in future – short ones. Pte Clayton died of enteric.

Skinner: [At Cairo with sick.] Punctually at 12 o'clock went to the canteen and indulged in a little beer which we had forgotten the taste of, the first English beer we had tasted since the 7th of January.

15TH MAY

Teigh: Church parade again this morning, but we were not there very long. We just had a few hymns and then the band played the Queen. I went to church again at night and Mr Watson again gave a very good sermon. After the service was over, he asked us if a few would stay behind and help him to collect the lanterns. So I helped him and then I came to my hut and went to sleep till morning.

Cox: Mail in, one from Mother and America.

16TH MAY

Teigh: We had our morning parade as usual at 5.30. At night we went on out post duty. While we were on the Captain of the company payed us out and I drew 2£. I did not do any sentry go, because my section did it last time we were on. So I got my night's rest just the same.

17TH MAY

Teigh: Route march again. We still keep them up as if we were at home, but as I came off post duty this morning at Reveille it did not take me for the route march, so I had a little more rest. We still have the old camp kettle in our hut and we are living alright today. They issued us out with our raw meat rations and I think it is much better because we can cook it when we feel hungry.

Cox:

17 TUESDAY (137–228) Rogation Day

THE Colonel has GONE !!!!!!

GOOD Oh !!

117

Skinner: Heard today that the Medical Officers and the Medical Staff Corps were to become one corps under the heading of Royal Army Medical Corps.

18TH MAY

Teigh: This morning we had a parade and were practising for the Queen's Birthday. After that we did a little Battalion drill and then we halted and piled arms. Major Simpson gave the order to fall out, and he told the band sergeant to play a few tunes, while we sat down and had a comfortable smoke. After we had finished our smoke we marched back to camp for breakfast. Then we were done for the day and could go where we liked.

19TH MAY

Teigh: We had a bathing parade this morning and the water was beautiful. The Nile is rising but very slow. We had a good dinner today, me and my chum, plain stew and a date pudding and I should not have believed how it would have been, if I did not taste it. Nearly all the Battalion seem to be making something extra for dinner.

20TH MAY

Teigh: It came out in our Regimental orders tonight that 20 picked men out of the Battalion would be allowed to go down by boat for a three-days trip down the Nile every Wednesday and Saturday to Abadia. The band was playing at the Officers' Mess so I went and heard them play a few tunes and then I went to bed.

Cox: Gymkhana today in which we won the tug of war in the inter-regimental final against the Camerons.[1]

---

[1] Cox would appear to have muddled his date – see Teigh, below.

21st May

Teigh: The Battalion went out this morning route marching and fired a few more rounds of ammunition. While we were on the move we came across a few deer and a lot of rabbits. So the General got a few men and fired a few rounds at the deers, but they did not hit any of them, as they were too far away. Soon after that we came in sight of the rabbits and the Artillery fired on them with the Maxims. They also did the same, they were too far away. We started for camp and got back about 8.30 am. Then we had our breakfast and were finished for the day.

22nd May

Teigh: 20 men of our Regiment left for Abadia this morning and the Captain of my company went in charge of them. They were men who felt a bit sick. This is done so as to keep them in good health. I went down to the Sports tonight. The Hurdle race was won by one of the Seaforths. There were two good pony races and our Adjutant came in second in one of them. Then the great event came off, the final tug of war with the Camerons and Lincolns of course. The Camerons pulled the Artillery last night. They had to pull our fellows tonight. They started as soon as the General said, "Take the strain". They pulled the Lincolns a foot first. It was a very good pull with teams hung on for a long time, but the Camerons were getting done and then the Lincolns gave a heave and pulled them off their feet. The prizes were very small. The tug of war was only 16/-. After the second pull one of our team fainted, but they soon got him a drink and brought him round again. After this event we made for our camps again and got back just in time for our tot of rum and six o'clock tea. Then of course the concert commenced.

After a couple of songs Major Simpson called for Lance Corporal Lockart, the tug of war coaxer and gave him the prize money that they won. The Major also gave a speech about the regiment, praising it up well and said he was very glad to see the Regiment winning. He said they were all Lincolnshire men except one, and that was Paddy Walsh of course. He was Irish. Major Simpson said he was not a Lincolnshire man himself but we all like to stick up for our own Regiment, so instead of giving the tug of war 16/- he gave them 200 piastres, which is equal to over two pound. So they did not do so bad at the finish. So he got a good cheer from the spectators at the concert. Then the band played a splendid piece called the Troopship.

We had one of the Camerons singing tonight and our Interpreter, Mr Hourie, gave a good bit on mesmerising. He got one of our men called McNeil and two native servants. He made them laugh, sing, cry, and dance and made them feel as if they were hot and cold, and several other bits he made them do. He amused the troops very well for they could not keep from laughing for about an hour. He made one of the niggers take his clothes off. He just fetched him round in time, or else he was going to take his trousers off. When he found out where he was, he picked up his clothes and ran for his life off the stage. Well of course with that being the last performance the concert was all over, so the Major called on the band and played the Queen. Then we went to our hut to sleep.

As soon as lights out sounded some one of our company threw a stone at the Greek's shop that is just outside our Compound. He came running along to see who it was, but he could not find out, so he said he would see the Major in the morning about the affair. However, he went back again and the men stopped throwing and then I went to sleep.

22ND MAY

Teigh: We had our church parade as usual, and we went very near to Darmali for the service. Everything went all right. We only just had the ordinary service. Mr Watson did not give any text, because after we had finished singing, it got rather hot, so the bands played the Queen and then we marched back to our camp. They have just got the telegraph poles put up a long way past our camp and they won't be so very long before they get the metals up here. The railway is only about 2 miles from Berber now.

We have got a native in our Compound and he is a very useful servant to us. He does our washing for us and fetches us water for to drink and make tea and he saves us a great deal of work for it is too hot for us to run about in the sun, all the day long. We are very kind to him and give him a little money and plenty to eat and drink.

Our new Commanding Officer arrived here today, Lieutenant-

Colonel Lowth and he is a smart and in every appearance of a soldier. He came from the 2nd Battalion now stationed at Sheffield and he seems very pleased with the 1st Battalion.

23RD MAY

Teigh: We had bathing parade this morning and the water was in a splendid condition. I had a nice swim and then we marched back to camp. I am on staff billet now, whitewashing. We went up to the other camp at Darmali to whitewash the stage ready for the concert tomorrow night.

24TH MAY

Teigh: This morning we paraded at 5.30 for the Queen's Birthday. We formed up into line. General Gatacre gave the command, Royal Salute present arms. Then we formed up again into quarter column and did our gallant march past before the General Officer. Then we started back for our camp. We got into camp just nicely for breakfast time. At night we expected a Brigade concert but as it happened a Major of the Cameron Highlanders died, so we had to postpone it. We also got an extra tot of rum the same night. While the parade was going on I was up at the other camp whitewashing the Brigade concert stage, and while we were having a rest we all had a nice drink of lime juice. Just as the Cameron and Seaforth Highlanders were marching into Darmali camp, General Gatacre passed the remarks to the Seaforths that they were a poor Regiment and he said to the Camerons, as they were dismissing, there is a Regiment that deserves credit. After they had dismissed we all finished for the day.

Cox: Ceremony parade for Queen's birthday – Lowth in command. a great treat to come off parade and still find yourself a gentleman!

Meiklejohn: Queen's Birthday parade and the troops marched past and cheered. General Andy Wauchope is to be our Brigadier, as Gatacre will command the Division. Another British Brigade is coming soon.

BUILDING STRENGTH

The months of May, June and July, 1898, must have been the most tedious Private Teigh had ever experienced, even when, at an evening concert, they sang:

'Then roll on, boys, roll on to Khartoum,
  March ye and fight ye by night or by day,
Hasten the hour of the Dervishes' doom,
  Gordon avenge in old England's way!'

Private Teigh's entries are rather repetitive. But this repetition gives some idea of the appalling conditions and difficulties experienced during the 'Long Hot Summer'. The sickness following the Battle of the Atbara was becoming less, though men continued to die in July. The Nile was beginning to rise; soon new troops would be arriving, and some, especially Egyptian, passed through southwards. The 'metals' were very close, but still the British Brigade sat in its camp waiting for the Sirdar to move south again. The heat was intense, the flies and insects terrible, but worst was the boredom. The men had to be kept fit, and so exercises were still routine, but because of the heat were always held early in the morning. Sometimes there were fatigues during the remainder of the day, but often there was nothing except to sit and wait. Concerts and sports continued, and the daily issue of rum continued to be a highlight. For some of the Officers, and even Sergeants, there were periods of leave, if only a short distance down the Nile. So boring did this period become that, as noted, Lieutenant Cox abandoned his diary till it seemed action was to begin again, except for the day he was promoted. Kitchener himself went to Cairo, where of course he had a house, and Gatacre spent a fortnight in Alexandria and Cairo.

During this period of waiting the Commanders were busy, although even they took periods of leave. Changes were made in the command structure. Colonel Lowth had arrived to take over the 1st Battalion Lincolnshire regiment, much to Cox's approval. A second British Brigade was formed under Brigadier the Hon. N.G. Lyttelton, Rifle Brigade, and included the 1st Bn. Grenadier Guards, the 1st

Northumberland Fusiliers, 2nd Bn. Lancashire Fusiliers, and 2nd Bn. Rifle Brigade. General Gatacre was to become the commander of the British Division now formed with two Brigades, while Brigadier A.G. Wauchope, of the Black Watch, took over from him as Commander of the 1st British Brigade. Some rivalry grew between the two British Brigades, the 1st feeling that they were old hands, having been several months in the desert, the 2nd claiming that they were fresh though less well-trained for desert conditions. Among the reinforcements were the 21st Lancers. They had never seen action and it was said that their motto was 'Thou shalt not kill'. Because of influential connections, a short, slight young man with a high opinion of himself, Winston Spencer Churchill of the 4th Hussars, had managed to get himself attached to the Lancers. Kitchener regarded him as nothing more than a damned scribbler.

At the same time the Egyptian Division under General Hunter was strengthened, including some companies of 'Friendlies', local troops, some of whom had even fought for Mahmud at the Atbara. Particular attention was given to the Artillery. The fire power eventually at Kitchener's command was significant, but most important were the gunboats.

For many years four had been in service on the Nile, the *Tamai, El Teb, Abu Klea* and *Metemma*. During the Dongola campaign three more had been added, the *Zafir, Nasr* and *Fateh*. Now Kitchener was anxiously waiting the launching of a further three twin-screw vessels of totally new design, *Melik, Sultan* and *Sheikh*, which had been brought up in sections and were being assembled on the Nile at Abadia. These were highly armed with guns of considerable power and with machine guns. Kitchener's plans could not proceed until they were ready, since they were needed for transport as well as fire-power. The work of assembling them was undertaken by Gordon's nephew, Major W.S. "Monkey" Gordon RE, a very competent officer. But Kitchener, unable to resist interfering, haunted the dockyard. Ultimately they were not to be the success that the Sirdar expected, although their massive fire power did enormous damage, but they were under-powered and their speed limited.

Equally important was the final stage of the railway. By 5 May, 1898, it had reached Abadia, north of Berber, and by 3 July Atbara. Within one week stores for three months had arrived. The Khalifa, his capital, Omdurman, and his army were as a result within the Sirdar's reach. The 'Long Hot Summer' was nearly over. The men were still singing a song written for a concert after the Battle of the Atbara. The tune is not known, but the first and final verses were:

> On Atbara's bank our forces
> Lay encamped at Umdabia
> Waiting eagerly for battle

For the dervish force was near.
When the joyous news spread quickly
That that evening we should go
'Gainst Mahmud's far-famed zariba
There to meet and fight the foe.

Once again "the advance" is sounded!
Then with steady step and slow,
Through that deadly hail of bullets
Soudanese and British go.
Sweeping everything before them,
Cool and steady as on parade,
Through zariba and through tuckle,
Over ditches, trench, stockade.

On they go with step unflinching
Till they reach the river bed,
Leaving ditch and trench behind them
Piled up thick with dervish dead.
Horse and man go down together
'Neath their fire so swift and cool
And their carcasses are whirling
In the Atbara's deepest pool.

Then our bugles sound "The Assembly"
And the troops from far and near
Gather round, and wake the echoes
With the victor's clam'rous cheer.
Soudanese, Egyptians, British,
Join in that loud wild "Hurrah!"
For our aye victorious army
And our general and Sirdar.

6

THE LONG HOT SUMMER

25TH MAY

Teigh: We paraded at 5.30 this morning for Commanding Officer's General Attendance parade. Instead of giving us a drill parade, he inspected the Battalion, as he had only just joined us. He wanted to look at the new faces. He inspected a company at a time and as he did so, each company marched back to their respective compounds and afterwards he came round and inspected the huts that we were staying in and said that they were pretty fair considering the way they had been put together. We also had our tot of rum at night and then proceeded to our Regimental concert held by a few of the Camerons and some of our men, with Major Simpson in the chair. Just as the concert was about to finish Colonel Lowth appeared and was only just in time to hear a couple of songs. The band played the Queen and we adjourned to our huts for the finish of the night.

26TH MAY

Teigh: We had our usual bathing parade this morning and when we got back to camp we had medical inspection. The Doctor passing round each rank both front and rear, but I don't think he found many men in bad health.

27TH MAY

Teigh: This morning we paraded at 5.30 for Commanding Officer's attendance drill and got off just as the breakfast bugle was sounding. We were finished for the day.
  At night the Brigade concert came off at Darmali Camp and

125

it was something splendid. The performers were in good condition, especially four Sergeants of the Seaforths. They gave us a very good Highland Fling conducted by the Pipe Major. There were also men of the Camerons that made a good performance, especially the 'Two Mac'. They made up conundrums about the battle of the Atbara. One item was why were the Cameron Highlanders, when they charged the zariba, like the Bank of England? Because Money was in![1] There was also a very good club team accompanied by the band of the Camerons. They put in all the practices and changes. Two Officers of the Lincolns sang. Captain Forrest and Captain Marsh gave a very good song each. Captain Marsh gave a song entitled, "I don't want to hear the bullets rattle in the Battle". The Scottish Regiments gave Recitations, Comic Songs and Sentimental singing. The performance was very long. It started at 8 pm and finished about 11. It was 12 when our men got into camp. It started thundering and lightening and very soon it started to rain. It came down in torrents. Every man that was sleeping out in the open had to be woken up and sent into the huts. With it being dark the troops could not see where to make their beds, but at last we found a little bit of candle and then we laid our blankets down and went to sleep.

28TH MAY

Teigh: The battalion paraded at 4.30 am for Brigade route march and we formed up between our camp and Darmali. We started off about 5 and marched for about 2 hours and then began to fire some more of our Dum-Dum away. Then we had to rest for a little time and very soon started back for our camp. We got in camp around 9 am, just in time for breakfast. Then of course we were finished. Tonight was our usual concert. It was not up to much. There were a few songs sung and the McNeil and his friends gave an amusing performance entitled the Cobbler. General Gatacre was at the Officers' Mess to supper. Of course he had to come to the concert. We also had our usual tot of rum. Today we got a tot of lime juice as well. The concert began at 8 pm and lasted till 10.30. The Band

---

[1]   Brevet Colonel G.L.C. Money, C.O. 1st Bn, Cameron Highlanders.

played the Queen and then we went to our huts and went to sleep.

29TH MAY

Teigh: We had church parade this morning and the General gave us a lecture about Khartoum and Omdurman. He said that there are about 40,000 Dervishes up there and he said it might be a hard fight, and when it is taken it will be the largest battle of the century, but he said he did not know who would win, but he knew who he would put his money on. We started putting up a large wash house for the Battalion for when the Nile is properly risen the troops cannot get down the banks to bathe. The natives have now got past our camp with the railway embankment, so it won't be so long before we get the metals up here.

30TH MAY

Teigh: We had bathing parade this morning. We started to make an oven and, as we could not get anything to make it with, we pinched some bricks from the natives building a hut for a Greek, who sells just out of our compound. We soon put it together. We are only waiting for pay day to come and then we shall have a few more extras.

31ST MAY

Teigh: Reveille at 4.30 am. We paraded at 5 for Brigade route march. We formed up about halfway between the two camps and the Brigade marched off towards the south for about half an hour. We then changed direction and marched towards the east. We marched across the desert in our usual direction and, after forming square a few times, we then formed into line ready to fire our few rounds of Dum-Dums. But we had to advance again a bit further and then the alert sounded and we doubled back into line and we got the order to fire two rounds by section volleys from the right of Battalions. We fired our two rounds and the General said let me see the Lincoln Regiment fire two more volleys at the same object. We did that and he said, very good firing indeed. We rested for a while and then we fired 2 rounds independent, and when the Brigade had finished the ground was properly riddled with bullets. In fact the centre was completely knocked out. We marched back to camp and reached there about 8 am.

After marching about 7 miles across the desert I felt properly fed up, as we had no sleep during the night on account of the rain, and we were sweating very heavily. In fact I don't think our blankets would have been much wetter if they had been out in the rain during the night. I was on boat fatigue, but as luck would have it, I did not have anything to do. We had an issue of lime juice at night and it was not strong enough to taste. It was properly adulterated before we got it.

The boat is expected in with the Sirdar on board, but the first post sounded and he hadn't arrived yet. However, about half an hour afterwards lights out sounded and we laid down on the two blankets in our compound on the sand to sleep. I had only been asleep about 2 or 3 hours when I was woken up with the howling of dogs and also donkeys making a horrible noise. I laid down again and soon fell asleep and I didn't wake any more till I heard the Drums beating the Reveille and then we had to fold our blankets up.

1ST JUNE

Teigh: We had to clean up our camp as the Sirdar is coming around. At 6.30 am our Captain came around and we had to keep our jackets on until the Sirdar had been around. He visited one or two compounds of different Companies and he said he was quite satisfied with them, and then he went towards the hospital and visited the sick. After a short stay at the hospital he made his way towards the next camp. We had a tin of Maconochie's bacon between every 4 men for breakfast, but we had to go short of fresh meat at dinner time. It was very hot during the day and another man died of my company; he was a man who had suffered a great deal and spent most of his time in the hospital. His name was Pte. Brannan. The Company paraded at 5 pm for the funeral. I being one of the firing party I had to parade at 3.45 for practice, but I was only on it for a quarter of an hour, then we got our tea; the Company arrived back about 6.15 and we got our usual issue of rum and it went down very high.

I was warned for guard and so I had to make preparations for it and by the time I had finished the first post sounded. Then I made my bed down upon the sand and went to sleep till morning.

Skinner: [At Abadia] Two of the gunboats that are being built here went up the Nile for a trial spin and to try her guns, the Sirdar being on board the *Melik*; these trials proved to be very satisfactory. When the *Melik* was near to the shore to her moorings, the telegraph from the steering room to the engine room went wrong, and the boat which was coming in at full speed at the time ran amidships of the *Sultan*, that was lying close in shore, the bows of the *Melik* were smashed clean in, and the side of the *Sultan* cut clean through.

2ND JUNE

Teigh: The Battalion paraded at 6.30 for medical inspection, but I was on guard so I had to mount at 6, half an hour before the Battalion paraded. I managed to get No. 2 so I had to go on sentry at 8, and I had been on about half an hour when the Orderly Officer came and I had to turn out the guard to him, and besides I had to give him my orders. I gave him one or two of the particulars and he said that will do, and he went away. I came off at 10, and I spent most of my time in the guard tent until dinner. I had a meat pie for dinner and it was very good considering as it was baked in an oven which we made ourselves of mud. However, it came my turn for sentry again. I had been about ¾ of an hour this time, when the Captain of the week came round. I had to turn out the guard to him, but he didn't want any orders. He seemed very much in a hurry, as it was very hot. I was glad when the cool of the evening came on and the moon shone brightly. The natives on the other side of the Nile were keeping their Xmas or something. They were firing guns off and tum-tumming nearly all the night until about 3 in the morning, until the moon disappeared and it was nearly dark. I went to sleep for about 2 hours when reveille sounded and I knew my time was getting short on guard.

3RD JUNE

Teigh: The Battalion paraded at 5.30 for Adjutants-General attendance and the guard mounted at 6, and so I got relieved about 6.15. It was very hot during the day and at night a terrible sandstorm came on and it rained in torrents; and it looked very dull the remainder of the night, but howsoever the first post sounded and I made down my bed in the usual place and laid down. I was soon asleep, I can tell you I didn't want much rocking and the next thing I heard was our drums beating off reveille.

4TH JUNE

Teigh: We paraded as usual at 4.50 for a Brigade Route March and we formed up between the two camps and then marched towards the east across the desert. After doing a few field movements we formed up in line and fired two volleys by Sections from the right of Battalions. After that we rested for a few minutes and then fired two more volleys the same as before. Then we fired one round independent all through the Brigade. Then we marched back and got to camp about 8.30. We got cocoa for breakfast, which we used to get twice a week. We spent biggest part of the day under cover in our mud huts as it was very hot. We had a draft of 8 men and 1 Captain join our Battalion from Cairo in the afternoon. We had our usual issue of rum and at night we had a bit of a concert in the other camp, but I happened to be on boat fatigue, so I didn't get a chance to go as it was getting late by the time we unloaded 8 barges of wood, khaki, socks, helmet covers, haversacks, flour and several other different articles for Darmali camp. I felt tired so I made down my blankets and had a lay down. It wasn't long before I fell asleep and I think I woke up once or twice during the night, but I soon went to sleep again till morning.

Meiklejohn: A sort of tornado swept through our camp last night causing much despondency. My hut was wrecked, cigarettes blown away and kit scattered. Frantic figures dashed wildly over the desert chasing blankets etc. and the language was emphatic.

We held the "Nile Epsom Race Meeting". The events were:

(1)   El Selim Hurdle Races.
(2)   Frontier Polo Scurry.
(3)   Atbara Derby.
(4)   Darmali Handicap.
(5)   Mahmud Sweepstakes.

Very few of us could raise any sort of mount.

5TH JUNE

Teigh: We had our usual church parade at 5.30, but the General didn't happen to be at Church so we didn't have our usual lecture. The Egyptian Artillery passed our camp this morning on their way to the front from Berber. We had another meat pie for dinner today. After tea the Soudanese Camel Corps passed our camp for the front. They are supposed to have been on furlough. I went to church in the evening at 7 pm and after that I took a walk across the desert with my chum.

6TH JUNE

Teigh: The Commanding Officer inspected the boots of the Battalion. It was about 6 am when he inspected my company. He told us to sit down so he could see our boots, which we did with the greatest of ease and then he walked round the ranks. We were to show a second pair, but there were very few who had a second pair to show on account of the rough marching we have done. During the morning Private Brannan's kit was sold but he only had what he stood up in, as he lost his kit when coming from Cairo.

There was a man come from Cairo today that transferred from my Company to Medical Staff Corps, his name is Angus. Some Friendlies passed our camp this morning making their way to the front.

7TH JUNE

Teigh: The Brigade paraded for Brigade Route marching as usual. General Gatacre is away on leave for a week, so Colonel Money took command of the Brigade. They marched across the desert to the usual place and fired four rounds of ammunition away for practice at some gazelles which were running across the desert. I was on fatigue drawing rations from the other camp for the battalion. They had no fresh meat and so we had to have preserved meat. It is a change once a week just to keep us in trim in case of emergency.

8TH JUNE

Teigh: The Battalion paraded as usual for Commanding Officer's General attendance and we done a bit of Battalion drill on the desert and we soon marched back. We got the order to whitewash our mud-huts, so we had everything to take out. After breakfast we got an order to show our kits and we laid down our waterproof sheets and shook out our kit bags. After we had done that we went on whitewashing. I happened to be ration carrier to a man on hospital guard, so I found plenty to do. We had our usual issue of rum this evening, and we also had our concerts, which we used to have twice a week but it is a fortnight since we had the last one. We had a few fresh songs and it went down well. Lieutenant Burrowes of our regiment gave us a recitation about the house that Jack built and I can tell you it made the troops laugh with the capers he cut on the stage. I think he had had an extra issue of rum as it was rum night.

9TH JUNE

Teigh: The Battalion paraded at 6.30 for Medical Inspection, and he gave us a lecture about men taking food to patients in hospital with enteric fever. He said it was a very dangerous thing to do. He said that a man that would do that was worse than a murderer and if anyone is caught in future he will be severely punished. My company finds the outpost tonight, 12 men and a Sergeant, and I am one of the 12. I done my two hours sentry between 2 and 4 in the morning and we finished at reveille.

132

10TH JUNE

Teigh: The Battalion paraded at 5.30 in shirt sleeves and drill order as it is very hot just now. We have been expecting the Nile to rise for this last month and I think we got the first rise last night. We had another meat pie today. Some of our Officers came off leave this morning and my Captain went on leave and he took his soldier servant with him, Private Tomkins. We had a small issue of lime juice just to keep us in good order. Soudanese and Friendlies are passing our camp nearly every day ready for our next advance on Khartoum.

11TH JUNE

Teigh: Reveille sounded at 4. The Battalion paraded at 4.30 and marched across the desert towards south-east and then formed up. Colonel Money was in charge of the Brigade as General Gatacre is on leave. They formed into line and fired two volleys and then had a rest and then fired two rounds independent at a distance of 1,000 yards, rather a longer range than usual.

My company got paid out at 5 pm. We also got our usual concert at 7. Our quartermaster was first to sing and he gave us one of the latest songs from Cairo, as he has just returned off leave. The concert finished about 11 by playing the Queen.

12TH JUNE

Teigh: Church parade at 5.30 am and after that the Band and 'B' Company paraded for a funeral to bury one of their men, who died of enteric fever. His name Pte Warriner, a strong built man, he was attached to my company when we were at Abbassiyeh, firing our annual course of musketry last August, 1897.

We had some small puddings for dinner, commonly called Norfolk dumplings, made in the Sudan, and we also had a plum cake for tea, but our oven was rather too hot. It was stuck at the bottom of the tin. I went to church in the evening and after that I took a walk towards the Nile to watch it rising. It rises about 18 inches every day and night.

13TH JUNE

Teigh: I was on hospital fatigue and I had to parade at 6 am over at the hospital to carry sick men down to the steam-boat, as there are a number of sick going back to Cairo. The man who I helped to carry was a Sergeant of the Warwickshire Regiment and he was pretty heavy. Howsoever I managed down to the boat and we carried him on one of our new barges made for the purpose of carrying troops up and down the Nile. I arrived back off fatigue about 7.30, just in time for breakfast. There were 5 men belonging to my company went on this boat; names Privates Broughton, Hunt, Pickwell, Watkin, Woolstencroft. The steam boat came right up to our camp this morning for the first time, so you can tell the Nile has rose a lot during the last 3 days.

14TH JUNE

Teigh: The Brigade paraded at 4.50 for Brigade route marching and General Gatacre took charge of the parade as he has come back off leave. He took us a good long way across the desert and then we formed a square and a few more movements and after that we formed into line and fired 4 volleys of the dum-dum ammunition away. Then we marched back to our camp, which we reached about 8.20.

We had some preserved meat for dinner, but it was not very good, so we gave it to the natives who soon devoured it and to see them eat it you would have thought they had not had anything to eat for weeks. In the evening I went down to the Nile and had a good wash, as we are not allowed to bathe now as there are so many crocodiles about here.

15TH JUNE

Teigh: The Battalion paraded for Commanding Officer's General attendance parade at 5.30 and after we had formed up a court martial prisoner was read out, Private Kedennick, who belonged to my company. He got one year imprisonment for insubordination and telling Captain and Adjutant Marsh that he would not do a parade for neither him nor any other officer of the Battalion. They marched the prisoner away. Then we done a few movements in Battalion drill across the desert for about half an hour. We were issued today with a helmet curtain each. We got our usual issue of rum at 6 pm, and after that I took a walk to the other camp to see a concert which was held by the Camerons. It was pretty good except one Sergeant. He got on the stage and started to sing and the men all started to hoot him and he soon disappeared off the stage. I got back to our camp at 11 pm.

16TH JUNE

Teigh: The Battalion paraded for Medical inspection at 6.30, but I was on fatigue so I did not attend this parade. We went out at 5.30 and got back at 7.30, just in time to get a wash before breakfast. The gun-boats go right past our camp now. Some more Egyptian troops and Soudanese passed our camp sometime during the night making their way to the front.

17TH JUNE

Teigh: Adjutant's parade at 5.30 and we marched across the desert and done a bit of Battalion drill. After that we marched back and got dismissed. It was about 6.30. Some more men went down the river for a trip and another man went back to Cairo. He was a prisoner. He was escorted by two men and a Colour Sergeant. A few sports took place in our camp tonight, wrestling on donkeys and such like. My company is going on outpost duty.

18TH JUNE

Teigh: A Brigade route march as usual with Colonel Money in charge. We formed up and marched towards the east and on our way we came in view of a gazelle and some men of 'G' Company doubled out to the front and had a shot at it, but unfortunately could not hit it. We marched a little further and formed into line and fired 5 rounds per man. When we had done that we cleaned our rifles and marched back to camp. We arrived back about 8.15 am. They have just got past our camp with the railroad and the first train passed this morning about 9 am. We got paid out at 6 pm and had our usual issue of rum and concert at 7.

19TH JUNE

Teigh: Church parade at 5.30. I was on wood fatigue so could not attend Church. We had a long way to go for our wood and I did not get back to breakfast until 9. It was very hot during the day. At night I went to Church. Mr Watson gave a very good sermon for the benefit of the troops. After church I went for a walk until first post, when I went and made my bed down on the sand, 2 blankets, a waterproof sheet that is our beds, but we are quite contented with that.

20TH JUNE

Teigh: Voluntary bathing in the wash-house. Mr Watson gave a prayer book to several of our men with the inscription on the cover, 'Nile Expedition 1898', but I never got one of these. He told them to take them to Khartoum with them when they go. We got an issue of lime juice at night.

Meiklejohn: Colour-Sergeant Doughty died of enteric and I had to take the funeral party. The smell at the Cemetry was awful. Then again the blanket came undone and had to be tied up at the grave. All this before Breakfast!!

Skinner: Railway has reached Darmali, it is very hot, registering at 12 noon 141° in the tents and 148° at 2 pm.

21ST JUNE

Teigh: Brigade Route march at 5.30 and each Battalion marched across the desert with their own Commanding Officers in command for about 3½ miles and then formed up. Here we fired 3 rounds per man and then marched back. We arrived back about 8.20. We had preserved meat again, but very few seem to eat it and I think the natives like us to have this meat as we don't eat it and they get a bellyful of it.

The Commanding Officer came round our mud hut this morning and one man was mixing up a pudding in an enamelled pot and he said, 'What have you got there?' and the man says, 'A pudding, Sir.' 'Oh,' he says, 'I thought it was whitewash.' But however we had the pudding for dinner, 8 of us, and it was very nice.

22ND JUNE

Teigh: Commanding Officer's parade at 5.30, but I was on Market Picquet so I had to parade at 6.30 with the guard. We then marched across to the market. We had to stay all day, but there was nothing to do, only sit watching the natives. We got off just in time for our usual issue of rum about 6.40 pm. There was a Brigade concert in the next camp, but it was rather too far for me to travel after being in the market all day, where it was very dusty and hot and so the evening is the best time to have a comfortable sit and smoke and talk about our next advance. The mail arrived about 8 pm and I got a letter from home. The mails come by train now instead of coming by steam-boat.

23RD JUNE

Teigh: The Battalion paraded for medical inspection at 6.30 and another Court Martial prisoner was read out for being drunk while on active service and also on duty. He was sentenced to 42 days imprisonment with hard labour and fined 1£.

The Nile seems to be at a standstill this last 3 or 4 days, but the boats can go for a long way past our camp up the river.

24TH JUNE

Teigh: The Battalion paraded for Adjutant's parade and we formed up and marched across the desert and did a bit of Battalion drill and manual and firing exercise. Then we marched back again and got dismissed. We had Maconochie's jam for breakfast. Some Friendlies passed our camp today. They were mounted on camels and I think there were about 200 of them, as near as I could say, if not more. They were all armed with the Remington rifle.[1]

25TH JUNE

Teigh: Battalion parade as usual. Our Battalion paraded at 5.10 and marched across the desert and formed up and fired 3 individual 2 volleys and then we marched back. It was about 7.45 when we got back. We received our pay at 6.30 pm, and also our usual issue of rum. At 7 we had our usual concert and this time it was very good.

26TH JUNE

Teigh: The Battalion paraded at 5.30 for church, and after the service was over, General Gatacre gave us one of his lectures. He had been to visit Atbara and the graves of Comrades. We had heard a rumour that the British soldiers' graves who had fought in the battle of Atbara were tampered with, but the General told us that they had not been touched as they laid in line just as we left them, and the battlefield is just as we left it, the ammunition and animals and different things lying all over. He told us that the sun had dried the dead Dervishes up and so there is not much left of them as the birds had eat all the flesh off the bones. There was one or two graves of our comrades which we buried whilst we were on the march which had been interfered with. Sergeant Mumby's was one at Ras el Hudi. He was drowned whilst bathing in the Atbara river, and Private Taylor's was the other. He was buried at the Atbara fort after the battle. He died through the effect of a wound in the thigh. He told us that the other Brigade were expected up very soon and of course we being in the Sudan all this time and having got used to the country, we weren't to

---

[1] This old rifle had been staged out of the British Army, and in 1885 the Egyptian Army had been re-equipped with the Martini-Henry .450. However, the Khalifa's *jehadiya* were still armed with the old Remingtons, many of which were without sights. Some of the Friendlies had fought at Atbara on the Dervish side.

forget to let them know who were the best of the two Brigades.

I went to Church again at night, but it was a short service lasting only ¾ of an hour.

Meiklejohn: Dixon and I decided to use the free afternoon trying for Gazelle with Army rifles. We separated after a bit and I spotted one some way off. Did a long stalk and eventually got within 300 yards. He started off and I saw my first bullet kick up the sand behind him. Fired again and he fell dead, my bullet having got him fair in the shoulder. Then had to drag him over two miles in the great heat. However, I received quite an ovation as it was the first anybody had got, and most welcome to the Mess. We play Whist in the afternoon as this passes the time and it's too hot to go out. We have also occasional concerts. There is a mud stage and the men get up theatricals. The scenery is made by black and red ink with curry powder for the green tints. The place is sometimes wrecked during proceedings by a passing "dust-devil".

27TH JUNE

Teigh: I was on ration fatigue and paraded at 5.15 and went up to the next camp to fetch the Battalion's rations. I arrived back about 7.20. After breakfast we had Commanding Officer's kit inspection and he walked round the ranks and just looked at the kits. That was all. Some Dervishers prisoners passed our camp this morning from the front making their way to Berber. They were escorted by some of the Soudanese camel corps. As near as I could say there were about 50 of them. It was very hot during the day and dusty. At night the wind blew all the tents down in the compounds.

28TH JUNE

Teigh: The Brigade was cancelled as it was too windy and dusty to take the troops out on the desert. We all got ready for parade but we received the order about 10 minutes before the parade formed up that there was no parade and there was a lot of shouting amongst the troops for a time. There was preserved meat again for dinner, but I bought some fish instead. Another man of our Regiment died today belonging to 'G' Company.

29TH JUNE

Teigh: Commanding Officer's Parade at 5.30 on our usual parade ground on the desert. We got dismissed at 6.30. We had some of Maconochie's bacon for breakfast. We used to receive our letters twice a week but now they come by train, we get them 3 times a week. We had our usual issue of rum at 6.30 pm and also a concert at 7. I went but I did not think it was up to much.

30TH JUNE

Teigh: Medical inspection at 6.30 and he walked round a company at a time and as he inspected us we marched to our compounds. The Nile is gradually rising again. The days are very hot now and the evenings are very close.

1ST JULY

Teigh: The Battalion paraded at 5.30 for Adjutant General attendance and he marched them across the desert and over the railroad and then let them fall out for a few minutes. After that he gave them a bit of battalion drill and the manual and firing exercises. Then he marched them back and dismissed them. I was on Officers' mess fatigue and I had to fetch 6 buckets of water from the Nile for cooking purposes, and when I had done that I washed up a few cups and saucers and plates and then finished before breakfast. I went back again after breakfast and I did the same as I did before and then peeled a few onions and then I finished for the day.

2ND JULY

Teigh: Brigade route march at 5 and we took our usual route across the desert and formed up and fired 3 rounds at a bush in front of us. After that we ceased fire and cleaned our rifles out and then marched back about 7.30. It was very hot during the day and our company was paid out early in the morning. At night we had an issue of rum. Another man of our Battalion was buried today ('C' Company). Concert at night, this one was very good.

3RD JULY

Teigh: Church parade at 5.30 and when we got back one of our men was taken to the Hospital very bad and another one died. We are losing a lot of men now. I was on Quartermaster's fatigue and I had to go round the camp picking up paper that was all I did. It was very hot during the day and at night, I went to church.

4TH JULY

Teigh: The Battalion paraded at 6 am for Commanding Officer's Inspection of serges. We paraded with khaki trousers and putties and red frock serges, and that is the way we are supposed to take Khartoum, when we make our next advance. Another of our men died today and was buried in the evening, Pte. Cage of 'D' Company.

5TH JULY

Teigh: Brigade parade at 5 am and we took the usual route march across the desert and formed up. Four men of the Seaforth Highlanders received the Humane Society medals for saving a comrade's life whilst coming up the Nile. The man fell overboard and his comrades dashed over after him and that way saved his life. It was a very dark night and a strong current was running. But the Nile is a very dangerous river and the currents are strong at the best of times. After that had been awarded we marched towards the east and then we formed into line and fired 3 volleys and two rounds independent making a total of 5. After we had cleaned out our rifles we then marched back to camp. It was about 8.10 am. We were deceived today instead of having preserved meat we had fresh meat. It was very hot in the middle of the day. In the evening we received an issue of lime juice.

6TH JULY

Teigh: Commanding Officer's general attendance parade at 5.30 am and we did a bit of Battalion drill and then we marched back and got dismissed. We had Maconochie's bacon for breakfast and so we had to go short of fresh meat for dinner. I have gone on the new Act today and so I shall receive 3d a day more in future making a sum of 1/4 per day.[1] We received another issue of rum at 6 pm. There was a concert at the next camp. It was held by the Seaforth Highlanders and this was very good.

7TH JULY

Teigh: The Battalion paraded at 6.30 for Medical Inspection and after that I took a walk across the Nile and spent about an hour fishing. I caught one weighing about 5 lbs. While there I saw some nice sights with natives floating about on pieces of wood and some swimming. The mail arrived in this evening and some of our Sergeants came off leave from Cairo, who had been to see their wives.

8TH JULY

Teigh: The Battalion paraded at 5.30 for Adjutant General attendance and they marched across the desert and did a little drill such as manual exercise and a few more movements. However they were out about an hour and got dismissed for breakfast about 6.45. We had Maconochie's jam for breakfast this morning, which we generally have twice a week. It was very hot during the day and I was on hospital fatigue at 2 pm, waiting for the train to take some of our sick men back to

[1] This is recorded in his records: 'Elected to come under Regulations governing issue of Messing allowance in accordance with provisions of para: 5 Army order 65 of 1898.' The effective date was the 1st of June, and his signature is shown.

Cairo. There was 10 of ours and 10 of the Warwicks.

There was a fearful sandstorm came about 3 pm and after that it rained for about 2 hours and there were every signs of it being a wet night. 'D' Company buried one of their men tonight, Private Rushby. He died of enteric fever. The funeral party got caught in the storm and was wringing wet through when they came back to camp. We had a small issue of rum at 6.30. We had to sleep inside our mud huts during the night because it was too wet outside.

9TH JULY

Teigh: Brigade parade was cancelled on account of it being so wet after the rain we got last night. So I took my fishing line and went down the Nile and spent an hour or two fishing. I left my line in the water while I came for my breakfast, but when I returned there was a fish on it. So I took it into camp and cooked it for my tea. We got paid out at 6 pm. This time I drew 130 piastres. We also had another issue of rum. We had another of our concerts which started at 8. It started very well but it finished up a bit rough and rather sooner than we expected, as there was a heavy sandstorm came on and blew out the lanterns and also tore down the canvas and scenery.

Meiklejohn: Lt. Bacchus has joined us. Sanderson has been kept in Alexandria for depot work – a proof of the danger of going on leave.

10TH JULY

Teigh: The Battalion paraded at 5.30 for church and they formed up in the same place and the service only lasted about half an hour, and then we marched back again and got dismissed about 6.30. In the evening another of our men was buried belonging to 'D' Company, his name was Dawson. He was a very fine and smart fellow, his home was in some part of Lincolnshire. At night I attended voluntary Church service.

11TH JULY

Teigh: I was for guard and the guard mounted at 6 am and I got second relief again, so I went on sentry from 8 to 10 and it was very hot, but I got through it alright and I managed to get dismissed the next day about 10 am. Our Company found out post last night, twelve men and a sergeant and they finished at Reveille.

12TH JULY

Teigh: Brigade route march as usual at 5 and Major Simpson was in command of our Battalion. They marched the usual route (East) and fired 5 volleys and marched back as near as I can say it was about 8 when they arrived back. In the cool of the evening I went fishing, but had no luck, so returned to camp and went to sleep till morning.

Skinner: I was admitted to hospital with enteric fever.

13TH JULY

Teigh: Commanding Officer's parade at 5.30 and took the same old route across the desert and done a few movements and soon marched back and got dismissed. One of the new gunboats came up the Nile past our camp this morning about 9. The Sirdar was on board of it. I was on wood fatigue and I can tell you it was a terrible job. I did not get back till 8.30. In the evening we got our usual issue of rum, and we also saw them trying the searchlight on the new gunboat. It was shining across our camp and across the desert.

POETIC LICENCE

On 14 July Lieutenant Cox started his diary again: "First signs of advance so I start again". For a further reason this was a significant day in his life; he also writes, "I am a Captain from today." This was actually gazetted from 11 March, 1898. He was soon to be appointed the Divisional Signalling Officer responsible to General Gatacre, and also became responsible for 'G' Company.

However, his initial enthusiasm to restart his diary immediately waned, as everyone continued to wait for the Sirdar to decide that the time was ready to launch his final offensive.

The utter boredom, particularly for the men, was incredible. The Officers at least could continue to go shooting, if not on leave. Private Teigh obviously enjoyed the concerts, and apparently even tried his own hand at writing a poem:

> Defaulters drill whats that you'll ask,
> I'll tell you is a kind of task,
> Or punishment for soldiers who
> Have done what they ought not to do,
> Such as for instance getting tight,
> Or staying out too late at night,
> For which complaints there is a pill,
> By us called hump, by you pack drill,
> To illustrate it I will pack,
> A soldier's straps upon his back,
> Fix bayonets, shoulder arms I shout,
> Quick march and then he moves about,
> Four hours of this he does a day,
> Go as you please: oh no I say,
> How then you ask, well do not smile,
> and then I will describe the style,
> Right turn, right form, touch up in the rear,
> Front turn a little sharper there,
> Left turn, left form, just stop at that,
> Or else I'll shift you out of that,
> This is the Sergeant's mode of drill,

And of it he gives them their fill,
From half past six to nine at night,
It is a most amusing sight,
To see them show their running power,
To reach the guard room each half hour,
I've heard it said twixt you and me,
Mind this is on the strict 'Q.T.',
That they can do the drill alright,
But not answering their names at night,
The reason obvious for you know,
Night is the time to courting go,
And do the amiable with Sal,
Or any other pretty gal,
Then oh how cruel when the dears,
At home in anguished, bathed in tears,
Are pining for their Sal and Jack,
Who can't come out till they've done pack,
You who may read this bear in mind,
Though the above can't be called kind,
It's only right and justice fair,
Should be dispensed else who would care,
Which proves that those who does this game,
Have only got themselves to blame.

G.E. Teigh L.R.

Private Teigh may not have been a poet, but he was only following in the example of Colonel Verner, wounded at the Battle of the Atbara, who had written:

A thousand miles from everywhere
They marched that hero band
Above the desert sand
Frozen by night, and scorched by day
Weary and footsore too
Still on they toiled to find a fight
Their fierce fanatic foe
How oft in that long desert march
To their hot aching eyes
Did visions of their country homes
In Lincolnshire arise
Those village homes among the wolds
In marsh or heath or fen
The dearest spots on earth to each
Of those true Englishmen
Oh to exchange for one brief hour

146

The desert dust and glare
For Lincoln's dull and temperate skies
And fresh life giving air
To see her woods and pastures green
Her fallow fields so brown
Her churches grey her cottage homes
In hamlet thorpe or town
It might not be they must press-on
The Soudan must be freed
From the fierce Khalifa's dark rule
Of tyranny and greed
The galling fetters must be struck
From many a captive slave
And from the town where Gordon died
The British flag must wave
So on till by the Atbara's bank
They found the foe at bay
And well the Lincolns bore their part
That memorable day
God grant them still success throughout
Their arduous campaign
And bring them safe through all their toil
To England shores again
For oh the hour may come and that
How soon we know not when
Begrit by foes on every hand
England may need such men
When all her sons must as one man
Together stand or fall
God shield her in that trying hour
And bring her safe through all.

Rudyard Kipling may have been more inspired:

'Fuzzy-Wuzzy'
(Soudan Expeditionary Force)

We've fought with many men acrost the seas,
    An' some of 'em was brave an' some was not:
The Paythan an' the Zulu an' Burmese;
    But the Fuzzy was the finest o' the lot.
We never got a ha'porth's change of 'im:
    'E squatted in the scrub an' 'ocked our 'orses,
'E cut our sentries up a' Suakim,
    An' 'e played the cat an' banjo with our forces.

So 'ere's to you, Fuzzy-Wuzzy, at your 'ome in the
    Soudan;
You're a pore benighted 'eathen but a first-class fightin'
    man;
We gives you your certificate, an' if you want it signed
We'll come an' 'ave a romp with you whenever you're
    inclined.

The final few weeks of preparation included the now so familiar parades each morning, marching in columns and forming squares. This was, in the eyes of the Generals, of extreme importance, since when the army went into its final attack this would be the formation, and the men had to be able to respond to commands instinctively. In addition, since the first part of the next stage of the advance would be on barges up the Nile, it was necessary to practise embarkation. However, once the daily exercises had taken place before it became too hot, there was, for Private Teigh at least, nothing to do for the rest of the day except brew and drink tea.

7

FINAL PREPARATIONS

14TH JULY

Teigh: Medical inspection at 6.30 am and after that the Sirdar came round and after he had been round our compounds he went across to the hospital and gave them an order to shift as it was too near the water and that is what is causing all the sickness. I notice they always find these things out too late. I was on fatigue and I had to go up to the next camp with the Mounted Infantry Equipment and hand them in to the O.C. stores and we also had to bring some matting back with us. We arrived back about 8.30 am just in time for breakfast.

Cox: First signs of advance so I start again. Orders confirm that the battalion in the presence of Sirdar will practise embarkation for the advance – 2 steamers, 4 barges allocated to each battalion. Each man carried 1 ½ blankets, 1 waterproof sheet, 1 pr canvas shoes, 1 Lascar cap, 1 pr socks, 1 flannel shirt, 1 pr boot laces, 1 towel, 1 piece soap. Chargers and a proportion of brigade staff and stores to be included. There will be a frightful squash. However, better than walking!
   I am a Captain from today! S. FitzG Cox Capt. 10th Regt.

Skinner: Sirdar visited El Selim today and at once gave orders that the hospitals were to be shifted further into the desert, which was carried out the same evening, also hear that the move of the Khalifa moving south all rot, that he was making his stronghold 10 miles north of Omdurman, where he intended to make strong resistance.

15TH JULY

Teigh: Adjutant's parade at 6.30 and they marched across the desert in different squads and each doing different movements. Some done firing exercise, some bayonet and some manual exercise and so on. After that they were marched back and got dismissed. It was 6.50. We had Maconochie's jam for breakfast. We had another man die this morning of fever and was buried in the evening. This man also belonged to 'D' Company, Private Johnson. We got an issue of lime-juice at night about 6.30 and after that several of the men went to the next camp to a concert.

16TH JULY

Teigh: Reveille at 4 and we paraded at 5 for Brigade parade. Major Simpson was in charge of the Battalion as the Commanding Officer has gone to Shabluka. After we got across the railway we formed sections and we marched across the desert in column of sections. The Brigade formed up in the same place and after that we had five minutes' rest. Then the alert sounded and we formed into line and fixed bayonets and fired 3 volleys by sections of half companies from the right. After that we cleaned out our rifles and then marched back to camp. It was 8.5 when we got dismissed. We then got our break-fasts. They are packing the stores close to the Nile ready for our next advance. I was on fatigue unloading stores off barges and it lasted about 2 hours. After that we fell out. There is great traffic up the Nile today.

In the evening we got our usual issue of rum and also got payed out at 7 pm. We had another concert and as near as I can say it was about 10 when this finished. This was a very good concert and the band took a great part in it. They also played the troopship. They finished up by playing the Queen.

17TH JULY

Teigh: Church parade at 5.30 and we had the service at the same place between the two camps. We arrived back about 6.30. After breakfast I was on filter fatigue and I had to bring the water from the filter tent to our compound. In the evening a convoy went back to Cairo and all boys was sent back. Our Regiment was the only one that brought the boys up.

18TH JULY

Teigh: Commanding Officer's parade at 5.45 and we paraded in mobilization order, just the same order as we advance in and that was marching order with emergency kits and canteen strapped at our back and coat bandolier-fashion with water bottles and haversacks. We embarked on board a barge just to see how many they could get on one of these barges. I think as near as I could tell they got 240 troops on board and there was hardly room to move. The parade lasted about 2 hours and I think we got dismissed about 7.30. It was very hot during the day and in the evening we had another issue of lime juice.

Skinner: The number of deaths from enteric fever here has reached 300.

19TH JULY

Teigh: Brigade parade was cancelled and Major Simpson had a parade at 5.30 in clean fatigue dress and he gave us a lecture and told us that we were going to have an experimental embarkation just to see what time it would take us to put on all the stores and embark ready to shift. After that he dismissed us and I was on Officers' mess fatigue, so I had to go and do a bit of graft for about an hour, while the remainder were having a sleep or something of the sort. We paraded in the afternoon about 5 in marching order, rolled coats and emergency kits, canteens, haversacks, water bottles and we also had 100 rounds of ammunition per man. We marched across towards the gunboat and barges in half-battalions and we got the order to pile arms and take off our equipment and we also took off our jackets. After that we got the order to start to load. There were two companies to each barge and each company was told off in 3 sections, one section working at a time. So we took our turn. There was a set time to load them in and be on board. The time was two hours but after working very hard we had the order to get dressed, unpile arms and we marched on board. All was done in 45 minutes and it was done very quietly. After we had been on board a few minutes, and got nicely settled down the bugles sounded the retire and we marched off the barges and Major Simpson told us he was very pleased the way the men worked and the good conduct of the men and Non-Commissioned Officers and also the Officers, the way they conducted themselves. He also told us that we were going for a voyage in the morning for a short trip up the Nile to try the engines on the new gunboats. When we got dismissed it was 7 am.

20TH JULY

Teigh: Reveille at 4 and we paraded at 5 in the same order as yesterday and we marched to the barges and embarked and got down. We put our rifles in racks made for the purpose and hung up our equipment on a beam in the centre of the barge with our canteen straps. After that we started our trip up the Nile. We were about an hour going up, but we came down much faster as we were with the stream. I think as near as I could say we went about 6 or 7 miles. We arrived back about 7.30 and then we disembarked and piled our arms and undressed, and we had to unload all the stores that we loaded yesterday. We unloaded them and I think it took us a bit longer than it did to load them. The Warwickshires came to give us a hand, but the Lincolns were too independent and so we unloaded them ourselves. We got dressed and we got dismissed about 8.30. We got our break-fast about 9. We had some sliced bacon for breakfast. Our Commanding Officer arrived back this morning from Shabluka. He has been up there for a fortnight on leave.[1] In the evening we had our usual issue of rum and we also found the out post duty, 12 men and a Sergeant of my company. The Seaforth Highlanders had one of their concerts at Darmali and so most of the men made their way up to see it. It was very showery and it kept thundering and lightning, so I never went to see the concert.

---

[1]   It is most unlikely that Colonel Lowth went to Shabluka for leave.

21ST JULY

Teigh: Reveille at 4 am and we paraded at 4.30 and while we were forming up the 9th Battalion of Soudanese troops passed our camp making their way towards Khartoum. We marched off in an opposite direction to what they went and took our usual route across the desert and after marching for about an hour we formed square and then we knelt down for a few minutes. Then we reformed line and unfixed bayonets and got in our usual position. After that the alert sounded and we formed into line and fired 5 volleys from right of sections and after that we cleaned our rifles and marched back. It was about 7.45 when we got back.

The day was very warm and in the evening I was on wood fatigue and it took 3 of us about 2 hours to get a camel load. We lost our sergeant, he went to look for camels and he was gone so long that we took up our wood and made our way up to camp. I think it was about 7.15 pm when we arrived back. We also got our usual issue of lime juice when we got back.

22ND JULY

Teigh: The Battalion paraded for Adjutant's general attendance at 5.30 and we done the manual exercise and a few other movements and then we got dismissed. It was 6.45. It was very hot during the day, and in the evening another sick convoy went back to Cairo, but it was very late when the train arrived. It must have been about 7.45. We also had another issue of rum.

23RD JULY

Teigh: Brigade route march was cancelled and so there was no parade, but I was on Quartermaster's fatigue. I had to fall in at 5.30 am and we had to make a shelter to shade the sun from the men in the middle of the day. I also had to parade again at 5.15 pm for fatigue. After that we received our pay and we also had one of our concerts which we have every Saturday night.

24TH JULY

Teigh: Reveille at 5 and while we were getting up the Egyptian Artillery went past our camp with their Maxims making for the front. We paraded at 5.30 for church and marched to our usual place half-way between El Selim and Darmali camps. General Gatacre was there as he has arrived back from Cairo off leave, and after the service was over he gave us one of his usual lectures. He told us he had arrived back from Cairo and that the sick and wounded which had arrived from the front were doing well. Some had gone home to England and the others will go when they get better. He also said that some of them wanted to come back again. After that he told us as far as he knew about our next advance on Khartoum would be very shortly. He said that the Khalifa force was in either 3 or 4 Divisions and that the first lot would be about 13,000 rifle and spearmen and the second would be about 25,000 women and children and the 3rd would be 4,000 horsemen and cavalry and the 4th would be the strongest of them all. It is believed that both Brigades will be completed by the 18th of August, but we will be further up the river. He also said that he was pleased to see us looking so well up here; and he told us that it was the last chance that he would get to give us a lecture as our new Commander of the 1st Brigade was expected out very shortly; and then we marched back and got dismissed about 7 am, and so we made ourselves contented until breakfast.

After breakfast I went down the Nile and got a bit of fresh breeze from the river as it was very hot in our mud hut. In the evening I took a walk as far as the cemetery where most of our comrades are buried, and I counted the graves and there were 37 in all and they have all died through fever since the battle of Atbara. After I had visited the graves of some of the heroes who fought bravely but died since, I returned back to my compound, which I reached about 7 pm. After that I laid down my blankets on the desert ready for my night sleep.

25TH JULY

Teigh: Reveille at 5. I was on fatigue at 5.30. We had to fetch the water from the Nile for the troops to wash with. After breakfast I went down to the Nile again as usual and tried my luck at

154

fishing and I had been down about an hour when I caught one and so I made sure of him and fried him for dinner. It was very hot during the day and in the evening I had to go on my fatigue and I didn't finish until 6.30 pm.

26TH JULY

Teigh: Reveille at 4 and we paraded at 4.30 for Brigade route march and we marched to our usual place half-way between the two camps and the Brigade formed up. The Lincolns on the right again as usual and then we advanced towards the east and after marching for about half an hour we formed square and after that we advanced in a square three or four times and then we got the order to reform line and unfixed bayonets and marched off. After marching for a short time we formed into line and fired five volleys by sections from the left of companies and when we had finished we cleaned our rifles and marched back to camp. We arrived back about 8.15 and we had cocoa for breakfast. We also had preserved meat for dinner in the evening. We had an issue of lime juice. It was about 7 pm and I laid down my blankets on the desert again as usual.

Skinner: Appeared in orders of the change of Medical Officers and that the officers and men are to be one corps under the heading of "Royal Army Medical Corps".

27TH JULY

Teigh: Commanding Officer's parade at 5.30 and they marched out and done a few movements but they soon got dismissed as it was very dusty. After breakfast we all received a pair of boots each and a pair of socks. I was on canteen fatigue and I had to fetch some water from the Nile for cooking purposes and during the day several of our officers came back from Cairo. The Captain of my company was one of them. In the evening we had our usual issue of rum and there was a concert at Darmali, but I believe it was not up to much.

Cox: We received orders today to hold ourselves in readiness to move to the Atbara Camp at an early date – 4 Egyptian

155

regiments have marched through here lately. All the fellows returned from home bar Forrest, they seem to have had a good time, some having taken a trip to the Bosphorus and Constantinople but £60 appears to be the minimum expenditure.

28TH JULY

Teigh: General attendance parade at 5.30 for running and after that Medical Inspection. We got dismissed about 6.30. A draft of 26 men of our battalion joined us from Cairo. It is a bit cooler than usual today in the evening. I was on outpost duty and I mounted at 6.30 pm and dismounted at reveille next morning, which was at 5 am.

Cox: Have started running drills again in the early morning. Today was our first and it hurt horribly, I was nearly sick and my heart went like a sledge hammer. Cumberland brought me up water to help my state. That brute Crozier has never sent my irons and I hear that he is off his head.

Meiklejohn: I am no longer Junior Subaltern now Jackson is here. Got a piece of grit in my eye and Hopkins, our doctor, had to extract it with a needle.

29TH JULY

Teigh: Adjutant General attendance parade at 5.30 and they done about ¾ of an hour drill and they marched back and got dismissed. A battery of Egyptian Artillery passed our camp this morning for the front. During the day the Captain of my company came round and inspected the mud huts and viewed the old faces once more. He said we were all looking very well and he also told us that we were all expected in Cairo before the end of September. In the evening we had some more lime juice.

Meiklejohn: Skipwith and Caldecott returned from leave. The latter had been ordered by Gatacre to grow a moustache and arrived with a very fine one, which fell off while he was talking to the Colonel. Much amusement.

Skinner: Have been allowed to get up a little today.

30TH JULY

Teigh: Brigade parade at 4.50 and we done the same old route as usual and the movements are getting properly stale to us. Colonel Money was in charge of the parade and General Gatacre was an onlooker. However, we done a decent old route across the desert and we formed into line and fired three volleys by sections from right to left of companies. We got back about 8.15 am. In the evening we had a concert and I believe it will be the last in the camp as we are on the point of shifting from this camp to the front.

Meiklejohn: Held a Gymkhana. The "Farewell Plate" and "Fed Up" stakes were run. An American dentist arrived and I made an appointment.

31ST JULY

Teigh: Church parade at 5.30 am and it was held in the usual place. After the service was over we marched back and got dismissed about 6.30. It was very hot during the day and in the evening a convoy of sick went back to Cairo. I think there were about 6 of our fellows went down about 7.30 pm. Three battalions of the Soudanese passed our camp for the front and we all turned out and gave them a good and hearty cheer for we knew they were good men for they fought side by side with us at Atbara on April the 8th, Good Friday.

Meiklejohn: The dentist had three unsuccessful attempts to destroy a nerve. Rather painful and I don't think much of him. His surgery is quaint and has become a sort of club. You get whiskys and soda between the acts!

Skinner: The new Brigadier Generals (Cols) Wauchope and Lyttelton with Surg. Gen. Taylor arrived today.

1st August

Teigh: Reveille at 4 am and we paraded at 4.40 and marched to our usual place and formed into line for our new Commander of the first Brigade.[1] He inspected us ready to take over. After he had inspected us we marched across the desert in battle formation and we had not marched far when we got the order to fire three volleys from the right of companies. After that we advanced and had not marched above 100 yards when we got the order to fire 3 volleys by companies and we still advanced and after that they sounded cavalry and the Brigade formed square the best and smartest I have seen it done lately. After we had formed square we got the order to reform line and we fired 3 more rounds independent that making us 9 rounds altogether. Then we marched back to our camp and it was 8.30 when we got back. In the evening we got another issue of lime juice. Two of our new gunboats came past our camp up the Nile today ready to take up troops to the front.

Cox: New Brigadier, Wauchope arrived yesterday – funny wizened little man with funnier ADC. Brigade parade this morning at which Gatacre handed us over to Wauchope. Yesterday the 9th Soudanese passed through to Atbara Camp – one brigade had in the ranks 700 who were dervishes at the Atbara!! Guards started from Cairo yesterday. That damned ass Crozier hasn't sent up my stirrups and girths. I wonder when we shall be off, the 7th they say.

2nd August

Teigh: The Brigade paraded at 5.15 for a double in clean fatigue dress and we doubled about a mile and back again. We were dismissed after breakfast. Two more gunboats passed our camp up the Nile. In the evening 'F', 'G' and 'H' companies paraded under Lieutenant Cummins, a Medical Officer, for a lecture on dressing wounds and stopping the blood in case of getting wounded but I was taking a walk across the desert so I never went.

---

[1] Brigadier A.G. Wauchope, Black Watch.

Cox: No mail in – it's disgraceful the way they let the mails rip. They don't seem to care a damn about them. Running drill this morning.

3RD AUGUST

Teigh: Reveille at 5. It should have been Commanding Officer's parade at 5.30, but on account of it being so windy and dusty there was no parade. So after breakfast several of our men went for a walk to the Nile and done a little fishing. some went in search of rabbits and killing birds, but owing to it being so very hot they soon returned minus of anything. We had our usual issue of rum at night and afterwards I went to Darmali camp to a concert, which was held by the Cameron Highlanders. It was very good and I got back to our camp about 11 pm.

4TH AUGUST

Teigh: Doubling parade at 5.15 and after that Medical Inspection which I think was about 6 am. When we got dismissed our new general was around our camp in the morning looking at movements of the troops. It was extra hot during the day and in the evening it was a bit dull and rather inclined to be a bit stormy. It thundered and lightened a great deal through the night and a little rain fell.

5TH AUGUST

Teigh: Adjutant's General Attendance parade at 5.30. We formed up and marched across the desert and done a bit of Battalion drill and then marched back. It was about 6.45 when we got dismissed. After breakfast some of the new Brigade of British troops passed our camp and went a few miles further up country. In the evening we had an issue of lime juice. My company found 12 men and a sergeant for outpost duty.

6TH AUGUST

Teigh: Brigade route march at 4.30 and we formed up in our usual place and before we marched off our new commander of the Brigade told us that he had got a very pleasant duty to perform. He gave us a good lecture on bravery and one thing or the other. He also told us that before very long the British flag will be flying over the ruins of Khartoum and then we shall all be going home to our friends, some to England, Ireland, Scotland and other countries mentioning Lincoln where those bells chime so sweet. He then presented two men of the Warwickshire Regiment with testimonials for saving a man's life on the Eleventh of January last. We then marched towards the east and fired four volleys. We then advanced in battle formation and then formed square. We then reformed line and fired 4 more rounds. We had just fired the last when our Captain said very good; the cease fire sounded and we unfixed our bayonets, cleaned our rifles and marched back to camp. It was about 8.10 when we got dismissed. In the evening we received the usual issue of rum. We also had one of our concerts.

7TH AUGUST

Teigh: Church parade at 5.30 and we held our service in the usual place. It was a very short service and after we had service we marched back. It was about 6.30 when we got dismissed. It was very hot during the day and in the evening we had to give in our blankets and then we got served with 2 for every 3 men. We made our blankets down on the sandy desert once again but I was soon asleep.

8TH AUGUST

Teigh: We paraded at 5.30 for pitching canvas which lasted about 2 hours. After breakfast we packed up our kits and moved out of our huts under tents. We were on fatigue nearly all the day clearing up different places and carrying baggage to the side of the railway ready to pack on the trains. After tea I was on Quartermaster's fatigue which lasted for two and a half hours. Then we got an issue of rum and after that two trains came past

160

with British troops. Some of the 21st Lancers and some of the 32nd Field Battery of Artillery from Cairo. We then made down our beds and went to sleep.

Cox: Regt. ordered under canvas – we pitched camp alongside the village and put all heavy kit and stacked it by the railway line, where eventually it goes to Atbara. Our chargers went off last Saturday, marching all the way. ½ Batt. passed through last night. Strolled over to see the cemetery in the afternoon. Many graves, 13 of which belong to us. They have built a wall round and erected wooden crosses on each grave. G.O.C. doesn't want me to ride on the staff, so I shall have to command 'G' Comp. and do all the other work as well.

9TH AUGUST

Teigh: Reveille at 5 and we paraded at 5.30 in clean fatigue dress. We only had a roll call and got dismissed. After breakfast I was warned for a fatigue and I was falling in and out for nearly 24 hours and at the finish I had to take my blanket and go and sleep on the side of the railway ready to load the baggage on the train when it came. But it never came until 7 am next morning.

Cox: Europe morning for officers. Howitzer battery came through last night – all heavy kit goes today, so once more on the move. 2nd half of Guards passed through in the afternoon. In evening went for a "stagger" with Cumberland and found that all the natives who live in this village are collecting to re-occupy on our departure. We expect to start tomorrow at least two companies, one of which is mine and the brigade staff.

Skinner: I was discharged hospital to-day fit for duty.

10TH AUGUST

Teigh: The Battalion paraded simply in embarkation order at 6.30 and got dismissed at 7. I helped to load the baggage which I had been sleeping against beside the railway. It took us about an hour. It was very hot during the day and in the evening we had to strike half our canvas and carry them across to the Nile

161

ready for embarkation as we are expected to shift any minute. We are waiting for the gunboats and then we are going to start.

Cox: Stood by nearly all day with no result – the steamers not arriving and signalling all night. ½ batt of the 6th (Warwicks) passed through in the afternoon.

11TH AUGUST

Teigh: The Battalion paraded for Medical inspection at 7 am and then we got dismissed. We are still waiting for the gunboats. We were out in the sun all day today, and still in the old camp.

Cox: No news of the steamers yet. Hear they are loading them at the Fort, in the meantime "standing by" is distinctly "off". Tremendous rise in the river this afternoon – came over the bank in places.

12TH AUGUST

Teigh: The Battalion paraded at 6 am in embarkation order and Colonel Lowth inspected the right half-Battalion and Major Simpson the left. There were a lot of men brought up for not wearing their best boots, they nearly all got 3 days' defaulters. I was told off for a fatigue and I was fell in 2 hours too early. Then we had to load a few stores and got dismissed.

Cox: Squadron 21st and ½ batt 5th Fusiliers passed through early this morning. Disturbed in the night by a pariah quietly drinking.

FINAL ADVANCE

Even after four months in the desert, there was still a period of waiting; rumours of an imminent move never came true. Weeks were spent practising getting in and out of barges and arrangements made to leave kit behind. Once again Captain Cox, as he now was, found life too boring to write about. By the end of July, 1898, everyone who had gone on leave was back and the new Brigadier-Generals were in place, with General Gatacre commanding the British Division. Then followed a tense period when blankets had to be handed in, mud huts abandoned for tents, and the baggage being left taken to the railhead.

On 17 August, 1898, Gatacre wrote from Dakheila, "We are very busy now with embarkations and detrainments of troops arriving from the north; we are up nearly every night, as trains arrive at most unearthly hours; this is of course unavoidable. My first Brigade has gone on, and the embarkation of the second commences at daybreak tomorrow. . . . We move by steamers towing barges to Wad Bishara about 145 miles, and thence by route march."

Since these boats were wood-fired, wood-cutting parties had gone on ahead to leave huge piles of timber near the banks ready to be taken on board. The Sirdar's plan was to move his army up the Nile to Wad Hamed by water, which was about 58 miles from Omdurman. The various accounts miscalculate this distance. While the Egyptian Army had gone on ahead, Kitchener did not know to what extent the Khalifa would attempt to harass his progress south. The Dervishes had some strong forts on the Nile, and there were places, such as Shabluka, where the Nile narrowed and considerable delay and damage might be caused to the fleet. However, the Khalifa had decided to conserve all his strength for a fight at Omdurman, and as these fortified places were reached they were found to be deserted. Some have suggested that the Khalifa had dreamed that it would be disrespectful to Allah to seek battle other than on the plains of Kereri to the north-west of Omdurman. Probably he feared another Atbara, and may even have felt that the Madhi's tomb must be protected at all costs, since it was the repository of sacred relics, and no infidel invader would succeed in attacking it.

By the middle of August Kitchener had assembled his army at Wad

Hamed and made the final preparations to march on southwards. The kit carried for each person was again reduced, and then on 23 August the Sirdar reviewed his army. He had, after eight months of activity, assembled, at a distance of 1,260 miles from Cairo, 8,200 British and 17,600 Egyptian and Soudanese troops, 44 field guns and 20 Maxims on land, 36 guns and 24 Maxims on the gunboats, 2,470 horses, 870 mules, about 4,000 camels and 230 donkeys. The review stretched for at least two miles as it lined up in the burning sun.

The next day the first sections moved off, on foot for the men and on horseback for the cavalry and officers. By 30 August the army had reached Egeiga, about six miles from Omdurman and from where Kitchener could launch his final attack. He despatched a message under a flag of truce to the Khalifa, advising him to remove all women and children from Omdurman, which he proposed to destroy by bombardment, and to overthrow the Dervish throne and government "in order to save the country from your devilish doings and iniquity".

Kitchener had formed a zariba to the west of the Nile at Egeiga. Gunboats lay to the north and south, and immediately to the east there were barges fitted up for the wounded, as well as a hospital near the bank at the back of the zariba to the south was a hill, Jebel Surgham, from which Cox as Signalling Officer was able to view the Kereri plain below and Omdurman in the distance. Close to was a ditched area, Khor Abu Sunt, but between the hill and ditch the Kereri Plain was open south-west to Omdurman. Here the Khalifa paraded his army on 31 August and called his troops to a Jihad, a Holy War, to drive the infidels from his land for ever.

On 1 September the gunboats opened the bombardment of Omdurman, tearing great holes in the gleaming white dome of the Madhi's tomb. But the Dervishes did not advance further towards the British at Egeiga, and Kitchener decided that his troops would bivouac that night behind the protection of the zariba. At 3.30 am on 2 September the army stood to arms, and even had breakfast. At 6.45 the field artillery opened fire on the Dervishes formed in a semi-circle south-west, as they advanced in attack on the British force. A great number of casualties resulted among the Khalifa's troops, but they continued to advance in a wide crescent to within 900 yards of the British, when fire was opened. The Dervishes were decimated, and the first phase of the battle was over.

The Khalifa expected that Kitchener would immediately march on Omdurman. He had a large number of troops to the south and west of Jebel Surgham, and others who at the start of the attack had gone to the Kereri Hills to the north-west of the British zariba. He hoped to crush the advancing army between these two forces. At 8.30, as Kitchener advanced, he had trouble with over-enthusiastic Soudanese troops who were busily shooting wounded Dervishes and wasting ammunition. Meanwhile the 21st Lancers having crossed the eastern

164

end of Jebel Surgham hill rode into a trap at full speed, and in line. This was the work of Osman Digna who had placed his men in a ditch, Khor Abu Sunt, to the south of Jebel Surgham. A short and bloody fight resulted, and in two minutes five officers, sixty-five men and 119 horses out of 400 had been killed or wounded and three Victoria Crosses won. The action was totally irrelevant to the battle.

During the advance some parts of the British force got out of position. Kitchener had never previously commanded an army of this size. Gatacre moved the British Division too far east and a gap opened between the Lincolns, on the right of the line, and the Egyptians. The Lincolns were ordered to go to the help of the Xth Soudanese, whom they had adopted. But, in spite of some difficult moments in this second phase as the British Army moved forward, the Dervishes retreated in their thousands across the plain towards Omdurman, pursued and slaughtered by the cavalry. Surveying the scene, the Sirdar told his officers that the Khalifa had been given a 'Good Dusting' and he resumed his march into Omdurman, where he found little resistance. The Battle of Omdurman had been won. Once again the wounded on both sides were not dealt with well. Many of the Dervishes were shot or bayoneted, the rest left to shift for themselves.

Two days later a memorial service was held for Gordon among the ruins of the Governor-General's Palace in Khartoum. The Reverend Watson, so liked by Private Teigh for his sermons, caused an interdenominational controversy by objecting to participation in the service by representatives of the Roman Catholic, Presbyterian and Methodist churches, since Gordon had been Church of England. The Sirdar gave him short shrift.

8

THE BATTLE OF OMDURMAN

13TH AUGUST

Teigh: Reveille at 5 am and we got the order to strike canvas and be ready to shift at 7.45, but the boats didn't arrive until 10 and when they did arrive it didn't take us long to put our little baggage on board that we had got. We loaded up and was ready to start in an hour's time. Just as we was ready to start the boat passed us that was going to take the Warwickshire Regiment. Anyhow we started up the Nile and when we arrived at Darmali we saw the Seaforth Highlanders getting ready to embark on board their steamer. In the afternoon the boat which the Warwickshire Regiment was on passed us as there was something wrong with our boat. On our way up to Dakheila we passed some very nice country which was well cultivated and plenty of inhabitants. Just before we arrived at Dakheila we saw a train loaded with troops making its way to railhead. We arrived at Dakheila about 6.30 pm and by the side of the river we saw several gunboats and on the opposite side we saw a lot of cavalry horses and mules. We still kept advancing up the Nile and it soon turned dark. It was about 10 pm when we stopped and anchored for the night. We got a blanket each and laid down but we were packed like sardines in a tin. The boat started about 4 am and reveille sounded at 5.

Cox: At 7.30 the fall in sounded and we found that 2 of the steamers were in – 6 comps. left at 1 pm and 2 are still waiting, myself included. They didn't look very comfortable, frightfully crowded. No news of our boat in the evening.

14TH AUGUST

Teigh: The boat stopped about 8.30 am and 'C' Company was on fatigue loading her with wood as they never use coal. All the Battalions went on shore and the companies' cooks boiled eight camp kettles of water per company to make tea. We were only on shore ¾ of an hour and then the retire sounded and we soon got on board again ready for another start. It is rather bushy country up to the present but never mind we have got what we have been looking for this last 5 months, that is our final advance on Khartoum. We have had a very fair voyage today and we passed plenty of scenery but few inhabitants. The Seaforth Highlanders passed us during last night. The boat stopped about 10 pm and anchored for the night.

Cox: Steamer arrived at 1 pm full of doctors! Embarked with 2 comps 6th and picked up Seaforths. We have 4 field hospitals and 2 communication hospitals on board, they certainly are not going to run short of help this time – got X rays on board.

15TH AUGUST

Teigh: Reveille at 5 and the boat had been travelling for about an hour. I was orderly man, so I had to draw rations and we had biscuits and Maconochie's jam for breakfast. We stopped about 10 am and took on enough wood to last us about 4 hours. After that we started off again and we had been going for about 4 hours when we stopped again and took a good old stock of wood on board. I being orderly man I had to fill the camp kettles and the cooks made some tea. After tea was made we had to carry it on board ready for another start. We started off again and we had a good old drink of tea and it went down alright after having nothing to drink only water for the last 48 hours. It was very hot during the day and just after retreat we found we were in sight of Shendi, one of the Khalifa's forts. We anchored down for the night. It was very stormy and we expected a severe storm.

Cox: Arrived at Atbara camp about 10 pm last night, took on more stores. G.O.C. (Gatacre) too energetic for words, came along the bank and met us at each place and then interfered with everyone's work. Going all today. Very thick bush both sides. No cultivation. Saw three hippopotamuses swimming about close to us in the evening, caused great excitement and nearly capsized one of the barges by men running to the side. Quite nice trip, got a good breeze all the time getting men burnt again. Night and day only stopping at places to pick up wood.

16TH AUGUST

Teigh: We started off early and we had been on the move about an hour when we passed Shendi. It is a very straggling sort of a place and there was a small look out and a small fort. It is in ruins, just as it was taken early in April. In another hour we came to Metemma on the opposite side of the river. It was a very large straggling place two or three miles in length and there was a large mud wall round it and it also reached well out across the desert. It was a bit windy and we stopped about 2 pm and got another stock of wood and the cooks made some more tea. We started and were travelling for about 7 hours when we halted again for the night. There were hills on the right and woods on the left side of the Nile.

Cox: On watch last night, ran ashore at 10 pm on a submerged island, dark night and strong wind – didn't get off till 5 am. Not so hot, sighted and signalled to steamer behind us with head-quarters officers. Saw three more hippos in the evening. We thought they were going to ram us but they turned off when close. I shan't think much of a salmon rise after a hippo one! Country more hilly – getting much more tropical – all sorts of birds, geese. Meroe pyramids sighted in the evening but dark when we passed them.

Skinner: This part of the Nile banks is very thick with wood and shrub, in a great many places the wood has been cut and stacked close to the Nile for use as fuel for the boats going up and down. A few crocodiles were seen along the banks but only small ones.

Meiklejohn: Arrived at Wad Hamed, our place of concentration, at 6 pm. It is a huge camp and most of the Egyptian and Soudanese troops have already arrived. It is just below the Shabluka cataract.

17TH AUGUST

Teigh: We started off again at 4 am and reveille sounded at 5 am. We were in sight of troops and different camps before we arrived into our camp a long time. We arrived at our destination about 9 am and we disembarked and, after being knocking about for about an hour in the sun, we had to set to and unload our baggage, which lasted for another hour and a half. When we got it all unloaded it was 12 noon and then we had our camp to mark out and our canvas to pitch. We did that after piling our arms, taking off our equipment. After we had got all our canvas up we were told off to our tents, eight men in each. We then had some tea and after tea the Battalion paraded for fatigues carrying stores and ammunition up to camp and at 6.30 pm we fell in again to line the zariba and there we stopped for the night. We had our equipment on and our rifles by our sides in case any of the Dervishes came. We had one blanket to lay down on. I soon fell asleep, but woke up several times during the night.

Cox: Up at 6 am. Woke up with a jump in the night and found we were ashore. Tied up for an hour to take on wood. Passed Metemma in the afternoon, saw dervish position and forts, also remains of the massacre of last year where 1,200 Jaalins were killed. The whole place was strewn with skeletons of human beings and I also saw the gallows where some were hung, the whole fort being a most extraordinary sight. We ought to reach Shabluka tomorrow. Passed two empty gunboats going down to fetch the second brigade.

18TH AUGUST

Teigh: Reveille at 4.30 and we had to get up and stand by for about three-quarters of an hour in case of an attack being made. However, we got the order to pile our arms in line and fall out which we did. We hadn't been fell out half an hour before we got the order to fall in again for fatigues. It is very trying these times, but we have to put up with these things on active service, but all the same I shall be glad when it is over. We got our breakfasts about 9 am. We had to fall in again for woodcutting to make our zariba stronger. This lasted for about an hour. After that I found my way down to the Nile and had a good wash all

169

over and then washed my clothes. After that I found my way back to camp. We had preserved meat for dinner, but it was so very hot I didn't want any so laid down and had a sleep till tea time. After tea I had to go grass cutting and I finished at 5.45 pm and we had to parade again at 6.30 to line the zariba for the night. We had to sleep with our equipment on and 100 rounds of ammunition in our pockets and rifles by our sides.

Cox: I had a bad night last night, went ashore about 5 times and finally had to tie up. Simpson as usual lost his head. What a miserable ass that chap is. Today river has more islands and is much broader, left bank is getting rocky. We saw friendly patrols on the right bank and passed two Egyptian battalions, who have been woodcutting all the way up, they were zaribaed and had outposts out! We expect to get in this evening or early tomorrow.

19TH AUGUST

Teigh: Reveille sounded at 4.30 and after we had stood to our arms for about an hour we fell out and went to our tents. We had to fall in again for fatigues, carrying ammunition. After carrying it for half an hour we were told to take it back again and this made us very wild for it was a hard fatigue and ought not to have been shifted, but to make it straight they loaded us both ways, one with ammunition and the other rations. It was about 8 am when we got finished. After breakfast I went down to the Nile and had a wash and filtered some water as it was too dirty to drink otherwise. 'G' and 'H' companies arrived today. We left them at El Selim and there was no room on our boat. It was very hot during the day and we sweated a lot in our tents. We had preserved meat again for dinner. I had a sleep in the afternoon until tea came up at 4 pm and at 6.30 the Battalion fell in and lined the zariba as usual. The night passed very quietly until early in the morning when we had a false alarm, but as we had seen before, we took very little notice of it and so we laid down and had another sleep, and the next thing I heard was Reveille.

Cox: Got in last night at 9 pm, disembarked at 4 am this morning – rather a nice place, rocks and high grass. Only 45 miles from

Khartoum. We have had 13 Soudanese deserters, men who were captured at Atbara. They caught one and shot him. It's beastly hot under canvas. My servant was flogged today for swearing at Cpl. Colbean. All the gunboats seem to be here. No reliable news of the enemy – Shabluka is unoccupied. One brigade is complete up here now. We have outposts out but everything very quiet, considering we are so close to dervishes. Our mess is very comfortable. Old Lowth is a ripper, things go like clockwork with no worry. Strolled out in the evening to the top of a high rock where the camel corps on outpost duty – splendid view. Had another deserter, funny devils they are.

Meiklejohn: A Soudanese was shot for trying to desert.

20TH AUGUST

Teigh: Reveille sounded at 4.30 and we had to get up and stand to our arms for about ½ an hour and then we piled our arms and fell out. I was orderly man and so I did not have to go on fatigue because I had to draw rations at 7. We received bread and Maconochie's bacon for breakfast and we also had got preserved meat for dinner. In the afternoon we received our pay. In the evening at 6.30 we fell in again as usual and it was lightening very much and it looked stormy. At 8.45 the rain came down in torrents and the wind blew a lot of tents up. It kept raining for about 2 hours and nearly all of us were wet through, but we couldn't change our clothing because we only had what we stood up in and we did look a nice lot.

Cox: Boots and fully equipped once again last night for bed – the battalion lined zariba. We had a slight false alarm. Strolled out with Plunkett and after went to camel outposts. Dined with Gamble and got caught in a thunderstorm, everybody soaked through.

21ST AUGUST

Teigh: Just before reveille we wakened up to line the zariba in case of a daybreak attack and at 5.15 we fell out. I was put on Officers' Mess fatigue and I had to do a bit of work for our officers. I don't think it is hardly fair us men having to do every little thing for them. I think they should have to do all their own work the same as us. After breakfast the XX Lancashire Fusiliers came and pitched their canvas by the side of ours and in the evening the Grenadier Guards joined us at our camp, and well the 1st Brigade knew it, for each Regiment had to find 100 men to go on fatigue and unload their baggage for them. By the time this was done it was dark and we had to fall in and line the zariba. It came over very windy during the night, but we had to stick it out in the open till reveille.

Cox: Lyall, Rennie and Earle rejoined, came up with the 20th, old Charles just the same as usual. Guards came in morning.

Skinner: The Grenadier Guards arrived this afternoon. Deserters are continually coming in from the enemy, in the afternoon about 2,000 deserters came in and gave themselves up. They were sent to the other side of the river under strong escort of the Jaalins.

Meiklejohn: We got a ration of bread as a Sunday treat, a welcome change from the eternal bully beef and biscuits. The Lancashire Fusiliers arrived in the morning and the Grenadier Guards in the evening. These units, fresh from England, feel the intense heat greatly and 100 men from each regiment of our brigade had to help them unload their baggage. The Lancashires have a yellow badge on their helmets, and the Guards a red and blue grenade. We now put a VI of mimosa thorns in our helmet badge. Toogood had enteric and was sent back to Dakheila this morning almost in tears. An Officer of the "Queen's Company" of the Grenadiers (all over 6 ft) asked one of our men this morning if he had seen his company. The reply was, "I expect, Sir, they have got lost in the long grass"!!

22ND AUGUST

Teigh: Reveille at 4.15 and we had to rise up at once and stand to our arms where we stood till 8 when we got dismissed. I can tell you we did look beauties with our faces all dust which had been blowing about in the night. We had to pack up some things which we weren't going to take with us to Khartoum and leave

172

them on an Island for the Egyptians to look after until we come back.

Cox: 5th (Northumberland Fusiliers) and part of the Rifle Brigade came in today. The whole army including transport paraded this morning – a very fine sight and a huge force, the end being out of sight. We did one or two manoeuvres and then returned. They have got a lot of foreign attachés up this time and all the correspondents have arrived, but the camp is so huge that one sees none of them. Was on a very tiresome equipment board all day. Got to parade tomorrow in same order as today.

23RD AUGUST

Teigh: Divisional parade on this morning. The General Officer Commanding this Brigade joined us at El Selim (Colonel Wauchope). General Gatacre commands the British Division and we had a very large parade on and the Sirdar and his staff were there. We marched out at 5 am and marched about 5 miles across the desert and done a few Brigade movements. The 2nd Brigade happened to be on the right this time as we marched out and on the left as we marched back. We had a hard day and we arrived back about 7.30 and we were sweating very much and also very tired. We rested for the remainder of the day and in the evening we had our usual issue of rum and at 6.30 pm we lined the zariba again as usual for the night.

Cox: Woke up at 3 am. The whole battalion drenched with terrific thunder and sand storm, pitch dark and confusion, with the camels simply awful. I fell over a box and found myself staring a camel in the face. When we had all got thoroughly wet through the "No Parade" sounded. Edwards arrived early this morning looking very fit – we have 29 officers now with the battalion.[1]

Meiklejohn: The whole force paraded in the morning, some 9,000 British and 12,000 native troops, a fine sight.

---

[1]   This entry refers to the following day.

173

24TH AUGUST

Teigh: Reveille at 4.15 and we rose up and stood to our arms for about half an hour and then we got dismissed, which after that we went down to the Nile for a wash. We arrived back at breakfast time. The 21st Lancers joined us yesterday and the Rifles this morning. It rained very hard. The Division is now complete for the final advance.

Cox: The Charger convoy arrived today, mine looking very fit. Some of them were looking decidedly off-colour. The Soudanese division left this afternoon. 2nd Brigade goes tomorrow and we in the evening. Went for a ride all around the camp with Tatchell in the evening, very busy scene at the bank loading gyassas.

25TH AUGUST

Teigh: Reveille at 4.15 and the 2nd Brigade left this morning at 5 and during the day we had to pack up and be ready. At night we marched off at 5 pm and the country is very broken and it is very heavy marching. After marching for about 7 miles we halted and formed square and had to sleep for the night. Each company found a double sentry in front of their companies in case of an attack.

Cox: Reveille at 4. 2nd Bde marched off in the morning. We struck camp in the broiling sun – loaded all our heavy baggage in gyassas and marched off at 4.30 pm. Only 7-mile march; bivouacked for the night. Quite a large army of correspondents and photographers. Barring the cavalry we were the 1st people at Wad Hamed. Made use of my charger as a pack horse. The result of our stay in the Sudan certainly made itself felt during the march – we had 3 cases of sun, and 14 other fall outs.

26TH AUGUST

Teigh: We marched off at 7.30 am and we marched about another six miles and then we halted for the day in the shade, but it was very hot and I was glad when evening came on so we could lay down. This is where we caught the 2nd Brigade as left us yesterday.

Cox: Marched off at 6 am and went 5 miles and are in bivouac. We joined the 2nd Bde in bivouac in the bush. I hear that 95 of the Guards fell out on the march – one of the 5th died. G.O.C. Division (Gatacre) saw me this morning and told me I was to be signaller to division, so less footing it any more. I hand company over to Wilson.

27TH AUGUST

Teigh: Reveille at 5 am and the Division advanced about 7 am. After marching for about an hour or two we had marched about 7 miles, we halted and we were encamped in the heavy bush at about 500 yards from the river. We made shelters with our blankets and marched off at 4 pm in the evening. We travelled about another 7 miles and then we halted for the night. It was read out in this camp to us that any man falling out on the march would be sent back to Dakheila. The Soudanese are here and their bands played us in. We made a zariba round the camp and anchored down for the night.

Cox: Paraded last night at 5 pm and bivouacked half way round Shabluka away from the river – carted water in fantassas. Paraded at 5 am and marched on the river again – Soudanese played us in – very hot today. This is a beastly bivouac.

Skinner: Again started at 5 am, marching till 8.30. This time our camp was pitched on the bank of the Nile. Here the Egyptian and Soudanese were already in camp. This was the first sight of the Nile we had [since] leaving Wad Hamed. We were also served here with fresh meat, the first we have had since the 12th. of the month. There were several deserters brought into camp this morning, one Baggara horseman being captured by the Egyptian cavalry. The water here is very clear. There is a very high hill standing a little way out in the river from the top of which could be seen the ruins of Khartoum. There are situated about here large mountains of rock stretching for several miles inland as well as embracing the Nile, which if held by a body of soldiers would simply be impossible for an army to pass either by land or water. This natural stronghold is called Shabluka, a distance of 35 miles from Omdurman. The great wonder is how the Khalifa could think of leaving such a stronghold as with this place in his possession he could have played great havoc with our force.

Meiklejohn: Started at 5 am and marched till 8 when we reached camp. All the Egyptian and Soudanese troops were already there, and sent bands to play us in. The selection of tunes included "The boys of the old brigade" which, they say, the 2nd Brigade did not find appropriate! On reaching camp we had to take the men to bathe by Gatacre's orders before getting our breakfast, so I had nothing till after 10 am. . . . The men have been "falling out" a great deal during recent marches, and General Gatacre threatens that he will leave the worst Battalion behind. But we think he overworks us, forgetting that the 1st British Brigade are pulled down by a summer up the Nile and the great heat, also indifferent food and sickness. The 2nd Brigade are not yet seasoned.

28TH AUGUST

Teigh: Reveille at 5. We had church parade at 7 and a short service and then got dismissed. In the afternoon several men of the 1st and 2nd Brigades who felt a bit sick were sent over to an island on the opposite side of the Nile and there they had to remain until we came back from Khartoum. The Division marched off at 4.30 pm and we marched about 8 miles and then camped for the night. Marching in this country is very heavy and those of us that has been up here since January are very weak and it is a common thing to see men drop exhausted on the march.

Cox: Reveille at 4.30 and church parade at 5, at which we had a sermon (by Rev. Watson) all about the ensuing fight, followed by a lengthy address by Gen. Gatacre in which he talked the usual rot and gave the Guards beans. Paraded at 4.30 and marched 8 miles to bivouac. Left Spailer and 50 weaklings behind at island depot.

Meiklejohn: On "wood fatigue" in the morning so did not attend Divine Service, but we heard part of Gatacre's speech which was very fiery as usual. He said that officers must now give up all idea of rest (this seemed to have been our lot for some time already!) and must always be with their Companies for the next five days. That the Khalifa had 60,000 men to meet us, but this only meant that we should kill the more.

29TH AUGUST

Teigh: We marched off at 5.30 am and a heavy sandstorm came on with a gale of wind. We marched a few more miles and then we halted. There are plenty of bushes and trees here for shelter but we are not allowed to make use of them. We had to cut down poles and rig up our blankets as well as we could in line and in rear of our piled arms. We also got the order to make a zariba, which took us about an hour to make.

Cox: We got in last night about 9.30 – I with a splitting head – sun I suppose – signalling to the island. A dervish was seen at the zariba last night and left a spear behind. Marched off this morn at 6 am. Marched 11 miles, bivouacked in square. Passed a dervish village recently deserted, beds, crockery, etc. all over the place. The 21st captured a prisoner.

Skinner: No move this morning, the wind is blowing very heavy and making it very uncomfortable for rest, the sand blowing in heavy clouds, causing plenty of desert pepper to be found in our dinner and tea. The marching of the British troops is not very satisfactory considering that we are only doing short journeys, great numbers falling out at every stage, and we have got our hands full to contend with them.

30TH AUGUST

Teigh: We marched off at 5.30 am and marched for about eleven or twelve miles and then halted. It rained very hard last night and us only having one blanket on us we got wet through. We passed through a large straggling village (Sheikh el Taib) in the bush and it looked as though it hadn't been long left with the Dervishes. We made a strong zariba and halted here for the night. We heard several shots fired during the night.

Meiklejohn: Started at 5 am and marched 13 miles, the whole Army Group now moving in fighting formation. Reached camp at 11.30 am and, having no tents, had to improvise grass or blanket shelters as best we could. Sun very hot! Passed several deserted mud villages, and one or two small palm groves. Heavy rain during the night, beginning at 2 am, and, having no shelter, we all got wet through, did not get much sleep, and were glad to see the dawn. I crawled under a bush, but it gave no shelter, and I found I was sitting in a pool of water, with a stream running down the back of my neck.

31st August

Teigh: Marched off at 5.30 am. Gunboats are keeping company with us on the river. We generally march near the river. After marching for 7 miles more we halted and after we had halted for about an hour we got the order to make a zariba and there we halted for the night.

Cox: Marched this morning, whole force . . . in fighting forma-tion – signalling used with messages . . . 21st position at Kereri and . . . their cavalry. Gun boats came into action, 8 of them are going along the Nile abreast of us. Bivouacked and zariba 1 mile from the river at 11 pm. Supposed to be about 9 miles from Kereri. Whole force in a huge square enclosed by a zariba.

1st September

Teigh: We marched off at 6 am and it rained very hard all last night and slightly this morning. It was very heavy and uncom-fortable marching. We travelled about 12 miles and halted in the desert in a village made of mud, which the Dervishes had occupied some time back. I went on out post. We had only been on two hours when the army had marched out on the desert and formed up ready to receive the enemy, who were supposed to be advancing to attack us. Now it was about 2 pm. While we were advancing this morning we heard guns of the gunboats firing at the enemy. The alert sounded and we formed into line and fixed bayonets. It was about 2.30. We have been waiting for about a couple of hours in the hot sun and no signs of the enemy, yet it was about 5.30. Then we got dismissed. We got the order to make a zariba in case they should make an attack during the night. Cavalry are still out. Several rounds were just fired, but they did not come during the night.

Cox: Marched off at 6 am through two recently deserted villages, some of the houses of which many were burnt – saw one burnt body and a half-starved woman, who cursed us as we passed. Found Kereri and supposed camp unoccupied, cloudy day so marched on and bivouacked 6 miles off Omdurman – gunboats went on – 8 abreast and shelled town – signallers out, got into communication with cavalry on a hill two miles west – whole dervish army reported by signal from hill to be marched out in battle array – everything carried out by signalling – had to take Sirdar messages every ten minutes – our force moved out and took up a position round stores and hospital, then zaribaed and bivouacked for night. Dervish army according to last signal 3½ miles SW, estimated strength 35,000.

Meiklejohn: Started at 6 am and we were "rear-guard" – the most trying and unexciting position. Spearman, always an optimist, tried to cheer us up by declaring that the dervish cavalry would very probably sweep round and attack from this direction. . . . The gunboats all went on to bombard Tuti Island and Omdurman. We heard the guns in the distance and everybody cheered up promptly. Our cavalry sighted some 400 horsemen and 1,000 infantry about 8 miles ahead of us. We reached a small mud village about 1 pm and were just getting some lunch when we saw a gunboat returning at full speed. It brought news that the whole dervish army was massing outside Omdurman, and meant to attack. We hastily bolted a little food, packed up and fell in at 2 pm. Then the whole army marched out, and took up position in a huge semi-circle about 500 yards outside the village, and sat down and waited. The two British Brigades held the left, or south, side of the semi-circle, the 2nd Brigade being on our left and extending to the river bank, since it was anticipated that the main attack would come here . . .
Heard that Colonel Forbes, who had taken over Command

after the Atbara, was doubtful about my being left in command, being the junior subaltern present, but Major Quayle-Jones . . . and others stood up for me, saying I had been in command at the Atbara and done well. The 21st Lancers reported some 60,000 or more of the enemy were halted just outside Omdurman, and apparently drilling. The Lancers had picquets on a hill south of us, whence they could see Omdurman. This was referred to as "Signal Hill". . . . At dusk we got orders that all lights were to be out by 7.30 pm and no smoking after that. . . . We had supper after dusk, half of us at a time, and "Lights out" sounded before I had finished, so I had to grope my way back. Could not have a smoke, but Major Cockburn and I managed to get a little water. Made a small hollow, put our waterproof sheets in this and took turns in having a bath. I also managed to change my clothes, so felt quite respectable. The 21st Lancers withdrew from Signal Hill at dusk to inside the zariba. Capt. Caldecott, Grenfell, and Etches came and we all had a chat. The two former declared we should not have a fight at all, but a Naval Officer from one of the gunboats, who joined us, said, "If you fellows had seen what I saw this afternoon you'd think it differently". Caldecott laughed and remarked that the "black swine" would all bolt during the night, to which the reply was, "Well, if you are alive this time tomorrow you will have a different opinion of these dervishes". Both Caldecott and Grenfell were killed: and Etches wounded, though only slightly.

Then Winston Churchill, who was attached to 21st, strolled up and we had a long talk. He was far less argumentative and self-assertive than usual. He said the enemy had a huge force, and if they attacked during the night, he thought it would be "touch and go" about the result. A massed attack against the Gyppies or Soudanese would probably break through, with highly unpleasant results. The Sirdar sent round word that he had two spies out, who would walk quietly up to the zariba during the night, and that we were to be careful not to fire on them. They would shout to warn us when they were returning. . . . Then while we were waiting, an unearthly yell was heard in front, and two figures came racing for the zariba. Nearly all the sentries came to the "present", but we shouted to them not to fire. It turned out to be the two spies, who had been chased some distance and were very frightened. . . . Caldecott came for a talk. He said he had not yet had any sleep, and the whole thing

180

was absurd, as the "niggers" did not mean to fight, and would never wait for us.

2ND SEPTEMBER

Teigh: This was a day of all days, the day that Omdurman was taken. Firing was heard during the greater part of last night in the direction of Omdurman, which is a few miles from here. From what we can hear the gunboats have shifted the enemy from Omdurman on to the desert.

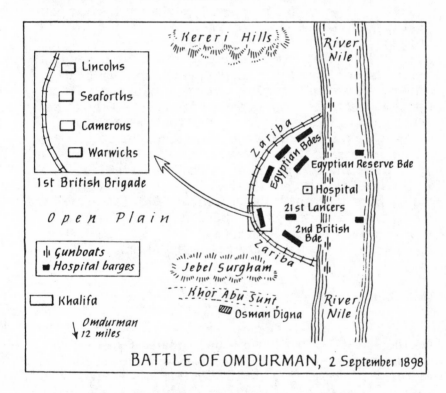

BATTLE OF OMDURMAN, 2 September 1898

We are now formed up waiting for them. It is about 6 am. There has been firing going on since daybreak. The Dervishes are advancing and have been in sight for about an half hour; the shells started bursting. The artillery started first, and then we started about 7 am and the whole force are now engaged, cavalry, Artillery, Maxims and Infantry and the Dervishes are

181

sticking it well up to the present. A Dervishes bullet has whizzed through the zariba and a twig of it struck me. A word has just been passed down to cease fire as the Cavalry are just going up to charge. The Lincolns were the first out of the zariba and we doubled out and formed to the west and then we advanced again. Our Regiment was ordered to the right to reinforce the Soudanese and here we had to double across the Dervishes' firing line, which caused us to have a lot of casualties. We formed up on the right of the Soudanese and formed into line, when volley firing was again given. It was between five and ten hundred yards we were firing. We fixed bayonets and fired about 30 volleys and then we advanced again across the battle-field and several wounded. We passed them and we also got the order to destroy all arms by breaking them on the rocks and some of our men were breaking them on the heads of the Dervishes. We passed over the battlefield and halted at 12.30 midday for a drink of water out of the fantassas. Then we marched on, after an hour's rest. We rejoined the Division which had been halted for some time. We had just taken off our straps when the half-hour dress sounded and we got served out with some corned beef and we refilled our water-bottles with white water similar to milk. After that we marched off and the 10th Soudanese cheered us as they passed and presented us with a large flag which they captured. They also played our Regimental march, which cheered us up. They call our Regiment their brother Regiment as both our numbers are 'X'. We marched through the outskirts of Omdurman and halted for the night.

Cox: Gaude! What a day! – see somewhere else.

Cox: Appendix: Battle of Omdurman.
On the 1st September left bivouac situated 6 miles north of Kereri and marched south. Enemy's advanced cavalry were reported to be retiring south. We passed through several deserted villages, which must have lately been evacuated. The force bivouacked outside a small village north of Omdurman. The gun boats had received orders to go forward and shell the Mahdi's tomb and Khalifa's Palace. The bombardment commenced as we reached bivouac. I rode on within 4 miles of Omdurman for the purpose of heliographing to Howitzer battery – gunboats, but failed to find a suitable place so rode

back to bivouac and got into communication with cavalry, who succeeded in getting communication with gunboats and Howitzer battery on Tuti Island . . .

Meiklejohn: We all got up quietly a little before 3.30 am and stood to arms till Reveille. Rather tense expectations, but nothing happened. It was light by 5.30. Since the enemy was not on the move, it was decided that we should move forward and attack, so we made gaps in the zariba to advance through, while the cooks prepared breakfast.

The 21st Lancers moved out, pushing forward patrols towards Signal Hill, while their main body halted in the hollow. We watched the scouts trotting up the slopes, reach the summit, then dismount and open rapid fire, while two came galloping back. Very shortly afterwards we heard that the whole dervish army were advancing on us. I think everybody gave a sigh of relief, since it was much better that they should attack. We fell in quickly and set to work filling in the gaps we had made in the zariba, and trimming it to fire over. We ate our breakfast while we were working, and everybody now in high spirits, for our wearisome "waiting" was over. Caldecott came up again and had a talk, but seemed preoccupied. We had finished off our work, and were chatting, when suddenly a subdued, but general, exclamation of surprise made us look up. We saw a really wonderful sight. All along the crests of the high ground to our right front a regular forest seemed to be springing up, which resolved itself into a dense mass of banners. Then a solid black multitude of men began to appear for over two miles all along the crest line, in considerable depth, while we heard distant shouts and war cries. Soon after another mass appeared all over Signal Hill ridge, and along the British front, but these hung back a little, as if waiting for the remainder of the mighty army to come up into line. Caldecott exclaimed, "That's the best sight I've ever seen!" I remarked that it looked like being a big fight, and he said he did not suppose all of us would get through it. He then said that he was owed some money for a pony, and would I see about it if he got a bullet in him. Was surprised as this seemed so unlike Caldecott, the least "nervy" individual in the world.

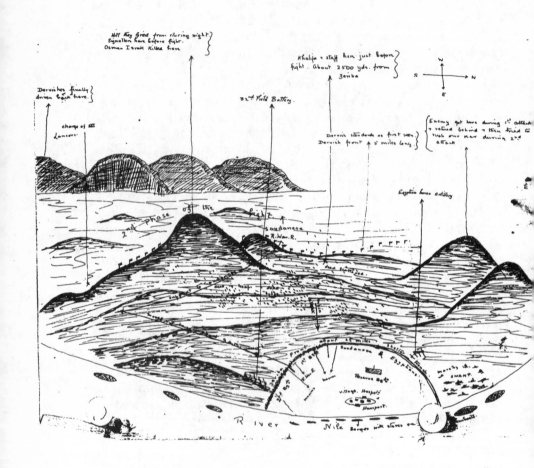

Sketch of the battlefield of Omdurman by Lt R. Meiklejohn.

General Gatacre came riding round and remarked, "You look very fierce, Captain Caldecott". He then pointed to a huge black flag in the middle of the dervish line and said, "I mean to have that flag before long".

Meanwhile the enemy masses were moving forward fairly quickly. Then suddenly slowed down, made a really very orderly "right wheel", then deployed into one huge and nearly uninterrupted line, and came straight at us.

Earle, our Adjutant, came galloping up and shouted, "Get into your places please, Gentlemen, the show is starting!" Caldecott said, "Remember about the pony, as I don't want . . . to score if I'm plugged," and we took up our stations.

The dervishes were now some two miles distant, their line being, I estimated, four to five miles long, and hundreds deep. It seemed to envelop our force altogether, and was a truly amazing sight. I heard the remark, "Thank God we have two British Brigades". As always in a battle, my description must be mainly limited to my own part of the front, for all one's observations are centred on this.

When the enemy were about 3,000 yards from us we were almost startled as our artillery opened fire. The first shell burst a little short, but the second fell amongst them. Then the gunboats joined in, and white puffs of shrapnel showed up all over the enemy mass, while columns of dust indicated common shell.

The enemy appeared to take no notice, except perhaps a slight quickening of pace, while, watching through glasses, one almost felt that nothing could stem his onslaught.

Suddenly they seemed to halt for a moment or two. A cloud of smoke came from them and an enormous rattle of musketry. I personally, and I think most of us, held my breath for a moment, expecting to hear a hail of bullets, as at the Atbara, but nearly all fell short, causing dust spurts well in front of the zariba, or passing over very high. They were now coming on fairly fast, firing every description of weapon, and I saw one man in the Seaforths go down, then another.

Then the order came to open "Company volleys" and I think the opening range was 1,500 yards. A volume of fire burst out from the whole length of the zariba. Continual repetition on my part of the words of command "Ready" – "Present" – "Fire" – "Ready" in this rhythm, only varied by a shortening range. Later the order came "Half-Company", and the "Section" take volleys and I was able to let my Colour Sergeant and Sergeants take over the word of command and try to correct distance. The brunt of the attack seemed to be falling on the Lincolns and Soudanese on our right, but a huge mass were streaming down the slopes of our fire. I could see little trace of "sand-spirits" from bullets in front of them, so concluded our elevation was correct, yet it seemed almost as if nothing could stop them. Then gradually their advance slowed down perceptibly and then stopped. They were now some 800 yards from the zariba, and, amid the rattle of musketry and machine guns (two per battalion), one heard their bullets increasing frequency. And now they seemed to be melting away in front of us, but a certain number got into a hollow much nearer us, and got in more accurate fire. They also got a couple of batteries into action under Signal Hill (captured from Hicks Pasha's force). One shell burst just in the air over Earle's head. One landed among the Camerons, killing two and wounding an officer and eleven men. One did some damage to the Seaforths, and we subsequently heard that two fell amongst the Egyptian battalion which had no British officers, and they "scattered". They were replaced by two companies of the Guards, who were in reserve.

I think we all felt sorry for the splendid savages we had to annihilate, even though we knew of all the barbarities in the Sudan.

About this time the enemy put in a most gallant attempt. Some 500 dervish cavalry suddenly swept forward and charged our force. A murderous concentrated fire was turned on them, and they were literally mowed down, yet they never faltered, riding straight for us with wild cries and brandished weapons. A handful got to within 300 yards of us, and I saw one solitary figure charging, so it seemed, our whole army single-handed for a few seconds, till horse and man collapsed in a heap.

Soon after this we got the order to fire Company volleys slowly. I was quite hoarse by now, and told my Colour Sergeant to carry on for a few minutes while I passed the order on to 'G' Company. I could not see Caldecott, so told "Bobby" Brewis, his subaltern, asking where he was. Brewis pointed to a figure on the ground with a red pool spreading on the sand, and said he was afraid it was all over. An elephant bullet had severed the jugular vein. Hopkins, the doctor, came up with a stretcher, but nothing could be done. I did not wait, but got back to my Company, feeling very sad. Caldecott was reputed to be the strongest man in the British army, and a champion heavyweight boxer.

Soon after this Etheridge's dog "Jack" and Day's dog "Smut", whom we were always trying to keep apart, seized the opportunity to indulge in a "battle royal". Etheridge separated them in the middle of the fighting, remarking that they clearly thought the whole thing was got up for their benefit.

By now the dervishes were retiring everywhere, and the firing slackened. Our artillery began shelling the small number who were in the hollow in front of us and the Lincolns, and after a bit they too began to retire, firing as they went. We got out the best Company marksmen (including myself) and picked off most of them. One man refused to retire, but kept on firing at us till three of us gave him a kind of volley, when he fell.

Then the firing ceased and the cooks prepared breakfast in place of our very scrappy one. So far our casualties are very few. Just before things started my gyppy servant, Abdul, appeared with a huge sword, saying he was going to fight beside me, and protect me. I had noticed him with the Greek interpreter snugly behind the biscuit boxes, but said nothing. Now he proudly appeared with his mighty sword, ready to protect me. He concluded by saying he was an Englishman and very brave, not frightened. I assured him I was grateful for his protection.

It was about 8 am. We had breakfast, and in about an hour the whole force received orders to advance on Omdurman. We were told there would probably be more fighting.

My company (about 70 strong) had already fired 5,543 rounds. We formed up outside the zariba, the 2nd Brigade on our left, and began the advance on Omdurman in echelon of brigades, the left leading. Sniping commenced very soon, but not very serious. The 21st Lancers moved off and, seeing what they took to be a number of disorganised enemy in front, decided to charge. When they were fairly started several hundreds more suddenly rose up all round, and they probably realised then it was a trap, but could not halt. The enemy were in, and around a deep donga, which the 21st did not know existed. The shock, we heard, was terrific as they drove into the enemy, and men and horses plunged into the donga, some being cut to pieces. However, the majority rode clean through, then dismounted and opened fire. Kenna and de Montmorency[1] very

---

[1] Both Captain P.A. Kenna and Lieutenant the Hon R.H.L.J. de Montmorency were awarded Victoria Crosses, as was Private T. Byrne.

gallantly recovered Grenfell's body. But we hear the charge was a great error, and K. is furious. They lost over 1 officer and 20 men killed, and 3 officers and 40 wounded, and 100 horses, and were not able to undertake the pursuit of the Khalifa, as Kitchener intended. Their fire, however, drove the enemy on to the Gyppy brigades, who wiped them out.

Meanwhile the firing away to our right was increasing, and soon a continuous roar of musketry. We saw Hector MacDonald's Brigade (Soudanese) wreathed in smoke, and forming round to meet large bodies of the enemy sweeping on it from three sides. Things looked a bit critical, but MacDonald handled the brigade superbly. Our brigade got orders to double up in support (it was a mile distant) and we wheeled round, and went full out under the blazing sun. Bullets came whistling past, and again wonderfully few casualties. Colonel Sloggett the P.M.O. fell badly wounded in the chest. I was talking to Hopkins, our doctor, when we halted, when a bullet passed under my arm and scored his horse's flank. Hopkins did gymnastics on its neck, and said another inch and he would have been playing a harp!

When we arrived the crisis had passed. The enemy fell back, and a Gyppy brigade stormed Signal Hill. Just before we got up I heard an ominous thud, and a man near me staggered and fell, holding his hand to his hip. A bullet had perforated his water-bottle, presumably giving him a bit of a shock, but he imagined the escaping water was blood!

Several dervishes whom we passed as dead, or beyond harm, slashed at our legs with their swords, or rose and charged. One hurled himself at an Egyptian company, speared two men, and created some confusion. Another charged the rear of the Camerons, but two sturdy Highlanders promptly bayonetted him. The Egyptian cavalry now made a grand charge amongst the retiring enemy, and we had a splendid view of this. They galloped right through them, their swords flashing in the sun, then reformed and back through them again, cutting them up.

Soon after 11.30 am our brigade reformed, and we marched on to Omdurman without any opposition. The battlefield was a terrible sight! Bodies of men, horses, donkeys, and even a stray camel or two everywhere, some horribly mutilated, a few burning.

About 2 pm we arrived at Khor Shambat, everybody parched with thirst, for the heat was terrific. There was a rush for water, which was very foul, and even had bodies in it. I drank through my very dirty handkerchief. Then we had some tea made, which in colour was hardly distinguishable from the water, and a ration of bully beef and biscuit. The subsequent outbreak of enteric was ascribed to this water! Later on we marched into Omdurman, the Egyptian bands playing us in. Everybody pretty weary. Two or three deaths from sunstroke, and one of our men suddenly started singing, went raving mad and died with five or six men holding him down. The Royal Warwickshires bivouacked near the Mahdi's tomb. We had saved a dozen bottles of champagne for this occasion so had about ¾ pint each, and it made me, and others, almost drunk. I think we all realised that we had taken part in one of the most spectacular (and perhaps "safest") battles ever fought.

AFTERMATH

Once Gordon had been avenged, Kitchener and his generals had to move the large army back to civilization as quickly as possible. First,however, the casualties had to be reckoned. On the British side numbers were very small, probably no greater than fifty from the whole Anglo-Egyptian Army, but including Captain Caldecott, friend of Lieutenant Meiklejohn, and a further 400 wounded. But the estimate of Dervishes killed reached 10,000, with probably double that number wounded.

As previously at Atbara the wounded were not dealt with well. There was confusion as to who was responsible for getting the wounded away from the battlefield, and Colonel Sloggett, the Principal Medical Officer, was himself severely wounded, which did not help. The barges brought up as hospitals had been moved so as not to impede the gunboats. Dead and dying lay in a temperature reaching 120 degrees in the shade. Major Adamson of the Lincolns records that: "As for Colonel Sloggett, we heard later that he had fallen lifeless, shot apparently through the heart. His corpse was picked up and placed amongst others on a gunboat and the Commander and the Medical Officer, tired after a morning's work, decided to have a little refreshment. As the whisky and 'sparklet' was being poured, so the story goes, the two officers were astonished to hear a voice from among the dead, 'Isn't there any for Arthur?' Colonel Sloggett had come to. His wound ran around the ribs instead of through the heart, and he is said to have recovered at the sound of the poured 'peg'."

Kitchener ordered the destruction of the Mahdi's tomb, since he felt it might become a focal point for some future revolutionary movement. His bones were dug up and thrown into the Nile. This was a blow to those who felt that he had gone on a visit to heaven and would return to resurrect his body. After his bones were removed, charges were laid and the already damaged tomb blown up. The Mahdi's skull was retained, and Kitchener is said to have considered having it mounted in silver as a drinking cup or inkwell, but abandoned the idea on realizing that it would not be popular, and instead offered to present it to the College of Surgeons. Queen Victoria was 'not amused' and it was buried at Wadi Halfa in the Muslim cemetery. This episode became something of a *cause célèbre* since he had made enemies among the press correspondents, who kept the issue open. Eventually he had to write to the Queen: "Lord Kitchener is much distressed that Your Majesty should think that the destruction of the Mahdi's tomb, and the disposal of his bones, was improperly carried out. He is very sorry that anything he has done should have caused Your Majesty a moment's uneasiness.

"A few days after the battle, I consulted with some native officers of the Soudanese troops, and spoke on the matter with some influential natives here; . . . and they recommended the destruction of the tomb and that the bones should be thrown into the Nile . . .

"Nothing in the matter was done in a hurry, but four days after the battle . . . I gave the order for the destruction, thinking it was the safest and wisest course; and this was carried out in my absence. There was no coffin, and when the bones were found the soldiers seemed all astonished, and exclaimed – 'By God! This was not the Mahdi after all he told us!' They had previously believed that the Mahdi had been translated bodily to heaven.

"When I returned . . . the Mahdi's skull, in a box, was brought to me, and I did not know what to do with it. I had thought of sending it to the College of Surgeons where, I believe, such things are kept. It has now been buried in a Moslem cemetery."

Meanwhile the officers and soldiers collected what souvenirs they could and embarked on boats and barges for the immediate return to Cairo. While going down the Nile may have entailed no marching, it was not a journey without incident, since many of the cataracts on the Nile, now in good flow, had to be negotiated. Then there was the final train journey into Cairo and, for Private Teigh and Captain Cox, arrival at Abbassiyeh camp. Private Teigh was awarded the Khartoum clasp to his Egyptian Sudan Medal, and Captain Cox the same.

As those who had taken part returned to Cairo, it is difficult to decide whether it had ever been necessary for them to leave. Certainly Britain's destiny as an imperial power had been vindicated, though with such superior fire-power it could not have been otherwise. Egypt was safe, and, more than anything else, Gordon had been avenged. Whether it had been done with the greatest military efficiency is debatable.

Captain FitzGibbon Cox had some reservations. He added to his diary:

'Failures Noticed on Campaign'

1) 2nd in Command immediately taken for other duties – consequences Officers Mess, Regt. institutions all hurriedly closed by other officers who knew nothing about them.
2) 2nd in Command taken for surveying – consequence – no canteens

191

– men not properly looked after in the interior economy line.
3) The allocation of ammunition.
4) Disgraceful state of the boots.
5) Field service dressings issued and when opened found to be absolutely rotten.
7) [*sic*] 4 Officers taken away from their Regt. – 3 surveying, 1 railway.
8) Cutting tools issued to the battalion absolutely rotten – both metal and wood work – evidently been stood for years.
9) Confusion as to baggage A.S.C. @ O.S.C. officers apparently not knowing how their own stores are marked – consequence Regt. @ departmental stores all mixed.
10) Water bottles found to be too small, new ones supplied to Regts.

Cox may then have been a very junior officer, but he was to go on to greater things.

Without doubt Kitchener had achieved success in bringing such a vast army with supplies so far south into the heartland of the Dervishes. While his army returned down the Nile to Cairo, he went south to make certain that no other European power was able to interfere in what was again firmly established as a zone of British interest.

Moving the army to Cairo was not a comfortable exercise.

9

BACK TO CAIRO

Teigh: We marched back out of Omdurman for about a mile and made shelters at about 9.15 am close to the Nile. We were not quite certain whether there was any more fighting to be done until tonight, when the following appeared in General orders: killed and wounded, 1 killed and 18 wounded. The Sirdar wishes to congratulate the Troops, British and Egyptian and Soudanese on their excellent behaviour during the action of yesterday, which result in the taking and the defeat of the Khalifa's forces and has worthly revenged Gordon's death. The Sirdar regrets the loss that has occurred and in worthly thanking the troops for their services, wishes to place on record his admiration of their courage, discipline and endurance. The name of the battle field is El Egeiga. We slept for the first time without our equipment since we left El Selim.

Cox: Rested all day. We marched out of Omdurman in the morning and bivouacked at the north end of the town, down by the river – a handy place for embarkations. Omdurman a much larger place than I thought. Deserters and prisoners coming in in crowds. Hear that Dever May of Guards to be tried by G.C.M. [General Court Martial] damn good thing. Khalifa appears to have got away, Osman Digna gone south.

Meiklejohn: I visited the Mahdi's tomb: Market place: and picked up some objects of interest. I got the Khalifa's State Banner, or what is said to be one of them. An elderly Arab was in the Tomb building, and looked rather threatening, probably longing to knife the "unbelievers".

We marched out of Omdurman about 10 am and bivouacked close by. I was sent on wood fatigue after lunch. The rumour

193

went round that much treasure was hidden in the town, and my fatigue party worked really hard removing wood from floors, but we only found scorpions and other insect life.

We then entered a shut-up fort, and when I went to investigate, I found several of our dead laid out in a row. Poor Caldecott's blanket had been partly removed, possibly by the wind, and I replaced this. All were buried that afternoon.

We had a really luxurious night all sleeping on angoreebs and actually being allowed to take off our boots, belts and coats!

4TH SEPTEMBER

Teigh: We are still encamped here waiting for the gunboats to take us back to Cairo. We had a church parade and the service was very short as the Rev. Mr Watson was called away to attend the ceremonial service at Gordon's Palace at Khartoum. All the Officers and about 100 Non-Commissioned Officers and men of each Battalion were present at the hoisting of the British and Egyptian flags at Khartoum, which is on the opposite side of the Nile to Omdurman. They arrived back about 12.30 noon and nearly every Officer had in his hand a memorial of some sort from Gordon's Palace.

Cox: Representations from each regiment numbering about 40 proceeded by gunboats to Khartoum where a square was formed round Gordon's palace. The Union Jack and Egyptian flags were hoisted simultaneously. Afterwards a memorial service – most impressive – the palace in ruins, must have been a very fine house in its time – all wounded went down river today. A gun was found at the palace which Sirdar gave to 32nd battery. Burrowes sent out with representatives of other regiments to count the slain. Number about 12,000. Lot of wounded still alive, crawling about on thin haunches!

5TH SEPTEMBER

Teigh: Divisional parade. We marched as far as the Mahdi's tomb, which was ruined by shells from the gunboats and the Artillery guns. We arrived back to our camp, where we were bivouacked. The transport of every Regiment went out yesterday to try and count the dead, but it was impossible; they were too numerous to count. We cannot get much reliable information about Osman Digna or the Khalifa. His forces are estimated at about 80,000 all told. The Warwickshire Regiment fell in at 2.30 pm and embarked on gunboats ready to go back from the Sudan and take up their Quarters at Alexandria, after a period of about eight months in the country.

Cox: Reveille at 4.45, paraded at 5.30 and marched with division round the Madhi's tomb and showed ourselves off in the town. Crowds of prisoners, who appear damn sulky – the women seem delightful – Newfeld says he is going to stop here. Guns appear to have done a lot of damage to the tomb and Khalifa's palace. Hear we go tomorrow, only hope its true. That counting party counted 10,820 killed on the field, and there are 25,000 wounded prisoners in Omdurman and yesterday a large force was seen in the hills west. Got a piece of Mahdi's tomb today. Warwicks left today by barges and steamer.

6TH SEPTEMBER

Teigh: The Lincolnshire Regiment embarked on gyassas at 11.30 am and we started off at 1.30 pm and making our way down the Nile with the stream. The 'X' Soudanese Band played us out. There were 50 men in each gyassi and we were packed like sardines. We passed a strongly made Dervishes fort that had been shelled by our gunboats. We also saw a peculiar steamer going down the Nile, which the Dervishes had captured some years ago. There is no wind. We are drifting with the stream and it is tiring. Some are standing up and some were down below the bulwarks. The flies and ants are enough to drive one mad. We have just received an order to take down the blankets which we had up for shelter, as there is going to be a storm. The horizon in the south is completely overwhelmed with a sandstorm. We have stopped now until the storm is over. There is a very moderate bridge belonging to the boat as the Natives seem afraid to adventure on it. There are flocks of large white birds on the side of the Nile and they are in droves of thousands. The cooks made tea and after that we went on board again and it rained slightly and we started off at 12 M.N. when the moon came to show itself.

195

Cox: Reveille at 5. We embarked for Dakheila in gyassas, 11 of them, most frightfully uncomfortable and crowded. I am on a boat with 57 men. There is no wind and we simply drift. We had an awful sandstorm last night. I wish we could have gone down in steamers and barges, but they say the whole of the river transport has got disorganised. We kept on the go half the night by moonlight. How ripping it is to be on the move again. We passed through Shabluka pass, wonderful scenery but rather weird going, we kept catching in whirlpools and circling round like a top. Saw the dervish fortifications, good but sites rottenly chosen. The fleet tied up at 6 pm at our old bivouac Wad Hamed, slept on shore, a just rest as half the men have been standing the last 24 hrs.

7TH SEPTEMBER

Teigh: We spent a miserable night last night as there was no room to lie down or even sit comfortably. We are now drifting along with the current. This is about 6 am. We stopped at 10 am and made tea at Royan Island, south of the Cataract where the sick men were left behind before the taking of Omdurman. It was here we received our emergency kits and waterproof sheets. After we had got everything on board we started off again and made our way through the Cataract, which took us an hour and half to get through. We were twisting and twirling all over the shop, sometimes going sideways, another time going headlong against the stream. It put me in mind of being in a Circus for a few minutes. The Niggers were shouting at one another and I can tell you we were alright. Every minute I was expecting to go to the bottom of the Nile, but as luck would have it we got through safe after a great struggle with the different currents. There were high hills and rocks on each side and it was well fortified. There were several forts and if the Dervishes had had enough sense to make a stand there it would have been impossible for us to pass through there with any of our boats. Shabluka was the largest fortified place the Dervishes had, whether it was high or low Nile. After getting past Shabluka we travelled for several hours downstream until it grew dark and then we halted for the night. The cooks made tea and after that we had a good sleep until 4.30 am next morning.

Cox: Reveille at 4.30. The fleet sailed or rather started at 5. We are getting quite good at fleet tactics, the Colonel's boat carrying the Admiral's flag consists of our regiment on blue and red "tin". I wish we could get a decent breeze, we have been drifting most of the time. Got to Nasri Island at 9 am, took on rations and baggage. Find that all the officers' kits we left here were upset in the river and a lot of stuff missing. Luckily I had nothing on board.

8TH SEPTEMBER

Teigh: We started at 5 am and went down the stream. After travelling for a few miles we passed Wad Hamed our old camp on the left at 8 am. We halted again and had coffee and breakfast. This place happened to be the Nasri Island where our spare kit was left in charge of the Egyptians. We took on our kits and stores and rations enough to last us for a few days until we get to Dakheila, where we would have to leave the boats and take train. We started off again and we had a fair voyage down the river. We travelled several miles during the day with the wind and stream together until it grew dusk, and then we halted for the night.

Cox: Day lost somewhere. I can't remember what the day is up here to save my life.

9TH SEPTEMBER

Teigh: Started off at 5 am, light breeze owing to the turns in the river. Then there was a dead calm heat, and we were floating down the Nile at the rate of 2 miles an hour with the Niggers on board. Here they eat twice a day. Their food consists of meal made up in the form of a pancake and a drop of oil on the top to season it. They also have some kind of vegetables similar to ground peas, which they mix up with their paste to eat it with their fingers and seem to consider it a famous feed. We stopped at sunset and had tea and stopped for the night.

Cox: Reveille 4.30, sailed at 5. C.O. blew us up for not keeping station. We had a bad time last night. First we had a collision with the C.O.'s boat and then nearly capsized in a squall. The damned Reiz, as is usual with natives, lost his head and could do nothing but yell. Ed Fowey saved the situation, otherwise I really believe we should have capsized. Took a dervish on board just now, swam alongside and begged to be allowed to come on board. Tied up at 6 pm in a beastly muddy hole.

10TH SEPTEMBER

Teigh: We started at 4.30 am and had a fair breeze and we arrived at Dakala lately known as the Atbara fort about 6.30 am where we landed and had breakfast. After breakfast the left half of the Battalion moved into Barracks or mud huts as I should call them and 'A', 'B', 'C', 'D' and part of 'E' companies left in the train for Wadi Halfa at 10.30 am. It is 385 miles by train. We got paid 25 piastres each. About 10 miles from here is El Selim our old favourite camp where we spent 4 months in the heat of the summer.

Cox: Got to Dakheila at 8 am this morn. The place has grown into a regular town. Rt. half battalion have gone on by train, we follow tomorrow. The men are in large mud huts and the officers in the rest house, very comfortable mud houses with straw verandahs made by the Egyptian troops.

Meiklejohn: Engine broke down at No. 6 station. Began to wonder if we would ever get back to civilization.

11TH SEPTEMBER

Teigh: Violent sandstorm before daylight this morning. The wind blew so hard it was impossible to stand up even with your back to it. The tents outside where the 21st Lancers were camped were blown down and one could hardly open our eyes. It was about the worst sandstorm we had ever seen. The left half Battalion entrained at 4 pm and we travelled nearly all night with a few stops at different stations.

Cox: Reveille at 5. Frightful sandstorm last night, expect to leave today at 11 am. 17 correspondents and about 12 officers coming down with us.

12TH SEPTEMBER

Teigh: We travelled all day, more or less. We were crowded in these covered trucks and packed like sardines. There were about 42 men in each truck, similar to a cattle truck in England. We travelled across the desert until sundown when we stopped and made tea. This was about 10 miles from Abu Hamed. After this we started off again and travelled for the remainder of the night at the rate of about 18 miles an hour.

Cox: Train left Dakheila yesterday at 4.30 pm. 7 officers and 7 angoreebs in a truck. Very comfortable but rather crowded. Another frightful sandstorm in the night – nearly buried us. Slept like a top.

Meiklejohn: Arrived at Luxor, had a bath and a luxurious breakfast at the Hotel.

13TH SEPTEMBER

Teigh: We arrived at Wadi Halfa at 6 am and embarked on board a steamer and a barge. We started off down the Nile at 9 am. The right half of the Battalion left here night before last. We passed a temple on the left bank of the Nile and on it were four seated figures with their hands on their knees. The 3rd from the right was totally destroyed except the knees. Further down we saw two more statues sitting in a sort of cave quite near the water edge and the water was washing their feet at times. We travelled all night and it was very rough. The waves kept washing over the front of the boat and I was like a drowned rat, and my two blankets were wet through and I had to go and sit with the stoker for the remainder of the night. I can tell you I wasn't sorry when morning came.

Cox: All day in train.

Meiklejohn: Reached Alexandria at 4.30 pm. Heard at Cairo that we leave for India in a month, and everybody very disgusted. No chance of getting home, and I have done two years without real leave.

14TH SEPTEMBER

Teigh: The morning came and we arrived at Shelal about 4 am and disembarked our stores and then went under canvas for a few hours. I had not been there very long when I was told off for baggage guard by the side of the railway and I had to take charge of all our luggage, and there were three or four boxes of money which I also had to take charge of. I think I done about 2 hours sentry go at the finish, and then they packed the baggage in the train, so I had an easy guard for once. The C.O. allowed volunteers to visit the Island on the opposite side of the Nile. There was a large building with tombs and all kinds of different figures in it. We arrived back about 2 pm and we had our tea and then got into the train ready for another start. We started off at 4 pm. There is one thing I missed telling you and that is that I had the best dinner today that I have had since I have been on the expedition. We had Maconochie's rations and mixed vegetables and also fresh meat. The right half of the Battalion left here at 6 last night. The country is well cultivated along the river. We travelled all night and we arrived at the station early in the morning, where we had to change trains.

Cox: Arrived at Wadi Halfa at 6 am. Got on board post boats with barges each side. Left Dyke behind at Halfa with dysentery. Takes about 24 hrs to Assouan, then by train all the way.

Arrived Assouan at 3 am, disembarked at 6 am. Train leaves for Luxor at 4 pm. Ripping breakfast – bloaters and eggs and bacon.

15TH SEPTEMBER

Teigh: We arrived at Luxor at 4.20 am and after changing trains and transferred our baggage on another line for Cairo we had breakfast. The station here is built of wood and bricks and the people are very civil and very pleased to see us come back and looking so well considering the hardships we have put up with and the long time we have been up the country. We came across one of our men who transferred from our Regiment to the 'A.S.C.' and we had a chat with him for a few minutes and then we made our way into the train and we started off at 9.30 am. We travelled in the direction of Cairo. We were travelling several hours and during the night I woke up and we were travelling at the rate of 21 miles an hour. However, we arrived at Cairo early in the morning.

Cox: Left by train for Luxor at 4.30 pm. Very comfortable really, men in trucks, officers in 2nd Saloon carriage, very crowded, but slept very well on the floor at night. Getting back into civilization. Cooled our drinks in canvas buckets hung outside between baskets.

16TH SEPTEMBER

Teigh: We arrived at Cairo at 6 am and after a short stay we proceeded to Abbassiyeh. We arrived there at 6.30 am. When we got off the train Major General Grenfell and his staff were there and he shook hands with the Officers and walked around the ranks and then we marched off to Polygon camp and the band of the 21st Lancers was there and played us into camp. We piled arms and took off our equipment and took our canteens in the shade of the trees and had breakfast. After an hour or two of rest we went and pitched our camp which took us about 3 hours, and to make the best of it when we had finished that we had to lay under the shade of the trees all day. We didn't get told off to our tents until just before dark. We received our kits during the day, which we left behind at the Citadel and mine was all safe and sound, nearly as good as it was when I left it. However, we found our way to our own tents and got settled down just before dark.

I can tell you we were all tired and so we didn't take much rocking to sleep once we got laid down. We had a good night's rest and no one did disturb us while about 7 am the next morning. The Battalion all had 'Dhi' [diarrhoea] for the first week after they got back and we lost a great lot of our men through sickness and all kinds of fever.

My experience of the Sudan, one who was through it all from 4th January 1898 until 16th of September 1898, a Private Soldier of the 1st Battalion, Lincolnshire Regiment. Polygon Camp, Cairo, Egypt.
Signed Private G. Teigh.

16 FRIDAY [259–106] ● 0h 10m A.M. (Greenwich)

arrived Luxor at 5 am. hot breakfast awaiting the men on platform. Officers went to hotel on donkeys – I had a huge one who galloped just like a pony passed all the others when the girths broke + I came an almighty purler – darling boy on top. had a ripping bath – big bath – got shaved. omelette, coffee + eggs + rolls for breakfast My GAUDE!! Changed trains + started 9.30 proper 1st Class carriage with only 2 officers in each! Canvas basket on the floor full of beer + soda with lump of ice on top My Gaude!!!!!!!! went over temple of Luxor. arrive Cairo tomorrow.

17 SATURDAY [260–105] Jewish Year 5659 commences

I'm all over the place – today is Friday really – however we arrived at Cairo within 100 yds of our camp at 7 a.m. everything very quiet + no excitement Lord ripping. —— diary here!

18 SUNDAY—15 after Trinity [261–104] Ember Week

Cox: Arrived Luxor at 5 am, hot breakfast awaiting the men on the platform. Officers went to hotel on donkeys. I had a huge one who galloped just like a pony, passed all the others, when the girths broke and I came an almighty purler – donkey lay on top. Had a ripping bath – big bath – got shaved, omellete, coffee and eggs and rolls for breakfast. My GAUDE!! Changed trains and started 9.30, proper 1st class carriage with only 2 officers in each! Canvas bucket on the floor full of beer and soda with lump of ice on top. My Gaude!!!!!!!! Went over temple of Luxor. Arrive Cairo tomorrow.

17TH SEPTEMBER

Cox: I'm all over the place. Today is Friday really. However, we arrived at Cairo within 1200 yds of our camp at 7 am. Everything very quiet and no excitement, food ripping. – diary bus![1]

23RD SEPTEMBER

Skinner: The remainder of the journey was very quickly done. . . . We arrived at Cairo station at 8.30 am. Here the transferring of the sick and wounded together with the baggage to the ambulances and wagons did not take long, so that we were soon able to make our way to the Citadel, which was reached at 10 am, and very glad I was to be in a place where once more we could get proper food, a washup, bed and clean clothing. . . . When I left Cairo on January 7th 1898 I weighed eleven stone twelve pounds but on my arrival back to Cairo 23rd Sept. my weight was reduced to 9 stone 2 lbs.

[1] Cox mis-spelt 'bas', a colloquial Urdu word meaning 'ends'.

EPILOGUE

The Khalifa had left the battlefield early in the afternoon and, after a vain attempt to collect men for street fighting in Omdurman itself, went to the Mahdi's tomb, or what remained of it, and prayed to Allah. Then he mounted a camel and escaped from the city before the Anglo-Egyptian army entered. In spite of his defeat, the Dervish Emirs remained faithful to him, as did the routed remnants of his army. For the next fourteen months he was a hunted man. He made for El Obeid, two hundred miles south-west of Khartoum, where there was a garrison. The Sirdar gave the responsibility for hunting him to his brother, Walter, who was made Governor of Khartoum, but he was not successful. However, late in 1899 General Wingate mounted a large force and attacked the Khalifa's forces at Um Dibaykarat. Wingate reported that the Khalifa "Seeing his followers retiring, he made an ineffectual attempt to rally them, but recognising that the day was lost he had called his Emirs to dismount from their horses and seating himself on his *furwa* or sheepskin – as is the custom of Arab chiefs who disdain surrender – and in this position they had unflinchingly met their death." Their bodies were reported to have been facing Mecca. Kitchener, in a letter, summed it up, "Well, at last we have settled matters out here, and the Khalifa is done for."

Osman Digna, who had eluded Gatacre at the Battle of Atbara and the 21st Lancers at Omdurman, was captured near the Red Sea in 1900 and held prisoner for eight years, before being allowed to return to Wadi Halfa. In 1924 he made a pilgrimage to Mecca and died two years later aged 86.

While there had been some criticism of the Sirdar, particularly over the treatment of the wounded on both sides, this did not prevent accolades on behalf of the grateful nation. Horatio Herbert Kitchener was elevated to the peerage and granted £30,000, with the thanks of both Houses of Parliament, unanimously in the Lords, but with twenty against in the Commons. It is said that Kitchener wanted to refuse the peerage but the Queen 'was not amused'. His brother Walter advised him, "You'd better accept as you won't get another chance". He took the title of Lord Kitchener of Khartoum and Aspall, in Suffolk, which

204

had been his mother's home. There was also the Grand Cross of the Order of the Bath.

His military career continued in India until 1911 when he was appointed British Agent, Consul-General, and Minister Plenipotentiary in Cairo. He was the virtual ruler, though the Khedive was in name. In 1914 he was appointed Secretary of War, much against his wishes. He was the first serving soldier to sit in the Cabinet for centuries. In this position he inspired the now famous poster showing him in Field Marshal's cap, with hypnotic eyes, bristling moustache and pointed finger: 'Your Country Needs YOU'. In 1916 he was invited to visit the Czar of Russia and set out in H.M.S. *Hampshire*, with destroyers as escorts, but the weather became too bad for them and they turned back. Shortly afterwards the *Hampshire* struck a mine and sank within fifteen minutes. Very few survived the intense cold, but not Kitchener, whose body was never recovered.

Major-General Gatacre was made a Knight Commander of the Order of the Bath before the end of 1898, as well as being awarded honours by the Khedive. Omdurman made the nation feel that the tragedy of Gordon had been overcome, and Gatacre was even invited to stay at Windsor. He then took command of the Eastern District at Colchester. However, in 1899 with the worsening situation in South Africa, he was appointed a Lieutenant-General in charge of a Division in Natal and sailed to Cape Town. The following year there was a failure to relieve a detachment at Reddersburg for which Gatacre was blamed, whether justly or not is disputable. He was relieved of his command and returned to Colchester, where he remained until 1903 when he ceased to be on the active list and retired two years later. But William Gatacre was unable to remain still for long. He joined the board of the Kordofan Trading Company and found himself exploring rubber forests in Abyssinia, east and south of Addis Ababa. Unfortunately, in January, 1906, he "Camped in a swamp – horrible water". A few days later he contracted fever and died on 18 January, 1906, at Iddeni. He was buried in the Abbyssinian Christian Cemetery.

Corporal George Skinner, within three weeks, was sent to Crete, then to Malta where he re-engaged in the Royal Army Medical Corps in 1899 to complete 21 years service. He arrived back in England at the end of 1899, but was almost immediately sent to South Africa until 1903, where he served with some distinction, being mentioned in despatches, before returning to England with a hospital ship. He was promoted Sergeant in 1905 and with a view to his future moved to the 'Cooking Section' of the Corps, and took a Certificate of High Class Cookery at the National Training School of Cookery in 1906, before his discharge on completion of 21 years service in 1910, when he returned to Ingleley Cottage, Elm Road, Kingston.

Lieutenant Meiklejohn continued his career in the Army, serving in

South Africa, Eastern Command, Scottish Coast Defences, and then in the Great War, in which he was wounded. After the war he saw service in Russia and Finland, and then was employed in the rank of Lieutenant-Colonel by the Foreign Office. He retired in 1927.

After Omdurman Captain Cox transferred to the 2nd Battalion Lincolnshire Regiment, which went to South Africa, again under Kitchener. He was very active in a number of areas, and awarded the Queen's Medal with three bars, and the King's Medal with two bars.

In 1908 Cox was promoted to Major and, serving in the Great War, commanded the 2nd Battalion as Lieutenant-Colonel from 1915. He retired on half-pay in 1919, when he would have been nearly fifty.

Private Teigh was sent, without home leave, to India in early November, 1898, and remained there till March, 1905. It is extremely likely that it was in Poona or Trichinopoly that he wrote the fair copy of his diary. This was a quite usual occupation for soldiers in India to help relieve boredom. Often the journal left the soldier with spare pages, and Private Teigh filled his volume with poems, and also a long account from a local paper of 'The Execution of Private O'Hara', who had, under the influence of the demon drink, shot two soldiers. His execution was remarkable for the long speech made by the condemned man. It is to be found in other journals of the same period. It is also possible that it was at this time he learned to embroider, again not an unusual occupation for soldiers. Two of his embroideries survived many years, one a fire-screen with flowers, and the other his Regimental Emblem. He also continued to improve his education, and in March, 1904, gained a Second Class Certificate in Education. He was also a member of a Lodge of the 'Royal Antedeluvian Order of Buffaloes' and received attendance medals from Lindum Lodge 1077.

Within five days of returning to England in March, 1905, he was discharged, having served twelve years and twenty-six days, being nearly thirty-one years of age. He returned to his home area Money Bridge, near Pinchbeck, and settled down in agriculture. He married Emma Eady, who was thirteen years younger, and had eight children. His wife died in 1948, and George Teigh in 1956 and is buried in the churchyard of Pinchbeck Church, where he had been baptized eighty-two years previously. Except for his twelve years in the Army, he never left the area.

BIBLIOGRAPHY

Some published sources

W.S. Churchill: *The River War*, 1899
B. Farwell: *For Queen and Country*, 1981
B. Gatacre: *General Gatacre 1843–1906*, 1910
H. Keown-Boyd: *A Good Dusting. The Sudan Campaigns*, 1986
A. Lee: *History of Tenth Foot*, 1911
P. Magnus: *Kitchener*, 1958
P. Ziegler: *Omdurman*, 1973

Manuscript and unpublished sources

Army Lists and Records, Public Record Office
Journal of Private G. Teigh, The National Army Museum
Diary of Lieutenant S. FitzGibbon Cox, The Royal
    Lincolnshire Regimental Museum
Diary of Lieutenant R.F. Meiklejohn, The National Army
    Museum
Diary of Corporal G. Skinner, The National Army Museum.

INDEX

Abadar, 73, 80
Abadia, 102, 111, 118, 123
Abbassiyeh, 133, 201
Abu Dis, 39, 40, 43, 44
Abu Hamed, 17, 20, 23, 43, 100, 199
Adamson, Surg Maj H.M., 9, 16, 22, 28, 35, 42, 80, 107, 110, 190
Adowa, 3
Adye, Gen J., 26
Alexandria, 2, 109, 195, 199
Assouan, 11, 18, 200
Atbara (Fort) 44, 50, 63, 167
Atbara, (River) 43, 45, 49, 63, 64, 67, 71, 73, 94

Bacchus, Lt J.B.R., 143
Bailey, Pte, 78
Baillie, Capt A.C.D., 111
Bainbridge, 111
Ball, Renissi, 67
Barlow, Lt C.C.L., 41, 42, 57, 68, 103, 104
Barter, Maj B.St.J., 79
Bateman, May, 35
Beatty, Lt D., RN, 74, 82n.
Berber, 43–48, 50, 54, 55, 63, 97
Berfeld Filter, 113
Boxer, Lt H.E.R., 20, 29, 48, 59, 76, 101, 103, 110
Brackpool, Col Sgt, 92
Bradell, Surg Maj M.O.'D, 9
Brannan, Pte, 128, 131
Brewis, Lt R.H.W., 36, 37, 186

Brooke, Capt R., 7th Hussars, 74, 75
Broughton, Pte, 134
Bull, Rene, 85
Burleigh, Bennet, 85
Burnham, Pte, 110
Burrowes, Lt L.A., 132, 194
Burrows, Pte, 61

Cage, Pte, 141
Cairo, 97, 200
Caldecott, Capt G., 37, 51, 83, 92, 156, 180, 183–186, 190, 194
Cameron Highlanders, 29, 59, 89, 186
Carr, Surg Maj H., 14
Christie, Lt W.C., 51
Churchill, W.S., 24, 123, 180
Citadel Barracks, 1, 203
Clayton, Pte, 116
Cockburn, Maj C.J., 15, 65, 83, 180
Colbean, Cpl, 171
Constantinople, 97, 156
Cox, Gen J.B., 2
Cromer, Lord, 4
Cross, Pte, 74
Crozier, 156, 158
Cumberland, Capt R.O., 109, 156, 161
Cummins, Surg Lt S., 158

Da Baka, 44, 54
Dakheila, 63, 68, 101, 103, 163, 166, 172, 196–199
Dale, Pte, 108, 109

Darmali, 44, 58, 59, 78–80, 97, 101, 103, 106–9, 113, 116, 120, 125, 130, 152, 154, 159
Dawson, Pte, 143
Day, Lt D.A.L., 89, 187
Derea, 51
de Rougemont, Capt C.H., RA, 77
Dixon, Sgt C.J., QM., (hon Lt), 91, 92, 139
Dongola Campaign, 98
Doughty, Col Sgt, 136
Dyke, Lt O.M., 200

Eady, Emma, (Teigh), 206
Earle, Capt F.A., 36, 185, 186
Earle, Lt P.D., 53, 172
Edefere, 10
Edwards, Lt L., 173
El Egeiga, 164, 193
El Obeid, 204
El Selim, 97, 105, 173, 198
Ellis, Pte, 110
Eritrea, 3
Etches, Lt C.E., 180
Etheridge, Maj C.deC., 15, 187

Fashoda, 4
Field Battery (32nd), 161
Findlay, Capt C., 88, 93, 95
Fitzclarence, Lt E., 17n.
Forbes, Col W.E.G., 179
Forrest, Capt J., 8, 78, 109, 126, 156
Fowey Ed., 109, 198
Freeman, (QMS), 48
Friend, Maj H.B., RE., 9

Gamble, Capt R.N., 110, 112, 171
Gatacre Lt-Gen Sir W., birth and early life, 25; bullets, 26; Forced March, 43; the Atbara, 72–77; Omdurman, 163–165; final years, 205; mentioned, 31, 32, 37, 45, 48, 49, 56, 65, 66, 68, 80, 83, 97, 121–123, 126, 132, 134, 138, 154, 157, 158, 167, 176, 185

Gavian Hills, 13
Geneinetti, 43, 45, 62, 103
Girouard Lt E.P., 99, 100
Gordon, Gen C., 3, 88, 165, 190
Gordon, Maj W.S., RE, 123
Gore, Lt P.A., 95
Gorst, Pte, 108, 111
Greatwood, Lt F.W., 114
Greer, Lt MacG., 95
Grenfell, Gen F., 201
Grenfell, Lt R.S., 180, 188
Guards, Grenadier, 122, 172
Gunboats
    Abu Klea, 123
    El Teb, 123
    Fateh, 123
    Melik, 123, 129
    Metemma, 123
    Nasr, 123
    Sheikh, 123
    Sultan, 123, 129
    Tamai, 111, 123
    Zafir, 123
Gurheish, 17, 20, 23, 32

Haines, Sgt, 16
Hatasoo, 15
Hill, Lt R. d'E., 29, 30, 106
Hodgson, Lt H., 107
Holland, Pte, 107
Hollins, Lt C.E., 103, 106
Hopkins Surg Lt C.H., 156, 186, 188
Hourie, (Interpreter), 120
Hubbard, Capt A.E., 38
Hudi, 45, 102
Hunt, Pte, 134
Hunter, Gen A., 72, 75, 78, 86, 100, 123
Hunter-Blair, Maj W.C., 90–92

Iddeni, 205

Jaalins, 88, 169
Jackson, Lt F.A., 156
Jebel Surgham, 164, 165
Johnson, Lt A.H., 34, 53

Johnson, Pte, 150
Jones, Pioneer Cpl, 95

Kedennick, Pte, 134
Kenna, Capt P.A., 187 @n
Kereri, 163, 164, 179
Khalifa, 3, 43, 149, 163, 164, 176, 193, 195, 204, *et al.*
Khalifa's Palace, 182
Khartoum, 3, 97, 165, 171, 175, 176, 194
Khor Abu Sunt, 164, 165
Khor Shambat, 188
King, Lt R.N., 109
Kitchener, Gen H.H. birth and early life, 24–25; strategy before the Atbara, 43–46; Omdurman plans 163–165; after Omdurman, 190–192; later years and death, 204–205; mentioned, 4, 16, 36, 48, 54, 69, 73, 78, 79, 83, 95, 98, 112, 122, 123, 128, 149, 179, 180, 193
Kitchener, W.S., 75, 204
Korosko, 13, 19
Korti, 31, 37
Kunur, 45, 61, 78

Lancashire Fusiliers, 123, 172
Lancers (21st), 161, 164, 174, 180, 187, 198
Lee-Metford Rifles, 26
Lockhart, L. Cpl, 119
Long, Col, 89
Longbourne, Lt Col F., 34
Lowth, Col F.R., 121, 122, 125, 152n., 162, 171
Luxor, 9, 14, 199, 201
Lyall, Lt C.G., 172
Lyttelton, Gen the Hon N.G., 122, 157

MacDonald, Gen H., 81, 89, 188
Mahdi, Mohamed Ahmed, 2, 3
Mahdi's Tomb, 163, 164, 182, 190, 193

Mahmud Ahmed, 43, 45, 46, 49, 58, 59, 72, 74, 76, 79, 83, 86, 88, 89, 95, 96
Mainwaring, Maj H.B., 60, 61, 78, 106, 108, 109
Malone, Sgt, 76, 85, 87
Maraut, 9
Marsh, Capt J.R.M., 88, 126, 134
Matana, 10
Maxim, H.S., 26
Maxwell, Gen J.G., 89
Maxwell, Capt R.P., 42, 60, 88, 106
May, D., 193
McNeil, Pte, 120, 126
Meroe, 168
Metemma, 168, 169
Money, Col G.L.C., 126n., 132, 133, 135, 157
Money Bridge, 1
Montmorency, Lt, Hon R.H.L.J. de, 187n.
Mumby, Sgt, 70, 138
Mutrus, 74

Nagh Hamadi, 9, 12, 15
Nakheila, 45, 73
Napier, Maj R.F.L., 95
Nasri Island, 197
Northumberland Fusiliers, 123, 173
Nubian Desert, 98

Omdurman, 3, 45, 163, 179, 181, *et seq*
Osman Digna, 43, 45, 59, 63, 64, 76, 88, 90, 165, 193, 195, 204

Pearce, 81
Perry, Pte, 41
Peters, Lt P.M., 18, 34, 109
Philae, Isle of, 18
Pickwell, Pte, 134
Plunkett, Lt E.A., 28, 42, 88, 171
Power, Sgt, 91

Quayle-Jones, Maj M., 51, 52, 83, 92, 180

Ralbaca, 55
Ras el Hudi, 45, 64, 67, 80
Reddersberg, 205
Reiz, 198
Remington Rifles, 88, 138n.
Rennie, Lt C.J., 172
Rifle Brigade, 123, 173, 174
Royan Island, 196
Rushby, Pte, 143

Sanderson, Lt W.D., 143
Shabluka, 163, 169, 171, 175, 196
Shelal, 200
Shendi, 43, 45, 50, 59, 68, 79, 168
Shepheard's, 7, 11, 22
Shulock, Cpl, 110
Simcoates, Pte, 18, 21
Simpson, Maj C.R., 7, 9, 10, 34,
    76, 102, 106, 118, 119, 125,
    144, 150–152, 170
Sitwell, Maj W.H., North. Fus.,
    111
Skipwith, Lt F.G., 32, 65, 79, 83,
    156
Sloggett, Surg Col A.T., 188, 190
Smith, Capt (hon), A.G., APD, 9
Smith, Lt W.D., AVD, 9
Snow, Maj T.D'O., R.Innis. Fus.,
    25, 30
Southall, Pte, 91
Spailer, 176
Spearman, Lt A.Y., 179
Steevens, W.H. (*Daily Mail*), 26
Sydney, Maj H.M., 17n.

Tatchell, Lt E., 68, 174
Taylor, Pte, 102, 138

Taylor, Surg Gen W., 157
Teigh, J., 1
Teigh, L., 1
Thebes, 14
Tomkins, Pte, 133
Toogood, Lt A.S., 54, 172
Tuti Island, 179, 183

Umdabia, 73, 76, 96, 97
Um Dibaykarat, 204
Urquhart, Capt B.C., 95

Verner, Col T.E., 17, 37, 76, 114

Wad Bihara, 163
Wad Hamed, 163, 164, 168, 196,
    197
Wadi Halfa, 15, 20, 25, 198, 199
Walsh, Pte P., 119
Warriner, Pte, 133
Watkin, Pte, 134
Watson, Rev A.W.B., 30, 105, 108,
    111, 114, 117, 120, 136, 165,
    176, 194
Wauchope, Gen A.G., 121, 123,
    157, 158n.
Wellington, 97
Wilcox, Pte, 20
Williams, Pte, 20
Wilson, Lt R.H.G., 65, 77, 78, 106,
    175
Wingate, Gen R., 204
Wolseley, Field Marshal, 73, 97
Wood, Sir Evelyn, 3
Woodcock, Lt E.E., 38, 81
Woolstencroft, Pte, 134
Wyeth, Lee Corp, 74, 104